DATE DUE

Return Material Promptly

But What If She Wants to Die?

But What If She Wants to Die?

A Husband's Diary

George E. Delury

A Birch Lane Press Book
Published by Carol Publishing Group

A Birch Lane Press Book
Published by Carol Publishing Group
Birch Lane Press is a registered trademark of Carol Communications, Inc.

Editorial, sales and distribution, rights and permissions inquiries should be addressed to Carol Publishing Group, 120 Enterprise Avenue, Secaucus, N.J. 07094

In Canada: Canadian Manda Group, One Atlantic Avenue, Suite 105, Toronto, Ontario M6K 3E7

Carol Publishing Group books may be purchased in bulk at special discounts for sales promotion, fund-raising, or educational purposes. Special editions can be created to specifications. For details, contact: Special Sales Department, Carol Publishing Group, 120 Enterprise Avenue, Secaucus, N.J. 07094.

Manufactured in the United States of America
10 9 8 7 6 5 4 3 2 1

The cataloging data for this publication can be obtained from the Library of Congress.

For Myrna

To Gloria Howard
1931–1997
With our deepest gratitude

CONTENTS

Acknowledgments   ix

 1 The "Happiness Principle"   1
 2 The Tombs   9
 3 The Summer of Love   19
 4 Myrna's "Passage"   32
 5 Discovering Disease—Saying "I Do"   41
 6 The Good Years   55
 7 A Time of Faith and Good Work   66
 8 The Ragged Years   78
 9 Down, Always Down   94
10 Losing One's Self   107
11 Scorn, Lies, and Red Tape   124
12 A Tattered Knight   129
13 No Escape?   148
14 The Decision, the Act   168
15 The Media, the Law, and the People   183
16 Criminal Justice   202
17 How Will We Live?   211

ACKNOWLEDGMENTS

There is no way I can thank by name the several hundred people who made this book, and my life, possible with their quiet interest, moral support, and practical generosity over the eighteen months since Myrna's death. In fact, given the subject matter, to name some of them might harm their relations with others. So I will use only first names where such a problem might conceivably exist.

Above all, thanks are due to my synagogue in general and to Simcha in particular. He, more than anyone, understood. Observing the Orthodox separation of the sexes in this listing, I want to especially thank Nancy (now in New Jersey) for inspiration, and Shirley and Gloria for their warm commiseration. On the other side, thanks are particularly due Michael and Isaac and Jerry, Glenn, Richard, Bernie, Mark, Leon, Marvin, Lenny and Gary, and Alan (now in Los Angeles), and, of course, all the rabbis and the "Chaz". They are only a few of the many who forgave me and blessed me with their comfort.

Outside the synagogue, I want to particularly thank Rabbi Abba Borowich for giving me an engrossing task soon after Myrna's death, a task that became the beginnings of this book.

Sean, besides moral support, gave me a means of earning a living, with the full backing, I believe, of Gordon, whom I've never met.

Some of Myrna's family have been more than kind, especially Charlotte Liebov in Brooklyn and Charlotte Libov in Connecticut, as well as Chuck and Jodie Liebov, Bobby Liebov, and Arlene and Sandy Levine. Dan Wilkes, in particular, has been a help with sound writing advice and good company.

Myrna's college friends Holly Regier and Barbara McCarthy showed a special concern for my well-being and state of mind. Siva Myer, Joyce Sills, Ellen Lehrer, and others have also been supportive.

Hemlock Society members around the country flocked to give practical support, but I want to particularly mention two in Manhattan—Manhattan chapter leader Carolyn Monro and Joan Stillman. Joan, already dying herself, went far out of her way to ease my lot in jail. New York State Hemlock president Bill Batt, past Hemlock Society USA president Sidney Rosoff, Westchester chapter leader Nina Engel, Eric Spence, Art Charney, Anne Keleman, and a dozen others in the New York area all helped with contributions, with letters and books for the jailed felon, and with firm support in hard times.

At Rikers, Rabbi Kwalbrun stimulated a dulled mind once a week. One captain and one corrections officer helped me keep faith that humanity can survive in the worst of bureaucratic environments; they know who they are. Thanks are also due inmates "Monty," Ralph, Billy, Willy, Mark, and Randy for keeping an eye on me, and to Vega, who at some risk to himself made it possible for me to write parts of this book.

A special thanks goes to writer Suse Woodman, who drew me out for her book, *Last Rights: America's Struggle Over the Right to Die,* and to journalists Ian Katz of the *Manchester Guardian,* Lorna Grisby of *People,* and Steve Lipman of *Jewish Week* for their care with the nuances.

Here at home on West 85th, Tracey Sterne, Kate Draper, Alan Dickstein, Suzanne Prescod, and the building staff all pitched in to help me through.

Far away, my old friend George Eberl kept me posted on public opinion, and, of course, a dozen family members, including my daughter Anna and son Conrad and honorary family member Claudette Guerra, were continual sources of encouragement and love.

Finally, my agent Bill Adler and editor Hillel Black encouraged me in the writing, while both Hillel and coeditor Carrie Nichols Cantor raised significant questions that contributed greatly to the book.

But What If She Wants to Die?

1

The "Happiness Principle"

This book deals with death, a difficult topic at any time, but especially so in the United States today. It is a topic surrounded, even in the most rational of times, by discomfort and distaste, dread and sorrow. It seems to me wise to describe the atmosphere in which death is discussed today so that the reader will not be put off by the highly personal story that follows.

"Why write a book about it in the first place?" a friend asks. "Haven't you already caused yourself enough trouble, what with jail time, lawyer fees, media unfairness? And whatever you say, the people who object to what you did will still hate you. You have nothing to gain but money—maybe. The dog has gone back to sleep. Let it lie."

Is my friend concerned only for my good? Or does he, at least a little bit, want to get away from the topic, to avoid further discomfort? For the atmosphere in which death is discussed today is, frankly, highly irrational. Americans are crazy about death.

In any given week, there are several dozen violent deaths depicted on television and in movies. Advertisers pay top money for their commercials to be shown during television portrayals of death; and mass audiences jam theaters to see gunplay and flying bodies. Reports of death—serial killings, drive-by shootings, infanticide, and random murders—dominate local newscasts. The threat of death is always in the media air—death from cigarettes, from poor eating habits, from sunlight. . . . Almost everything seems to be life threatening. TV news reporters and advertisers thrive on giving viewers the frisson of danger, while posing as helpful advisers.

Yet for all this fascination with fictional and distant danger and death, the modern person seldom comes into immediate contact with real death. Real death is usually hidden away in hospitals and hospices and spoken of in hushed tones, if spoken of at all. Death has replaced religion and politics as the subject banned from polite conversation. It has replaced sex as the forbidden topic. Our TV talk-show hosts have no scruples about exhibiting the oddest kinds of sexual and political behavior, but seldom touch on death, unless it is violent, the kind of death we assume happens only to someone else.

Yes, we are crazy about death. Back in 1955, well before the advent of the "action movie" genre, British anthropologist Geoffrey Gorer wrote an article in which he likened modern attitudes toward death to Victorian prudery about sex and suggested that the depiction of death in TV shows and movies was a "pornography of death" that arose out of our secret fascination with the forbidden topic. More than two decades later, a French scholar, Philippe Ariès, in *Western Attitudes Toward Death from the Middle Ages to the Present,* wrote: "In our day, in approximately a third of a century, we have witnessed a brutal revolution in traditional ideas and feelings. . . . It is really an absolutely unheard-of phenomenon. Death, so omnipresent in the past that it was familiar, would be effaced, would disappear. It would become shameful and forbidden."

This "revolution," "brutal" because the denial of death is so psychologically destructive, was in large part a result of advances in medical science that, in the three decades from 1930 to 1960, virtually eradicated many of the most common causes of death in the developed world; from childhood diseases to epidemic killers, from diphtheria and polio to influenza and typhoid fever. Consequently, an unexamined idea arose in the public mindset: Not only was death a topic to be avoided, it was avoidable in fact. Death became unnecessary, a sign of a failure of technique and will, an embarrassment.

Ariès had another theory about Western attitudes toward death. He noted that from the High Middle Ages until the early nineteenth century, people were more concerned about the manner, the style, of their own death than they were about the deaths of others. It was important to our ancestors that they should die nobly if possible and that their nobility be displayed—to the family, including children, and to society. From this view arose the traditional deathbed scene, well-known in fiction, of the family patriarch dispensing, with his last breath, blessings or curses on his relatives and calling on God to save and vindicate him.

But in the nineteenth century, a new approach to death began to appear, promoted in part by the Romantic movement in the arts. There was, in Ariès's view, an increasing concern and focus, not on one's own death, but on the death of the "other," the loved one. With this change came the tendency to conceal from the dying the facts of their "horrible" condition, thus depriving them of the opportunity of dying with dignity, dispensing justice and wisdom from the edge of the abyss.

In the romantic view, Ariès says, "death was increasingly thought of as a transgression which tears man from his daily life, from rational society, from his monotonous work, in order to make him undergo a paroxysm, plunging him into an irrational, violent, and beautiful world." In this view, death became a rupture in the fabric of the ordinary. Death was transformed from a commonplace natural event to a dramatic crisis, an eruption of the unusual and outrageous.

It is not a giant step to go from thinking of death as something unusual and outrageous to thinking of it as unnatural, something to be condemned and avoided at all costs. In short, in a relatively brief time, our attitude toward death changed from an almost celebratory ceremonial acceptance of a normal and expected event to horror and denial of a grim intruder in our otherwise tranquil and optimistic social scene. The dying person was an unwelcome gate-crasher; our concern with the other's death became a peculiar mixture of sorrow and annoyance, even anger.

Ariès goes on to note that these changes ruled out any acknowledgment of death through a display of serious grief. Unrestrained grief became a "sign of mental instability or of bad manners; it is *morbid*." Unseemly displays of grief, once honored and, in some cultures, even required, were banned, "for it is henceforth given that life is always happy or should always seem to be so." According to Ariès, modern society created a "need for happiness—the moral duty and the social obligation to contribute to the collective happiness by avoiding any cause for sadness or boredom."

Nowhere on earth or in history is this "happiness principle" more ingrained than in contemporary America. From "happy face" buttons to "happy talk" TV news, from the inanity of "have a nice day" to the gross misinterpretation of "the pursuit of happiness" enshrined in the Declaration of Independence, "happiness" has become the prime moral obligation of our social life. To be unhappy is virtually un-American, almost treasonous.

"Happiness" is not only a moral obligation, it is an economic necessity, enforced by advertising and boosterism. Modern American prosperity is founded on the belief that "happiness" can be acquired. Thousands of products depend on the idea that annoyances and dissatisfaction can and *ought* to be eliminated with the purchase of the right hair rinse, the latest electronic gadget, lite beer, granola, or crack cocaine. How we go about getting and staying "happy" may depend on our education and economic condition, but that we have a right to be "happy" and *ought* to be "happy" goes unquestioned. America is the richest, strongest, and freest country on earth and in history. It is bursting with promise and opportunity. There is no excuse for being unhappy. To be unhappy is to deny the American dream.

Privately and intellectually, we know this is all baloney; we know that unhappiness is common and persistent. Nevertheless, the social pressure to conform to the "happiness principle" invades and infects our private lives and attitudes. The culture's focus on "happiness" makes it hard for us to face and deal with personal difficulties and to face and accept those real problems which have no solution. In fact, the idea that a problem has no solution is antithetical to the American "can-do" tradition—another betrayal.

This national cult of "happiness" and our private misgivings about it infuse and warp our views of health, illness, and the role of medicine. Health is seen as the prerequisite of "happiness," so that ill health is almost a faux pas. It bespeaks bad habits; it suggests sin. Just as there is no excuse for not being happy in our wonderful country, so there is no excuse for not being healthy, especially given our supposedly first-rate medical system. Nevertheless, sickness, hypochondria, and even chronic ill health, are so commonplace that we have an entire industry devoted to offering questionable remedies to those embarrassed by their real and supposed illnesses. (The unrecognized hypochondriac is in a peculiar position—on the one hand scorned for his continual poor health, on the other praised for seeking out every possible cure.)

Our view of the seriously ill is a difficult combination of mixed feelings. We are embarrassed over not knowing what to say or do, and often fall back on sentimentality and pity to hide that embarrassment. We admire the person who dutifully affirms our "can-do" tradition by doing everything possible to recover, and are uncomfortably displeased by those who appear to be slacking in this regard. We admire the courage of the hopelessly ill, but are, if we would admit it, annoyed and even angered by their affront to "happiness." Above all, there is anxiety—personal and social—the dread of falling into the same condition, feelings of helplessness, and embarrassment for the person who has violated the "happiness principle."

Because we avoid thinking concretely about serious illnesses and disabilities, we too often fail to note the immense variety and differences among them and the even more varied personal experiences of the afflicted. Even in our public policies toward the very ill and disabled, this immense variety is lumped together in a few general categories. We fail to distinguish clearly between the able disabled, such as an employed paraplegic, and the utterly disabled and homebound. We don't think about the difference between the kind of disability that is stable and can be accommodated and the kind that is progressive, requiring constant new adaptations. Even many disabled people fail to make these distinctions.

All these mixed feelings are intensified in the face of death. Death is a problem without a solution and the most grievous betrayal of our social "happiness." All terminally ill persons are seen as more or less the same though the personal experiences of different terminal illnesses are as varied as the illnesses themselves.

At the same time, there is widespread recognition that the process of dying today has been immensely complicated and prolonged by our medical "miracles." People are vaguely aware that doctors and nurses too often thwart death simply because they can.

Any discussion of death, let alone of a chosen death and euthanasia, therefore takes place in an atmosphere of dread and fear, disgust and anger, approval and admiration, horror and pity. In the worst case, this stew becomes a hysteria that makes rational discussion impossible.

I beg the reader to cling to reason as he or she reads this book. For emotional balance, please try this exercise: Try to think of circumstances in which you personally would prefer death to continued life . . . and then try to imagine your reaction to anyone who tried to force you to live in those circumstances.

I wrote this book above all to vindicate my wife's decision to die and to contribute to a rational discussion of the issues. In the prevailing atmosphere surrounding death, the death by choice of a young woman, however ill she might have been, so disturbs people that they want to distance themselves from it by turning her into an object of pity. As one newspaper columnist put it, "Myrna Lebov herself became a vague, pathetic figure," as the media and general public tried to make a victim of a courageous and generous woman who chose death as the last exercise of her independent will.

Unlike the pathetic many who drag on out of a vague sense of duty, or fear, or sheer inertia and lack of will, Myrna looked the inevitable in the face, examined her options, and chose the one she felt was best for her. Vague and pathetic she may have been to the opinion mongers, but she was not vague and pathetic to those who knew her.

On the contrary, she was a heroine of the highest order. She had waged a valiant and constantly losing struggle against multiple sclerosis for more than twenty years, with little complaint or self-pity. She was always considerate of others, trying to make them feel that she was all right, in good spirits, and ready to fight on. She seldom faltered in her resolve to make the struggle her problem, hers alone, and to present to the world at large and to those close to her an unassuming nobility of spirit. To use one of the highest accolades of the ancient world, she was a "woman of valor" (Proverbs 31:10).

She had adapted to each loss of function, accepting each new limit on her freedom and independence and displaying an astounding capacity to cope. She did not curse her fate; she did not get lazy and fat; she did not take out her frustrations and fears on other people. She took full responsibility for her condition and never used it as an excuse or a weapon. She continued to pursue her various interests in film, theater, art, and literature. Above all, she maintained her fierce drive for independence, the core of her life project.

Her suffering was largely psychological and easily dissimulated. Most of the time she disguised the fact that she chafed terribly at the restrictions on her life and at the necessary but boring concentration on the physical details of managing her handicaps. In that, I suffered with her. As her mind showed increasing signs of decay, I mourned the slow disappearance of the woman I loved— the lively and insightful conversationalist, the perceptive observer of nuances, the amusing commentator on social foibles. But when she returned to full awareness, as she did periodically, I was again inspired by her grace and courage, as was everyone who knew her well.

She remained stalwart to the end. As she gulped down the bitter brew I had prepared that would end her life, she said little. Watching her, helping her hold the cup, and urging her several times to slow down lest she make herself sick, I saw the shyly bold young woman I had fallen in love with twenty-seven years earlier. She was beautiful and she was brave.

The living must beware lest their own anxieties about death lead them to dishonor the memory of those who face death with courage and dignity. The living must beware, also, of projecting their sorrow and grief onto the now-perfect mirror of vanished loved ones, turning them into pathetic victims.

I also have an obligation to present to the public a case of assisted suicide that illustrates in the extreme the many ambiguities in the discussion. For Myrna did not meet most of the criteria by which we are wont to measure the ethical validity of a chosen death. She was not terminally ill, and she was not in any physical pain. She frequently showed signs of severe depression, but, at the end, she rejected medication that might have alleviated it, saying it might change her feelings but not the facts.

She was under conflicting pressure from others to choose between life and death. She did not have good cause to believe that she would be well taken care of in the future. And she may well have chosen to die, in part, out of generosity to me. Finally, Myrna did not leave behind clear and convincing evidence to a "moral certainty" that she chose death of her own free will at the time of the act itself.

All these points are touched on by opponents of chosen death and of assisted suicide. There are those who, without knowing any further details, would condemn Myrna's suicide and my assistance for any one of these reasons alone.

This then is the story of Myrna's final months and of the earlier years of joy and freedom, bondage and sorrow, that were our life together. It is a tragic love story, in which there are no victims and no villains, only the strange and beautiful progress amid failures of two ordinary people learning how to love fully. It is a story, too, of our society, of our often inept attempts to help the desperately ill and disabled, and of our refusal to accept and value tragedy; a story of ignorance, fear, and secrecy.

My primary aim in writing this book, as I said, is to vindicate Myrna, and all others who make her choice at the right time for them, against the desecration of their memory by the sentimental, the self-righteous, and the fearful. In this age, when so many aspire to be victims and claim special rights, Myrna would deny she was a victim; all she would want to claim is her honor.

When you are done with this book, if you have a tear for Myrna, remember her as a heroine and honor her by striving for a whole life, an aware and responsible life of your own.

2

The Tombs

Noise and the constant light in my glass-walled cell woke me at about 5:30 A.M., July 5, 1995. I had slept fitfully on a cushioned, swiveling office chair, my feet propped on a similar chair, the only items of furniture in a filthy, musty-smelling eight-by-six-foot cell with a very high ceiling. Three walls, the floor, and the ceiling were concrete. The fourth wall, made of relatively thin glass brick, allowed the guards to observe me at all times. My feet were cold. I had to leave my moccasin-style shoes outside the cell because of the shoestrings. And my pants were down around my hips because the guards had taken away my belt.

Was I a suicide risk? Or did they just want to isolate me from the other prisoners? If I had been suicidal, the time to kill myself would have been the previous morning, July 4, before I called 911 to report that my wife, Myrna, was dead, a suicide from a fatal brew that I had concocted for her. With Myrna gone, after her long struggle with multiple sclerosis, I had little to live for beyond defending our decision.

I was in the Tombs, or Central Booking, the first stop for alleged felons arrested in Manhattan and awaiting arraignment. I had been there since about nine o'clock the evening before and had been dozing, off and on, since then. In the forty-eight hours since the morning of July 3, I had had about six hours of sleep, none of it restful. I had also, during those forty-eight hours, helped my wife kill herself, turned my incriminating diary over to the police, waited hours to be interrogated by an assistant district attorney, and spent two hours being questioned before being arrested and hauled to the Tombs. I had eaten only a tuna sandwich the day before.

The police had been decent, offering not rough stuff but rather a distant, cool solicitude. The interrogation had not been intense, just a slow accumulation of the facts and an attempt to discern my state of mind, which was numb, stunned, disoriented, and resigned.

But not quite resigned; I had a moment of classic prisoner's panic. What if my name drops out of the system? What if I'm just left here, forgotten? Don't be silly, I told myself. You're tired and uncomfortable. Wait it out. God knows where you are.

A television set without sound on the wall just outside my cell showed me on the news. I looked very seedy being led out of the precinct station the previous evening. There was also a shot of a body bag being trundled out of our apartment building on a gurney. That image remains strong in my memory—the reduction of Myrna to a shapeless gray lump.

"Breakfast" was served—two sandwiches, one bologna and one cheese, both made with dry slices of puffed-air bread, and a half pint of milk. I wolfed down the cheese sandwich and drank the milk.

They came for me at about 9:15 A.M. Handcuffed, I was led to a squad car and carted one or two blocks to the criminal courts building. It was clear that I was getting special treatment: the police officer in charge didn't seem familiar with the circuitous route we took through the building to the courtroom. After trekking up and down stairs (walking down stairs with your hands cuffed behind your back is difficult and dangerous) and backtracking at least once, we arrived at the side door of a courtroom and waited, while other prisoners, in a cage just behind me, quietly jeered my going to the head of the line.

Through a window in the door, I could see on the bailiff's desk a copy of the *New York Post*, a sensationalist tabloid, with a picture of a grubby-looking, bearded man taking up nearly half the front page and a large headline screaming "HUBBY HELPS WIFE KILL HERSELF."

That was my first taste of what the media would do with the story, and my first reaction has not changed—a little amused at the foolish hype, angry at the subtle errors and distortions, and shocked at the attention. I had not anticipated the media's interest in the story and cannot to this day clearly explain why I was surprised. If I had thought about the media at all before Myrna's death, I think I had expected a brief and bland item buried among the advertisements and soon forgotten. I believe I had put out of my mind any serious thought about the media, as well as the legal process I faced, because they were irrelevant. Regardless of the media or the law, if Myrna chose to die, I would help, just as I had promised years before.

At the arraignment I was charged with violating §125.15 of the New York State penal code: "Manslaughter in the second degree. A person is guilty of manslaughter in the second degree when: . . . 3. He intentionally causes or aids another person to commit suicide. Manslaughter in the second degree is a class C felony," punishable by five to fifteen years in prison.

A young public defender spoke for me, following a script I never saw, and in seconds I was released on my own recognizance and walking out the door into a phalanx of reporters and cameras. The public defender had advised me not to speak to anyone until I got a lawyer and I followed that advice. I did, however, cadge a ride home by promising a persistent and perspiring cameraman-reporter an interview that I reneged on when we reached my apartment building where another media mob was waiting for me.

It was there that I encountered the first reaction of private citizens to what I had done. Before I went up to my apartment, I had to visit the small grocery downstairs to get some staples. The grocery manager, who knew me only by sight, chased the reporters out of the store and, ringing up my few purchases, wished me good luck. Inside my building, the doorman and other staff also shooed the mob away and expressed their sympathy. I went upstairs to an empty apartment.

I think that emptiness would have been unendurable were it not for a note under the door. It was from Kate, a neighbor on the floor below, who had known Myrna well. In a lovely calligraphic hand, it read: "Dear George, Please know that you have my sincerest sympathy and *total support.* If the need arises, don't hesitate to give my name and number to your lawyer as I will gladly attest to the goodness, and strength, and courage of Myrna's and your characters as well as your marriage together. I know you will miss her deeply. We all will." I appreciated Kate's recognition of Myrna's courage, but I wished I could fully share her opinion of me.

As I went about cleaning up the mess the police had left behind—empty paper cups, odds and ends of unidentifiable investigative materials, the bed on which Myrna died, from which the bottom sheet had been removed—I thought about the trouble I was in with my conscience. Intellectually, I was firmly convinced I had done the right thing for the right reasons, but my heart told me that it was wrong for me to still be alive to gain from Myrna's death.

My thoughts were a muddle. I was shocked at the carelessness of the police work. Besides the sheet, they had taken the blender in which I had mixed the poison with honey; Myrna's purse, her pill container and all her pills, and the floppy disk from her word processor. But they had left behind the little custard cup and spoon I had used to give Myrna a taste of the poison to see if she could tolerate its bitterness. And while the police had taken several books on death and dying, they had overlooked the most significant one, *Final Exit* by Derek Humphry, on how to commit suicide. Nor did they find or, as far as I knew, even look for the cache of Baggies, the two-gallon size, that I had set aside to use if the poison didn't work.

I reviewed what the district attorney's investigation would find as they tried to determine if this might, in fact, be a murder. They would find no monetary gain. There was no money left, and I was deeply in debt. Within six months of Myrna's death, I would be officially bankrupt and would still owe more than $20,000 to the tax collectors. Nor was there another woman. I had no interest in other women and no time for them in any case. My only gain was that I could rest now and someday recover, more or less, from the grief that had haunted me for so many years. I was haunted, too, by the fear that I had pressured her into ending her life; I had certainly encouraged her to make that decision. But had she really wanted to die? Had I really wanted her to die?

Nevertheless, I had to remind myself that if Myrna had not really wanted to die, if I had pressured her into killing herself, if I was a villain, then she was a victim. Myrna would have hated that idea. She recognized that people can be victims, but she was fiercely independent and always insisted on taking full responsibility for her fate. My sense of guilt, with its implication that she was a victim, dishonored her.

The D.A.'s office took its time with the case, partly to allow public interest to die down and partly because of the press of cases involving real criminals, but also to take time for summer vacations. In December, the case was finally taken before a grand jury. My attorney had told me that the D.A. had ruled out murder and would only seek an indictment on the charge of assisting a suicide. We felt I had nothing to gain by testifying, so I didn't. On December 12, the indictment was handed down, and at the same time the D.A. released the diary I had handed over to the police on July 4.

The press loved it. But they hated it, too, because it showed all the ambiguities of life in the flesh and did not permit a snap portrayal of me as a hero or a villain. By increasing the complexity of the story, the diary made sound-bite drama impossible for responsible journalists. Most of the press preferred just to pick up and reiterate the most lurid phrases from the diary—and never mind context.

The D.A.'s view was revealed three months later in a letter to the judge handling the case. The letter is under seal and cannot be quoted, but its basic thrust was that while there was little doubt that Myrna drank the poison voluntarily, I had encouraged and even pressured her to do so. It said I acted out of a selfish desire to be released from the burden of caring for her. All true, but not the whole truth.

My attorney, in his letter to the judge, also under seal, noted that I had fully cooperated with the police, which suggested that

I believed I was acting in Myrna's best interests with her consent and active participation. Acknowledging that my diary contained some very damning passages, he noted that a selection of other passages would give a completely opposite impression, the impression of a man so deeply in love that he was prepared to risk everything to comply with his beloved's wishes. He also noted that he could fill the courtroom with Myrna's and my friends, who would confirm our love and the constant tenderness of the care I gave her. Again, all true, but not the whole truth. My attorney concluded that it was unlikely that any jury could agree on a verdict.

This exchange of letters was in preparation for a plea bargain, and on March 22, 1996, I did plead guilty to a reduced charge of attempted manslaughter on the promise that I would be sentenced to only six months in jail. Again, the entire process followed a script I never saw. My role was to say "Yes" or "I did" to whatever questions the judge asked me. I had told my lawyer that if the judge at any point even indirectly hinted that Myrna was a victim, I would not accept the bargain.

I believe that my attorney, the D.A., and the judge had agreed in advance that the questions would be bland and fact specific: Did you prepare the mixture that killed your wife? Did you help her hold the cup from which she drank it? There were also the required questions about whether I fully understood what I was doing in agreeing to plead guilty. I walked out of the courtroom still a free man—until May 17, when the probation department would file its obligatory report, the sentence would be pronounced, and my jail term begin.

I was completely satisfied with this resolution of the case. I did not want the case to go to trial, which I saw as a waste of time and money I didn't have. Unless I successfully persuaded the jury to completely ignore the law I had broken, I could end up spending at least two years in prison. The more likely outcome would be a hung jury, another year wasted, and an insurmountable mountain of debt. And a trial, with its legal rules and adversarial style, along with the inevitable melodrama created by the press, would only obscure the issues that are important to me.

I sometimes imagine how hypothetical jurors might react to the whole story and answer the questions raised here. If one of them believed that this physical life is sacred and that only God can take it, I would be condemned. If another believed that it is certain qualities—memory, self-awareness, hope, and above all the exchange of love—that make human life truly valuable, then I had brought Myrna the only cure available for the disease that was robbing her of these qualities, and I would be exonerated. But I hope and believe that most jurors would not have a heartfelt certainty about these things and would be unable to come to a decision that left them unscathed. For it seems to me that all the great ethical questions, the truly hard questions, must forever remain unresolved, or passion is only theatrical pretense, not the rich agony of real life.

When I am in the slough of self-doubt and guilt, I ask the question strangers ask, "Did she really want to die?" But when I look back on our years together, on our joys and sorrows, our hopes and disappointments, our years of peace and years of dread, I begin to see that the ending was in the beginning, that it was all a wholeness, complete in each moment of the passing stream, not just in the last one. And then I know a quietness of heart and a new quickness of spirit and say Amen to our life—and death.

In the first few days after my release from the Tombs back in July 1995, the media was on me like a rabid dog. For the most part they were respectful and decent enough. I gave one interview, to the *New York Times,* and refused all other opportunities to talk. One or two newspapers reported there was a twenty-nine-page suicide note, completely confusing the single-paragraph note Myrna had signed with the long diary I had turned over to the police. Once the media got the idea I was going to be silent, they began to leave me alone. Besides, the trial of O. J. Simpson had started up again, and they needed the space left over from advertising to cover that much-sexier story.

I stayed close to home, except for one trip by subway to the Wall Street area to pick up some work. (I work as a freelance editor out of an office in my apartment.) On the way to the subway, a street person, black, approached me. I checked my pockets for the quarters I usually give when asked for a handout. But this guy had a different kind of handout in mind. "You the guy did his old lady?" Hesitantly, I said, "Yes." He raised an open hand to the height of his head, and I flinched before I realized he was giving me a high-five. "Put her there, man. Guts!" I don't know if he was approving of my having helped Myrna to escape or, if he believed that wives in general should be offed. I hope he didn't go home and "do" his, if he had a home.

On the subway trip back from downtown, a young man sat down beside me and began reading the story in the *Post*. There I was, staring at my photograph in the paper, while the stranger beside me was too engrossed in the second-hand news to notice that the subject of the story was sharing his seat. Across the aisle, a woman noticed, recognizing me from the story in the paper. I must have looked very disconcerted, because she gave me a wink, a shrug, and an amused smile—New York sophistication at its finest.

The days before the funeral all ran together. On Thursday afternoon, July 6, my son from my previous marriage, Conrad, and his wife, Joy, arrived from California. My daughter, Anna, also from the previous marriage, had wanted to come, but she was five months along in her first pregnancy, which was difficult, and her doctor prohibited travel for her. It was a profound comfort to hug Conrad and Joy and have them take over the apartment and tell me what to do.

On Friday we loaded up a limousine with friends and family and headed for New Haven, Connecticut, where Myrna would be buried in the cemetery that held the graves of her mother and father.

The short service at the funeral home was quiet and dignified, attended by nearly one hundred people. I spoke first, to briefly comment on only one of Myrna's virtues: "In all the twenty-seven years I knew Myrna, nearly all her adult life, I never once heard her say anything cruel, anything mean, anything even insensitive about another person. In this trait alone, she was one of the Lord's unique creatures. She often said, only half joking, that she was naturally lovable. It was true: Everyone who knew her well loved her. A light has gone out in the world; it is a darker place now." I could not have said more without breaking down.

Myrna's sister Beverly spoke lovingly of her sister at greater length.

The cantor of Myrna's and my synagogue gave the eulogy, noting that he and Myrna had both been born and raised in New Haven and had gotten to know each other fairly well after the death of Myrna's mother. He emphasized Myrna's personal courage in her long struggle with multiple sclerosis and how she had dealt with her losses without complaint or despair. He concluded: "Myrna, your courage and strength have been an inspiration to all of us whom you leave behind. May your memory ever serve as a blessing to us and all those who loved you, whose lives were profoundly affected by yours."

At the cemetery, after Myrna's coffin was lowered into the ground and the other prayers and kaddish said, I rushed forward to be the first to shovel dirt on her grave. I felt it was my duty, an obligation not to hang back and let others begin the end of what I had started. Almost blinded by tears, I threw in my shovelful and nearly tumbled in after it. But I braced the shovel against the ground and fell back instead. Friends caught me and sat me in a chair.

Afterward, we went to a cousin of Myrna's who graciously fed us all. Because the Sabbath was fast approaching, I couldn't stay long. I and those who had come to New Haven with me piled into our monstrous limousine and were back in the city by four.

I wrote in my diary a few days later:

In the reflective peace of the Sabbath, I have been able to make some sense of my feelings, which include almost every feeling available: guilt, anxiety, fear, depression, loneliness, gratitude, and a numbing grief. The guilt is awful, though I know it's foolish. I just don't feel like the courageous hero some people say I am, more like a damn fool who wandered into a moral morass out of the habit of service. But I had no choice. Still, I am haunted by memories of that night. To anyone thinking of doing likewise, I would have to say, "Do not do it without preparing yourself for the aftershocks. Beware, beware."

Earlier in the week a comforting friend, who had often helped wheel Myrna back and forth to synagogue on Sabbath mornings, came by to protest my having told the *New York Times* that our rabbi had suggested, when we had asked months before, that suicide might be acceptable. My friend pointed out that the information would hurt a great many people who had refused to help loved ones die in the correct belief that Orthodox Judaism forbids suicide in virtually all circumstances.

I can't remember what I replied, but I know what I would say now: We who are asked to help are going to be hurt whatever we do, whether we help or refuse to help. Irrational primitive guilt feelings, the loneliness of the decision, and the memories of the act itself, if carried out, create a permanent, open wound that only God can heal.

3

The Summer of Love

Our meeting and marriage, like Creation itself, must have been made in Heaven, because the possibility of their occurring by accident defies simple belief.

I was born in Carson City, Nevada, in 1932 and grew up on the edge of the desert in the small town of Sparks, just east of Reno. I was the oldest of three children; my two sisters were seven and twelve years younger. Myrna was born nearly eleven years later in green New England in a good-sized city, New Haven, Connecticut. She was the youngest of three children, with a brother, Ronald, twelve years her senior and a sister, Beverly, seven years older than her. With the exception of my maternal grandfather, an Easterner, my grandparents were born in the Far West; Myrna's grandparents were immigrants from Romania and Russia. I was raised in the Baptist Church, part of the great stew of American Protestantism. Myrna grew up in the bosom of a tightly knit Jewish community.

Myrna's father was a prosperous businessman who made a small fortune in the tire business during World War II; my father began his working life as a cowboy and ended it as a common laborer. Myrna lived most of her life in the same house in a strong and stable family. By the time I was fourteen, when my father walked out on us, I had lived in at least six different houses in four small Nevada towns. Myrna traveled to Europe when she was thirteen;

19

my first venture outside Nevada came at age fourteen when we moved to the "big city," Oakland, California.

In elementary school, Myrna worked hard and got good grades; she always said she was a perfect child. I loafed and got good grades, except in "deportment," where I consistently rated an "Unsatisfactory." Myrna graduated near the top of her high school class; I had to repeat two courses, Spanish and American history, because I hadn't done any homework. She immediately went off to prestigious Smith College, one of the "Seven Sisters." Her family could pay all her expenses.

After a stint in the Marines during the Korean War, mostly as a guard in a Navy brig, I used the G.I. Bill to go to Redlands University, one of the very adequate colleges in Southern California's would-be "Ivy League." My long-term aim at the time was to teach the freshman and sophomore general civilization courses common in most colleges of the day. Because religion is a central element in Western history, because I had, from early childhood, a passionate interest in matters religious, and because I wanted a more sophisticated education, I chose to go to Harvard Divinity School for three years, 1956 to 1959. This was financed largely by my first wife, whom I married in 1955, and in part by a very generous fellowship from the Danforth Foundation. From Harvard, I went on to Stanford, now wholly supported by that fellowship, to study Modern European History with an emphasis on Germany. Why Germany? That will become clear later, when I explain why I converted to Judaism.

Myrna spent her junior-year-abroad in Geneva. I didn't get to Europe until a year later, 1963, to do research for a doctoral thesis on a topic in labor history in pre-Nazi Germany. Our paths almost crossed; Myrna took a vacation in Greece in the spring of 1963; I spent nine months in Greece a year later. Then, in an emotional and moral crisis that I will describe more fully later, I dropped out of the academic life, separated from my wife and children, and for lack of other available employment, turned to social work, first in Los Angeles, in South Central, before and after the "Watts riots" there in 1965, and then in Brooklyn in 1966.

Despite the many differences, Myrna and I had many things in common: loving mothers, an interest in history, a love of movies, constant reading, pleasure in ideas, a detached interest in politics, and a rather timid taste for the exotic. We were both quietly and cautiously adventurous. We were both loners, intensely private people, uncomfortable in most social situations; uninterested in the social whirl, even bored by it. We both had the academic, intellectual tendency to analyze everything, to second-guess ourselves, to weigh our feelings carefully, to question them, to seek balance. A friend tells me this is a quality of character that is little understood by others, much less appreciated.

It was our interest in history that brought us together. A history major who leaves the academic life has few prospects. Working as a writer or editor is one of them, and New York City is the publishing metropolis of the United States. So we both found ourselves finally in New York. On graduating from Smith in 1964, Myrna spent a few months as an employment counselor in Boston, then moved to New York where she got a job editing newsletters on the global petroleum trade. I arrived a year later and, after a few months of social work in Brooklyn, finally found a job editing telephone repair manuals and research papers for AT&T and Bell Labs. On Friday and Saturday nights I worked as a hotel clerk.

History majors are also generalists with a wide range of knowledge about politics, government, military affairs, social conflict, economics, etc. So they will seek out jobs that make use of this kind of knowledge. In the summer of 1967 Myrna found a job with a little outfit called Deadline Data on World Affairs. It was a mom-and-pop operation of about eight people who, each week, published updates of an ongoing chronology of political, economic, and social events in every country in the world. Each chronological entry was accompanied by one or two quotes from the world press. It was necessary that one be able to read at least two foreign languages in order to work there. Myrna was fluent in French and could read German.

On March 4, 1968, eight months after Myrna started there, I also went to work at Deadline Data, or DD for short. I was nearly fluent in German and could read French and Spanish. I had arrived at about the same place in my career as Myrna had in hers, but ten years later in my life. That March 4, though I didn't realize it, was the real beginning of my life.

I was not impressed, however, with Myrna Lebov. She struck me as too young, too flighty, a scatterbrain, a bit of a frump, and too earnest about doing a perfect job. She, on the other hand, confessed later to having had fantasies about this tall, bearded, blond *goy*, an "older man." We were both involved with other people: she with a childhood friend from New Haven, I with a Rubenesque blonde with a taste for poetry, booze, and nightlife.

DD had just been sold to McGraw-Hill and was to become part of another McGraw-Hill acquisition, Defense Market Survey, or DMS, which was hoping to establish a global version of its U.S. survey. The man in charge of this new venture, a former army intelligence officer (who proved that "army intelligence" is an oxymoron), lived in Towson, Maryland—so DD was about to move to the Baltimore area.

That was fine with me. My little studio apartment on East 25th Street in Manhattan, a fourth-floor walk-up, had been burgled three times in the previous eighteen months, and I was happy to leave the city until such time as I could afford an apartment in a more secure building. I also had the crafty feeling that my two immediate superiors at DD would not last long outside of New York and would soon leave to return to their publishing mecca. I would then, I imagined, by dint of age and my own slight military experience, become DD's managing editor.

Myrna had other plans. She was going to film school in the fall and would only move to Baltimore for the summer to help DD get settled and to make some money for the coming year. Myrna and I and our two immediate bosses were the only New Yorkers to move to Baltimore. Jack, the managing editor, returned to New York every weekend that summer. Ed, the associate editor, was married; his weekends were also accounted for. Myrna and I were the only people we knew in Baltimore; we were thrown together. To get around, I bought an old VW Bug. For company, I asked Myrna to go to the beach with me—a three-hour drive across the

Chesapeake Bay, eastern Maryland, and Delaware to Rehobeth Beach. It was on these long summer Saturdays or Sundays, at the beach and on the long drives back and forth, that Heaven's plans began to be realized.

The summer of '68. The last Summer of Love, the beginning of the end of hippydom in hard drugs, despair, and violent activism. The year had been packed with monstrous events: January, the Tet offensive that turned so many Americans against the war in Vietnam; March, the virtual resignation of President Lyndon Johnson, who announced he would not run for reelection; April, the assassination of Martin Luther King Jr. and riots and burning in central cities across the country (Baltimore was especially hard hit and the scars were evident all through the city); June, the assassination of Bobby Kennedy. In August, the Democratic convention in Chicago would see police beating students in the streets. In November, the country would elect Richard Nixon president and continue its long slide into a moral malaise from which it has yet to recover.

Myrna and I talked about all these things as we drove back and forth to the beach and on our trips to New York to see our respective lovers. We were not hippies: I was already beyond the age of trustworthiness ("Don't trust anyone over thirty."), and both of us were too oriented toward conventional living to do more than experiment with some hippy pastimes; that is, an occasional joint if, and only if, someone else did the buying. We were both liberal Democrats, however, and strongly opposed to the war in Vietnam.

We also talked about our pasts and our families and our hopes and ideals. She amused me with a wry, sly sense of humor, and astonished me with a profoundly realistic, unsentimental sense of political possibilities. Where my view of the immediate future was always distorted by my hopes and optimism, her view was cold, clear, utterly without illusions. Her hopes did not cloud her objectivity; she saw increasing chaos and repression down the road. I began to find her intriguing.

Intriguing was and is a word I use a lot. I find many things intriguing; the world is an interesting place, many things in it puzzle me, and I enjoy a good puzzle. Everything, from the lay of the land to the behavior of dogs to the myriad follies of humankind, can and usually does lead me to ask questions. Myrna found my "intriguing" intriguing.

During one of those long drives, we found an area of disagreement over a fundamental issue of life. The subject was cheating. Myrna confessed that she often cheated in games. It was only a game, after all, the aim was to win, and the rules were often obstacles to the aim. Cheating was not only permissible, it was almost required. But in life, not to follow the rules was to disappoint and hurt people; the rules are important and must be followed as best one can.

I argued, on the other hand, that a game is senseless if the rules aren't followed. No rules, no game; and winning is not the point of the game, the pleasure of playing the game is. Further, the rules of a game are not ambiguous and not in conflict. But in life, which has its own natural rules and, most important, ultimate stakes, breaking ambiguous and contradictory social rules may be necessary to bring about a desirable end for others as well as for oneself. It is not to be done lightly, of course, or brashly, but with due consideration and a full assumption of responsibility for the consequences, foreseen and unforeseen. We could not have imagined that the issue would become a matter of life and death for us.

I grew to admire Myrna. One of my favorite activities is to play with ideas—any idea, however outlandish or disgusting—to see where they might lead and what light they might throw on reality. Many people can't do this. Hitting on a shocking idea, they immediately condemn it or ignore it. They can't hold it in their minds as a "what if." Myrna could, sometimes making leaps of imagination that delighted me and, sometimes, dismayed even me.

I found she was almost always gentle in her judgment of people, even when they deserved a beating. She was measured in all things, a virtue I had come to value immensely in the abstract, and she was moderate, not out of fear or sentimentality, but as a matter of sound judgment. She was generous with her feelings, reserving very little. She was guileless and without pretension, utterly lacking in even the rudiments of a facade. She had true unselfconscious enthusiasm, so that when she was well into a topic, her usually slow speech turned rapid and her waving hands said as much as her tongue. At a restaurant table, I often moved aside the glasses of water and wine and anything else she might accidentally knock over while concentrating on her point.

She found out I was divorced after nine years of marriage and had left two small children behind in California with their mother. I explained that I had grown up church-mouse poor and had been an ambitious, unreflective social climber, who had married well because, in part, in the fifties, marriage was the thing everyone did. As I matured, I told her, I began to realize I was trying to live a storybook life, not my life. I was not and did not want to be the goody-good young man I had pretended to be. I had been hiding out in academia, afraid of entering the larger world with its bottom lines and rough competition, but I had grown sick of the pettiness of academic politics. I had not really loved my ex-wife, and I was ashamed of myself and my callowness. In short, I had been a fraud who had lost himself in the pretense. I had also been very depressed, to the point of suppressing nearly all emotion, a condition which three years of therapy after the separation had helped me overcome.

I also explained that I had serious self-doubts about being a father. Not having had a decent father of my own, I had no feel for the role. I told her I had even lost track of my children's whereabouts because I felt I had no right to interfere in my ex-wife's life in any way and she had not informed me when they had moved without leaving a forwarding address. I knew I could get in touch again through the grandparents when and if I could ever help them.

Myrna didn't know what to make of my consuming interest in religious issues. Religion for her, being Jewish, was an open-and-shut case. To her, questions about God had been more or less unsatisfactorily settled by rabbis long ago and didn't concern her. Religion was a comfortable set of customs and semiannual celebrations at Passover and Rosh Hoshana/Yom Kippur. "Questing," that nomadic drift from Western religion to Eastern mysticism to esoteric cult to mind-altering drugs, was simply not in the Tarot cards for her. She was Jewish and that was that. So we didn't talk religion much; it bored her.

We began spending time together some evenings after work, taking in a movie or play, or grabbing a bottle of wine and some Colonel Sanders chicken, which we would take to Loch Raven, a nearby reservoir, where we could find relief from the summer heat. Myrna learned that although I *might* marry my New York lady, I doubted she would move to Baltimore and was more relieved than not by that prospect. I learned that although Myrna *might* marry her New Haven boyfriend, she doubted she could be happy with an IBM computer salesman.

And so, inevitably perhaps, the day came, August 24, 1968, a Saturday, when I kissed her at the beach. Myrna kept a diary, in which she wrote of that event: "blanket—read—talk—laugh—tempting—silence—look—kiss—beard—play—laugh—eyes—look—surprise—gentle." We didn't jump into bed right away. Myrna wanted to observe some proprieties and think about it. So we drove back to Baltimore with the question hanging in the air.

The next evening we went to a forgettable movie and stopped off at the Western Union office to send telegrams to the Democratic convention in Chicago urging the candidacy of "Clean Gene" McCarthy. Then we were waylaid by a spectacular fire in a large retail paint store. The paint made for an exciting, colorful, and very hot fire, which the firemen could scarcely contain, let alone extinguish.

So with fire outside and in, we adjourned to my studio apartment and fell, as if from the natural force of gravity, into bed. But it was not gravity, it was levity. Our lovemaking then and almost always thereafter was as playful as three year olds in a sandbox or two puppies tumbling and tossing each other about. In Myrna's diary it was: "fire—heat—fun-filled—giggle—FIRST—stunned and shocked." I'm not sure what she meant by "FIRST," but since I was not her first lover, I can only imagine that it was her first orgasm. Thus always do dirty old men ensnare young innocence.

Our relationship at that point was unusually ambiguous. We were both slightly attached to lovers we were not too happy with. Myrna was headed for New York and film school, while I was planning to stay in Baltimore. I assumed, largely on the basis of our age difference and Myrna's strong family loyalty, that we were a temporary item. I could accept that, but it saddened Myrna. I didn't love her—yet—but she was infatuated, at least, with me. I remember feeling strongly that we had no future together. But then why did I show her "Revelation"?

Another effective snare used by dirty old men is to bare the soul of the poet in one's breast. I had begun writing poetry in 1963, when my Christian faith fell to pieces and my marriage began to unravel. Poetry was a way of ruminating on the meaning of my life and life in general. I began to read more poetry and to read about the lives of some poets I particularly admired—Yeats, Graves, Frost, Eliot. In Greece, a Greek friend introduced me to Rainer Maria Rilke with a gift of his *Letters to a Young Poet*. Rilke's sensibility—his tentativeness, his delicacy (effeminate at times), his images—resonated with my feelings and aspirations. I bought a translation of his *Duino Elegies*, and studied it as if it were a Bible. I began to write poetry, or snatches of poetry, with increased seriousness:

> Afraid of the barbarians,
> I built a Chinese Wall:
> words on paper in an empty room.
>
> They broke in anyway—
> through the semicolon,
> the half-thought,
> the pause for breath.

Back in Los Angeles I had joined a writing group led by a published poet, and in New York I attended poetry readings in Greenwich Village. I never read my work in public. I thought it too amateurish. I got into a poetry class taught by Adrienne Rich at the YMHA on the strength of a poem written earlier in the year. When the six sessions of the class were over, the group continued to meet to share and critique our work.

One early evening, in the fall of 1967, I was preparing to go out on a date with a new lady. I ran a bath (I had no shower), slipped into the tub, and lay back to grab a minute of relaxation. Then, "Heaven blazing into the head," I leaped from the tub, grabbed a pen, and wrote ten words. I had seen, in one sharp flash, the images and structure of a long poem that would crystalize four years of thinking. The ten words were triggers, each invoking a panoply of images for the ten sections of the poem.

I took my bath, dressed, and went off on my date, utterly confident that I could not forget an iota of what I had seen. When I returned from the date, not having thought about the poem at all, I scribbled it out in one sitting.

"Revelation" was the sum and substance of my soul then. Did I show it to Myrna a couple of days after our first bedding to ensnare her? Or to warn her off? The poem is as dark or darker than Matthew Arnold's profoundly pessimistic "Dover Beach." Where Arnold envisioned the possibility of love and trust—"Ah, love, let us be true to one another"—I concluded: "Only, now, let us glance at each other. Yes! We will be blind, and oh! half dead a long while on these strange roads."

But perhaps the poem merely came up as we discussed the chaos in the streets of Chicago, where police, oblivious to the television cameras, were brutally beating up young people protesting the nomination of Hubert Humphrey for president. For the poem, after questioning the sources of human morality and the nature of God, says of the divinity:

> Let's put pretense aside and name it:
> CHAOS!
> Blessed Father/Mother of us all,
> disguised for Carnival in time and space,
> the mask of forming power on its ugly face.

In her diary, Myrna wrote: "Humphrey nominated—police brutality against young protesters—Is U.S. headed toward police state? Read some of George's poetry—allusive, subtle, intellectual. . . . "

Myrna left for New York and film school on September 15. My New York lover came down to Baltimore the following weekend, looked the city over, and pronounced it impossible: "Return to New York or we're finished." What a relief! I had already concluded that I should never contemplate marriage again, that I should not inflict my craziness, my rootlessness, on anybody. I would manage as a permanent bachelor. But Chaos had other things in mind.

Three weeks later, Columbus Day weekend, Myrna came back to Baltimore for a visit. I drove her to a beautiful spot I had discovered—Harpers Ferry, and later in the day, turning at random into a narrow lane, we dead-ended in an apple orchard where we made love, fully clothed, on the ground among the fallen leaves and apples.

Myrna wrote of that weekend: "Baltimore—George—so beautiful and comforting to sleep with him—arms around him during middle of night—endless talk—[The next day] Drive to Harpers Ferry—beautiful scenery—rolling hills—Wide panoramic vistas—fun—comfort—apple orchard, tree—love—smell of apples—subtle wind sound—beautiful experience—oneness."

I wrote Myrna that Monday: "Just a quick note to share my ebullient feeling of deep satisfaction, luckier-than-thou smugness, and idiot delight with our weekend. I'm happy to the apple core. I've thought about it carefully and cynically and decided that if I ever think life has not been good to me, I'll have forgotten you. You are delight walking, real with tears, and in the unenviable position of being loved by anyone who knows you. Shoot high, you'll hit it—whatever future you can grasp or bear. Love, George."

Later that week, I wrote:

PAST PROPER TURNING

We made love in October
in an apple orchard
in West Virginia.
How came we there—
you from Romania and points east,
I from Dublin and points west?

except   as windfalls   in an autumn
time past   proper   turning of seasons
into a fall   of leaves   already burned
with sunlight   we made love

```
      back to front      like animals      returning
    to an old core      of warmth      winter ahead
      and you      face down      in the love leaves
  with spring      only a bite away      under earth-skin
            we rooted and bloomed

    Over us      bare branches      the waiting frame
        of time      work      far places
    apples of politics      and war      and art . . .

          Oh! my love,
    we were parted      when we dropped.

          And afterwards, you said
          you thought that
          Adam *found* the fruit
          and offered it
          to Eve.
```

It was only the next day that it dawned on me that I had fallen in love, the snarer snared.

Another week went by before I sent the poem off to Myrna with a very off-hand proposal of marriage, phrased so indirectly that she didn't have to take it seriously if she chose not to. Or was I angling for "deniability"? Most of the letter had to do with a recent fight she had had with her boyfriend. I was avuncular, advising her not to get drawn into his drama but instead to pursue her own happiness. Then I lightened up: "When I put aside my concern for you, I do see a considerable joke in your concern for that hefty hunk [her boyfriend] and your ridiculously human attachment to your first real lover. But I love you anyway and, if you will, *I'll* marry you. There. And comedy or no, I mean it."

Reading that nearly thirty years later, I wonder at myself—the obvious self-interest behind the cellophane of good advice and the almost insulting oddity of that "proposal." Myrna's comment in her diary shows her good sense: "George sends poem about apple orchard—love—chance—proposes—S.C. talks to our class—Dynamic, intelligent, enthusiastic about film." She didn't say yes; she didn't say no. I didn't really expect her to.

That spring, my hunch about my immediate superiors proved true. They both returned to New York, and I became managing editor of Deadline Data. The big issue was whether Myrna would come down to Baltimore the next summer and live with me. She did, and we had a delightful reprise of the previous summer, with the added fillip that we found we got along easily at close quarters for extended periods. Marriage now looked more reasonable, but there was a major snag—Myrna's family.

Myrna's father had strongly urged her to marry her boyfriend from New Haven, a mistake on his part. Urging Myrna, I was to discover later, was tantamount to telling her to do the opposite. So Myrna had broken up with the boyfriend. Still, I was not something she wanted to bring home to her father. A divorced Irishman, ten years her senior, without money and of no discernible profession, was hardly what he had in mind for his youngest daughter. She had not made my existence known to the family. That summer, in fact, I was forbidden to answer the phone in the apartment; Myrna did not want them to think she had a new boyfriend, let alone that she was "living in sin."

At the end of the summer, however, as I was planning a vacation trip to California, Myrna surprised me. Her sister, Beverly, had just moved to the Pasadena area with her husband, a hospital administrator. Myrna set up a meeting. It seemed to go well. I stayed overnight in Bob and Bev's home and we exchanged pleasantries. I returned to Baltimore, and nothing was said about meeting the rest of the family.

4

Myrna's "Passage"

A month later the question of meeting the rest of the family became moot. Myrna's father died of a stroke at age sixty-two. During the mourning period in New Haven, Beverly's daughter Alison, with a five year old's innocence and guile, asked Myrna, in front of the assembled family, "Where's George?" So George was out of the bag. I met Myrna's mother two months later.

Her father's death shattered Myrna. He had been a benevolent despot, an ever-confident, all-comforting leader of the "I'll take care of everything" type. But after a long and very successful career as a businessman, he died bankrupt, having desperately risked everything he had in an effort to save his business. He left almost nothing for Myrna's mother. Myrna's feelings about him became very mixed. Perhaps to make up for her anger at his ultimate failure to provide, she reverted to his ideas regarding a proper lifestyle.

Suddenly I was besieged with questions about where and how we would live if we married, and it was clear that Myrna's inclination now was toward suburbia, a lawn, a child, and a Jewish husband. She toyed with the idea of returning to New Haven to live and take care of her mother. She virtually dropped out of film school, although she did complete her degree the following year.

Myrna had already begun some light psychotherapy with a group. Now she plunged into one-on-one therapy, fortunately with a good therapist. For the next three years, therapy was nearly half her life. Work was most of the rest; I occupied a corner, a respite when she needed it.

I had been through the therapy process myself from 1965 to 1968, starting out with once-a-week sessions, raising it to two after a year, and going to an intensive three per week for the last nine months. I knew how it occupied one's waking and sleeping thoughts. I also believed that Myrna needed therapy. She needed to discover a core of confidence in her abilities, a real sense of freedom to act without constantly second-guessing herself, and she needed to gain some perspective on her family. From random comments she made about her therapy, I learned something about her father . . . and for the first time in my life was able to give some thanks for mine.

My father had been physically abusive. His temper had been erratic and too often violent, particularly when he had been drinking. I recall my mother intervening on several occasions when she thought a whipping had gone too far, and I had watched, grateful and helpless, as his rage turned on her. The big "breakthrough" in my therapy came the day I "awoke" on the couch in a fetal position, gasping for breath after reliving the grinding terror I knew from age six to thirteen.

Compared to Myrna, though, I had been fortunate. Red weals on the back and bruises on the face make it hard to believe that a physically abusive father means only the best, but the intentions of a psychologically abusive father are harder to understand. Myrna could recall being struck only twice in her life. One blow was a ritual slap from her mother when she announced her first menstrual flow. The second blow, much harder, was from her father, who was enraged one summer evening when five-year-old Myrna went to bed in the late afternoon to escape the veiled (and empty) threats of her sister, who was to babysit her that night. Unwilling to tattle on Beverly, Myrna could not explain her behavior to her father, who hit her and derided her "lazy dreaming."

Myrna often bragged to me that she had been a perfect child and then confessed that it had only been because she was afraid of drawing down on herself the verbal wrath her father so often visited on Beverly. Myrna said he would fly into shouting rages if defied or even questioned, something that apparently only Beverly dared to do. In therapy Myrna came slowly to realize that terror had been a major part of her young life also, that much of her father's behavior was "hostile."

Nevertheless, Benjamin Lebov could be a doting and caring father who, particularly in the summer, would spend hours with the children, first in a modest bungalow on Long Island Sound and later, when the cash flow was at its peak, at a more comfortable beach house on the New Jersey shore. Myrna recalled these childhood summers with great nostalgia.

Myrna's older brother, Ronald, twelve years her senior, did not figure prominently in her memories. By the time she was six and beginning to accumulate lasting impressions, Ronald was away at college. But her big sister Beverly, seven years her senior, played a major role in Myrna's life. Here is a scattering of Myrna's memories:

- She still felt guilty for digging out and eating the soft interior of a fresh-baked loaf of bread, because Beverly was blamed and punished for the depredation while Myrna remained silent.
- She saved her pennies to buy her father birthday presents or would make something for him; Beverly would "borrow" money from him to buy him something fancy. Myrna recalled that while her father never showed any preference for one gift over another, Beverly was scornful of her little sister's gifts.
- The family once returned home from a vacation to find their home had been virtually cleaned out by thieves. This left Myrna with serious anxieties. Until she was thirty, she had nightmares about Arab terrorists raiding her home or apartment.
- When Beverly was preparing to go to college, her first choice was Barnard, a women's college associated with

Columbia University on the edge of Harlem in Manhattan. Her father drove her down to New York for an application interview, but on seeing the college's surroundings, drove right home again despite Beverly's protests. Beverly went to Vassar.

There were other shadows of something odd in the family. The most obvious was "the girls," Benjamin's three maiden sisters who lived together in the house their parents had lived in. Zelda, Ethel, and Lillian, in order of declining age, were all, I think, younger than Benjamin. Three more vacuous and self-centered people would be hard to imagine. Their lives were fantasy-filled and revolved around TV shows, movies, and celebrities. I called them "the weird sisters," Myrna later came to label them "the Blights."

Whenever we went to New Haven to visit Myrna's mother, Anne, a visit to the girls was de rigueur. Myrna and I would steel ourselves for an hour or two of one-way exchanges of trivia expressed without a trace of real interest, let alone enthusiasm or excitement. Most of the talking was done by Zelda; Ethel would add a clarification now and then. Lillian seldom spoke; she was considered slightly retarded. My own view was that she was too lazy and fearful to be interested in anything beyond her own fantasies.

The weirdness of these sisters did not make me question the soundness of the family as a whole. The harsh and ragtag life of the Old West imbued most Westerners with a simple acceptance of skeletons in the closet; everyone had them. With three grandparents dead of alcohol (one a suicide), an aunt who was a certified paranoid schizophrenic with homicidal tendencies, an alcoholic uncle, and a gypsy aunt who was probably also an alcoholic, my own house was too glassy for me to even think of picking up a stone.

The house the weird sisters lived in had been, in some way I never understood, a bone of contention in the greater Lebov clan long before I met Myrna. Whatever the cause, it created such an unbridgeable rift that I was unaware of the existence of a large number of relatives named Liebov and a smaller group named Libov until several years after Myrna and I were married. On acquaintance, I found these "lost" relatives to be such lively and open-hearted people that I began to suspect something mean and petty in Myrna's father that required their existence to be hidden for so long.

Still another piece of the puzzle fell into place in the last years of Myrna's life. Not long after her mother's death, Myrna began to receive phone calls from Uncle George, her mother's brother. I hadn't known Anne even had a brother! And he seemed to be, over the phone, a very sweet man, whose calls to Myrna were intended to cheer her and let her know a vestige of her mother still cared. I suspect that George's estrangement over all those years, like that of the Liebov-Libov clans, stemmed from an inability on the part of Myrna's father to tolerate any feelings of affection that extended beyond his immediate family. One can only imagine the kind of terror he had grown up with that he should have so great a fear of betrayal.

Overall, I concluded that Benjamin Lebov enforced a strict code of family loyalty and secrecy that virtually excluded outsiders, even close relatives. The family rule of secrecy, intentional or not, enabled the benevolent despot to rule more firmly and securely by cutting family members off from outside influences and making it difficult for the rest of the family to question their leader and protector, to get advice from others, and to think and act independently of the boss.

The upshot was a tradition of family solidarity in all circumstances. No other value was greater. Personal inclination, fair dealing, basic honesty—all were secondary to family loyalty. Myrna's way of coping with this code was withdrawal and silence. She might not assent to some of the family ways, but she would not criticize them. In later years, Myrna found it almost impossible to say anything negative about her early family life or about any family member. I believe she often felt guilty about her inability to totally submit to her family's need for unquestioning approval of her father's values.

Even her private diaries, which she kept from 1966 to 1976, are almost devoid of criticism. Where the average twenty-five- to thirty-five-year-old Manhattanite in therapy is all too ready to blame every trouble on Mommy and Daddy, Myrna never did. Outside of a single entry mentioning her father's hostility, her diaries are silent on the subject. How much did she open up to her therapist? I hope she told him a great deal more than she told me, which was almost nothing. In general conversation, her childhood was mostly an idyll. Only by accident and inference did I learn much about the family's past or anything that might cast a shadow on its storybook perfection.

That childhood idyll may have been created by Myrna's mother, Anne. Open, generous, accepting of others and interested in them, and long-suffering without bitterness, Anne must have cast steady sunlight on an often stormy scene. She had been orphaned early in life and had survived, in part, by adapting to whatever was required of her. Nevertheless, she did not lose a bouncy liveliness and good humor, an unselfconscious pleasure in herself and others.

She was short, with the strawberry blond hair, high cheekbones, and wideset eyes that suggested a Russian ancestor in the distant past. Her family, I believe, hailed from Odessa on the Black Sea. Anne had an old-fashioned Brooklyn accent with a hint of "dem," "dose," and "youse." Her reports of conversations were laced with "So I sez, I sez ... And she sez, she sez. . . ." Her speech would never have pleased a grammarian, but what she had to say usually made good sense.

If Anne had a fault, it was a common one—she told her children how much she loved them by telling them how worried she was about them. Myrna could not begin anything new or even continue on a well-worn path without her mother expressing worried concern, usually over trivia. This had the effect of reassuring Myrna of her mother's love while undermining her confidence and independence. Myrna only escaped from this double bind after therapy and constant reminders from me that her mother's worry was not real, that she had great confidence in Myrna and pride in her. What seemed like worry was only a twisted way of showing affection.

Anne and I met for the first time on Christmas Day, 1969. I took to her right away. I liked her earthiness, her Jewish mothering, and her sly sense of humor that seemed to surprise her as much as it amused others. She was more cautious about me, telling Myrna out of my hearing that she doubted I was only thirty-seven and that Myrna should not rush into anything. There was, furthermore, some incident in the past involving an Irishman that had given the family an abiding distrust of the breed.

Nevertheless, Anne seemed dutifully impressed by my education and my superficial knowledge of Judaism. And, I suspect, she was just a bit thankful that a mature man was seriously interested in her twenty-six-year-old daughter with the wallflower past, who seemed to her to be well on the way to spinsterhood.

Another year passed. The Baltimore enterprise failed, and I moved Deadline Data, the only profitable part of it, to company headquarters in Greenwich, Connecticut. Myrna and I began to see a great deal more of each other in spite of the strain over her father's values. Over the summer of 1970, she slowly began to recover from the shock of her father's death. She decided not to go to New Haven, finished her master's degree in film, and began to flower anew.

But she had emerged badly scarred. Intellectually and emotionally, her view of the sum of life had now reached that nadir the German-British scholar Eric Heller called "the disinherited mind" in his book with that title. In *The Savage God*, a book about depression and suicide among artists, A. Alvarez describes this state of mind as continually asking "the perennial question 'What am I?' without benefit of moral, cultural, or even technical securities." The great portrayer of this condition is Samuel Beckett and its icon is his *Waiting for Godot*. At its worst, I call it "the passage," a narrow strait where one is constantly in danger of running onto the rocks of utter despair and from which one can never emerge.

I recently encountered the worst of "the passage" in a dream. I was visiting Switzerland and happened on an institution that cared for refugee children from Bosnia. The children were gathered in a fenced playground at the back of the building, a playground equipped with every imaginable apparatus on which children could entertain themselves.

But the children paid no attention to the equipment. They only stared into the distance, their bodies assuming odd postures, their faces frozen, their eyes empty. One boy made the hip-thrusting gestures of sexual intercourse against a wall. Another boy clung to a slightly older girl, gently tapping his tear-stained face against her shoulder as she blankly ignored him. These children had seen horrors beyond bearing. I was filled with rage, and I thought how good it would be to bring to these children the men who had created their agony so the children could tear them apart.

Later, awake, I realized the children would treat those monsters with the same indifference they had shown me. For in a world in which God is dead, everything may be permitted, but nothing is justified. In "the passage," even Solomon's "vanity" is of no avail. All is futility.

Myrna put it this way in her diary after attending High Holy Day services one year: "Yom Kippur—Kol Nidre—Essentially rhetorical questions [in the Kol Nidre service]—'What is our life and of what avail our strength?'—No answers for me—God indifferent—Not necessary."

This aspect of Myrna's thinking had been hidden from me. I first became aware of it, glancingly, in the summer of 1970, when I made a random comment about a particularly nihilistic point of view expressed in an article I was reading. Myrna responded with a shrug and said something that implied that the writer hadn't even begun to imagine how meaningless life is. On another occasion Myrna simply looked at me as if I were a fool when I momentarily entertained an idea of moral progress.

In "the passage," there is no use searching for the meaning of life; there isn't any. Wealth, social status, reputation, pleasure, even competence—all are trivial and unsatisfying. In "the passage," each individual must create meaning, finding a reason to go on, a way to cope with the constant threat of running aground on the rocks of futility. This is the subject of that other great icon of "the passage," Albert Camus's *The Myth of Sisyphus*, which both Myrna and I had devoured more than once.

Myrna did not talk about her "passage" and, outside of reading Camus, showed no need to understand it or "cope" with it. That worried me. I had a dozen different religious ideas and questions to put wind in my spiritual sails and strong poetic images mapping the rocks and shoals of the passage. Myrna appeared to have nothing. How did she manage to survive? It was only later, when she began to show an interest in returning to the observances of traditional Judaism, that I began to think that it was pure grit that sustained her, a grit bred in her Jewish soul.

5

Discovering Disease—
Saying "I Do"

When Myrna and I first met, she shared an apartment on the Upper East Side of Manhattan with a roommate. She lived there until about a year before we were married. I, on the other hand, was an Upper West Sider. Many people on each side of Central Park are snobbish about what they see as the virtues of their side and the failings of the other. From my point of view, an Upper East Sider is halfway to abandoning the city and moving to the suburbs. The area is predominantly white, upper middle class, and upwardly mobile or already very comfortably settled. It supposedly has less crime than the Upper West Side.

My side of Central Park is far more multiethnic and multiracial and populated not by executives and white-collar climbers, but by performing artists, literati, and people with only a secondary interest, if any, in money and social status. On the Upper West Side, intellectuals, blacks, Orthodox Jews, gays, Hispanics, atheists—all the variety of urban mankind—mingle in an atmosphere that is unusually appreciative of our differences.

The area stretches from Lincoln Center on the south, roughly 64th Street, to Columbia University, at 116th Street, on the north.

East to west, it extends from Central Park to the Hudson River and Riverside Park. The north-south avenues—Central Park West, Columbus, Amsterdam, Broadway, West End, and Riverside—are broad and busy roadways. The east-west streets are quiet residential areas dominated by old brownstones, many of which have been converted into flats. Central Park West, West End, and Riverside are also predominantly residential, with huge apartment buildings dating back to the early twentieth century. Some of them, such as the Dakota, where John Lennon lived and died, were built soon after the Civil War.

Columbus, Amsterdam, and Broadway, at street level, are largely devoted to retail business. An Upper West Sider can buy almost anything the world has to offer without walking more than a few blocks. Although the streets are jammed with cars, many Upper West Siders live for years without owning a car and its headaches. At 80th and Broadway, one finds Zabar's, perhaps the most complete delicatessen in the world—certainly the most famous. The area also boasts four multiplex movie houses, including one devoted to foreign films. From the Metropolitan Opera and New York Philharmonic at Lincoln Center to the vast libraries of Columbia (open to the public for a sizable fee), the Upper West Side reeks of high culture, while along the avenues and side streets, one hears the sounds of salsa and rap, Judy Collins and Metallica.

The place teems with humanity. On a sunny weekend day, the sidewalks are jammed with people shopping in stores that are nearly all open seven days a week, eating at the outdoor tables of the many restaurants (from Burmese to Moroccan), sifting through remaindered and old books offered by sidewalk vendors, and dodging the ubiquitous panhandlers. The variety and density of experience is intense.

I first became acquainted with the Upper West Side in the summer of 1966 when my girlfriend of the time moved there from Brooklyn Heights. Two years later, when I returned to New York from Baltimore, I sublet an unfurnished apartment on 82nd Street between Amsterdam and Columbus. For the first time I was living on the Upper West Side, and I loved it.

I also began to repair relations with my children. I found out from their grandparents where they were (a small mountain town east of Bakersfield, California) and began to send money for their support. At Christmas in 1971, Anna, then twelve years old, came to visit me for a week. It was not a comfortable reunion for either of us. It had been six years since I had seen her. She was now a moody preteen, not a little girl, but she was still a quiet, serious person with a streak of fey humor. And still a beauty, with dark red hair, alabaster skin, and big brown eyes with lashes some women would pay thousands for. Her reserve was intense, but she had obviously become a very intelligent, very self-reliant person, with a decided, if insecure, sense of self. Anna was understandably wary and as tense as I was, and I was rather at a loss as to how to entertain her. She was cool toward Myrna, and the feeling was reciprocated. Nevertheless, it was a beginning.

Soon after Anna left for California, I began hearing rumors that McGraw-Hill was going to sell DD's parent company, DMS. I began to look for another job and quickly found the best job of my life. On March 4, 1972, four years to the day that I began work at DD, I became the editor of *The World Almanac*, a thousand-page book of facts that sold about one million copies a year. The job presented exciting new challenges in a pleasant work environment and paid a good deal more that I had made at DD.

That same spring, I was very surprised, and both pleased and angry, when Myrna moved to the Upper West Side not long after my sublet had expired and I had taken new temporary quarters in Greenwich Village. Although I had long touted the Upper West Side to her, I hadn't the slightest idea that she was thinking of moving from her apartment, let alone moving to "my" area. Obviously she had not told me because she didn't want to be pressured into getting an apartment with me. At twenty-nine, she wanted to try living alone, in her own place, for the first time in her life. Living alone was a step Myrna had to take to complete her independence, her sense of self-direction, and competence.

I saw the move as a rejection, incomprehensible in light of my long-standing proposal of marriage and my new status as editor of a national publication. In fact, the move was toward, not away, from me. It showed an acceptance of my values in contrast to her family's and a new sense of freedom and experimental verve. It clearly marked the end of her long mourning for her father.

Myrna's new one-bedroom apartment was a cheery, sunny place in a large old apartment building at the corner of 83rd and Broadway. She didn't ask my help in the move or in fixing up the apartment; this was her domain, and she didn't want a "significant other" kibitzing. She repainted it herself with help from friends, had the parquet floors sanded and polyurethaned, and decorated the walls with her favorite art: a Daumier lithograph, an antique ivory bas relief of Tristan and Isolde, and odds and ends of posters. In the entry way, she mounted a series of three cartoon pictures cut from a greeting card that said a great deal about her view of the world and herself.

The first cartoon showed a small snail creeping along the bottom of the card. The second showed a massive block of stone falling toward the snail. The third cartoon showed the block of stone beginning to split in half and fall away on contact with the snail's shell. Myrna was saying that her vulnerability was stronger than the crushing weight of the threatening world around her. Her bleak realism and her zest for life had found a resolution, a unity, in courage. Was there also in these pictures a premonition of the crushing weight that would fall on her less than two years later?

We lived together in that apartment the following summer, the summer of 1972. It was a happy time for both of us. We fell easily into a pattern of cooking on alternate evenings; whoever didn't cook, washed the dishes. The old rules applied—I could not answer the phone. Myrna did not want her mother to know her daughter was "living in sin." But I knew Anne, and I believe she would have preferred to know that her daughter and boyfriend were normal adults.

We took a half-share in a Fire Island house together and spent wonderfully relaxed weekends there in a little beach community called Lonelyville, not far from Fair Harbor and within walking distance of Ocean Beach. We focused on doing nothing—simply lying around on the beach, reading, endlessly talking, and partying with old friends and new acquaintances at night.

When the summer came to an end, I returned to my new sublet in the Village, disappointed that Myrna did not want to continue the arrangement or marry me. I began casting about for an apartment of my own and began to contemplate a life without Myrna. I found a modern studio apartment in midtown, near Columbus Circle, and enjoyed planning its decor and furnishing. But the cold modernity of the building and apartment were not my style; I never really felt at home there.

That Christmas, my son, Conrad, came to visit me for the first time. He was ten years old, a bright and lively stringbean of a boy who took after his mother's family in looks but was more like mine in personality—imaginative, curious, reckless, and outgoing, while retaining, even at that age, a certain reserve or confident self-possession. We explored New York and took a trip to Washington, D.C., where he met a "big shot"—Ralph Nader, with whom I had a brief conversation over the possibility of publishing an almanac of American politics. Conrad and Myrna established an easy rapport rather quickly, based to some extent on their mutual amusement over my foibles.

The stalemate with Myrna, however, continued to anger me. My new status and the money that went with it led me to believe that these issues ought no longer to concern Myrna. I began to think that Myrna had psychological blocks that would, perhaps, forever stand in the way of marriage. I resolved to bring matters to a head, finally and conclusively.

I told Myrna I wanted a three-month separation, during which we would not see each other or communicate. When the three months were up, *I* would decide whether to renew the relationship. Myrna accepted this fiat with both disappointment and disbelief; she knew I loved her and had counted on my steadiness. My own feelings were very mixed. I hoped, on the one hand, that I would find another partner, and on the other, that the separation would make clear to Myrna that I was important to her, too important to lose. What I got in the meantime was a three-month reversion to my early days in the city—an unpleasant round of unsuitable dalliances, made all the more pointless, even disgusting, by my longing to be with Myrna.

Myrna did not let any grass grow under her feet. She had a whirlwind affair with a young, good-looking and well-off garment-district figure who took her to fine restaurants and on ski trips in Vermont. But her diary reveals that she found him withdrawn, immature, and a bit dull. He had no love of film, no intellectual interests, no passion for books, no interest in the language.

I hadn't talked to Myrna for three months when I finally called her, in early April 1973, and asked how she was doing.

"Awful. I'm off work. I can hardly walk or see and I can't button my clothes at all."

"What is it? What do the doctors say?" She had been through a string of doctors in the last couple of years—dermatologists, ophthalmologists, general practitioners, gynecologists, neurologists—to diagnose and treat a bewildering array of temporary symptoms ranging from hypersensitivity to touch, blurred or double vision, tingling in the lower legs, and a mild vertigo.

"A new doctor at NYU, a neurologist, says it's a 'demyelinating disease.' He says I need complete bed rest, so I'm going to Charlotte's for a week or two."

Charlotte was Myrna's older cousin by marriage. She lived in a big old house in Brooklyn. I got Charlotte's number and told Myrna I'd call her there in the next few days.

I hung up, walked around to the office of a medical writer, and borrowed his Merck manual, a compendium of disease descriptions. My guess on the spelling of *demyelination* was close enough, and I was soon looking at a list of symptoms I was too familiar with and had begun to think were psychological, a way of putting me off when I was particularly pressing about marriage.

It was multiple sclerosis, a disease of the central nervous system without known cause or cure that could, *but might not,* lead to progressive destruction of the brain with attendant loss of motor functions, eyesight, sense of taste, speech, and memory. In its initial stages, the disease is *usually, but not always,* marked by periods of indeterminate length when one or more symptoms appear, sometimes with severity, followed by similar indeterminate periods when all symptoms disappear and normal function is restored. This exacerbation-remission phase is *often, but not always,* followed by a chronic-progressive phase in which symptoms do not disappear and loss of function is permanent.

In both phases, the development of the disease is unpredictable, and in some cases, even the most severe, it will "plateau," inflicting no new symptoms or disabilities. The chief characteristic of the disease is its utter unpredictability. I thought of it as the quintessential disease of the existential twentieth century, as tuberculosis had been the appropriate disease for the romantic nineteenth.

So I had a big problem. I had been asking Myrna to marry me for more than four years, from October 1968 to December of 1972. For three of these four years, I could understand why she might not want to marry me, an editor who was just barely making a living as manager of an odd little publication that was just barely surviving. But I was now in a job that paid well and carried a modicum of prestige.

But now, even if she did refuse to marry me, could I just abandon her because of the multiple sclerosis? I questioned my capacity to bear with her the possibly terrible future she faced. On the other hand, could I live without her? So while Myrna stayed at Charlotte's for two weeks, I explored the problem from every angle, even taking the unusual step (for me) of asking friends what they thought about the situation. My friends were unanimous in suggesting that I was lucky in having begun to break off with Myrna and advising me to end it completely.

On the other hand, I was sick of the "meat market" of guys and gals putting on their best fronts, trying to sort out their feelings, falling into bed, and arguing over details arising from fundamental incompatibilities they tried to pretend weren't real. I believed I would never find anyone I felt as comfortable and happy with as I did with Myrna. I loved her and was beginning to find out what "love" really meant. If I walked away, I might never find out any more.

And there was the fact that I had already walked away from a previous marriage, leaving behind a wife and two children and creating for myself a persistent deep guilt that cried out for redemption. If I walked away from Myrna, the guilt would only be compounded. I would lose my chance to become fully human.

Most important and persuasive, however, was the simple fact that I could not walk away; Myrna and concern for her were now, willy-nilly, whatever I did, a permanent part of my life.

So when she returned to her apartment in Manhattan, I wrote her a note and sent it to her with a potted cactus. The note, which she kept with all my old love letters, read:

April 23, 1973

Dearest Myrna,

I've thought long and hard about you and me and us. I think we know each other as well or better than we know anyone else in the world. We know how to please each other and how to irritate each other. We know our strengths and weaknesses. We pretty much know what we can expect from each other.

But we each need certain assurances.

You need the assurance that I will be a reliable father, knowing that I am not eager to have another child. All I can say is that I was once a kind, firm, fair, and loving father—and I can be again, with your help. And while I may not want a child in the abstract, I can be a sucker for one in the flesh.

I need to be assured that you love me, want me, and trust me. You can provide that assurance by answering "yes" to this question:

Will you please marry me?

Your answer (yes or no) doesn't have to be given now, or next month or even next year. I've waited; I'll go on waiting.

    Faithfully,
    George

P.S. Try as I might, I can't stop loving you.

The cactus, Myrna would know, represented me—surviving and thriving in the most arid conditions, not much to look at and prickly on the outside, but full of the cool, sweet water of life inside.

To my utter surprise, Myrna called me quickly to say simply, "Yes!" I've always believed there were two reasons for that answer. The more important one was that a very close friend of Myrna's, her former roommate, whom she admired for her independence and boldness, had recently decided to marry, which told Myrna that even the most independent woman could remain her own boss in marriage. Second, Myrna was taking prednisone, a corticosteroid that provides protection for nerve cells under attack and may, as a side effect, induce either feelings of anxiety and depression or of confidence and self-satisfaction. Myrna may well have been feeling the latter effect. So, for two reasons, Myrna had new hopes for marriage.

A few days later we went together to see her neurologist. I had said nothing of what I knew about the disease and her threatened future. I wasn't a doctor; it was not my place to say anything. I could only cause her anxiety and doubt of me until she heard the truth from a doctor. Besides, I could be wrong; I hoped I was. So when the doctor said "Your symptoms are consistent with a syndrome called multiple sclerosis," Myrna gasped and I only nodded. The doctor explained the oddities of MS, reassuring Myrna that the disease was not fatal (not quite true) and that it was not unusual for people with MS to live all their lives with little or no disability.

We asked the doctor about having children. He responded that there were no real obstacles, that women with MS did get pregnant and have children without complications. But there was the danger that the physical strain of pregnancy and infant care could seriously exacerbate the disease. Subsequently, Myrna decided she did not want to take the risk or subject a child to what, quite possibly, might become a very difficult situation in years to come.

Afterward, as we were walking out of NYU Hospital, Myrna was not too stunned to turn to me and say, "You already knew, didn't you? How did you know?"

I explained.

"You knew before you sent me the cactus," she said, as if that were obvious.

I nodded.

She just looked at me, and I think it was then that she began to truly trust me. I was proud of myself; for once I had exercised good judgment and restraint, and our future was off to a good start. Myrna had accepted my last proposal without knowing that she might have great need of me; and I had made the proposal with a fairly clear knowledge of what might lie ahead.

In the months that followed, we learned a great deal more about MS. We found out that it was thought to be caused by a virus that lay latent in the body until activated by a high body temperature (Myrna's measles in 1968) or by severe emotional stress (the impact of her father's death). The virus then supposedly moves into the cells of the myelin sheath, the insulation around nerve pathways, changing the cells in some way that causes the body's immune system to believe the cells are foreign and need to be destroyed. Sometimes the myelin restores itself; if it doesn't, the destruction leaves behind hardened (sclerotic) scar-like tissue that impedes, misdirects, or completely blocks nerve impulses. *Multiple* refers to the fact that the scar tissue appears at random in various places in the central nervous system, leading to a variety of different symptoms.

We learned that the disease is not fatal in itself, but that complications it creates can lead to death. Among those complications are spasticity in the bladder sphincter that makes it impossible to void the bladder, with consequent kidney failure. Other fatal complications (e.g., an embolism or pneumonia) can arise from the patient's loss of mobility. MS only rarely causes pain, although most patients suffer occasional uncomfortable tingling or numbness in their extremities.

There are about 250,000 cases of MS in the United States. It is the third leading cause of serious disability among adults, after arthritis and trauma. The most noted cases in recent years include: Jacqueline Du Pré, the noted young cellist whose story was told in a movie with Julie Andrews; Barbara Jordan, the noted black congresswoman and legal scholar from Texas; and Annette Funicello, of Mouseketeer and "beach blanket" movie fame.

MS tends to strike in young adulthood, the late twenties or early thirties, but it occasionally appears in teenagers and in people over fifty. Two to three times as many women as men contract MS. (An early symptom in men is impotence, a crushing blow to a young man in his prime.) In rare instances, MS moves swiftly, severely crippling or, more rarely, blinding within a few months. Usually, if the particular form of MS is severely chronic and progressive (about 15 percent of cases), it moves very slowly, taking twenty to twenty-five years or longer to wreak any serious havoc on the brain. In some people, about 20 percent of cases, there are few or no symptoms. Sometimes the presence of the disease is only discovered when an autopsy reveals the characteristic scar tissue in the brain. The remaining 65 percent of cases will show moderate to severe disabilities over the course of a normal lifetime.

There is a genetic element in the origins of MS; people from temperate climates are far more likely to get it than other people. In South Africa, persons of Dutch and English descent contract MS more frequently than persons in the black population; in Israel, Ashkenazi Jews, with their origins in northern and eastern Europe, are more subject to the disease than Sephardic Jews, who stem from North Africa and the Middle East. But genetics is not the whole story: It can strike just one of a pair of identical twins. Environment, or some form of casual contact, must also play a role in the disease's origins.

In fact, MS is probably not a single disease. Technically, it is a "syndrome," a set of symptoms and physical signs that, while similar in each case, may not have exactly the same cause in all cases. It is quite possible that several different viruses with similar effects are the cause of the syndrome, a possibility that makes research on the causes and treatment of MS immensely difficult and expensive.

There has not, in fact, been much progress in either understanding the cause or developing an effective treatment over the last three decades. The fact that the disease may be several diseases and can exhibit long remissions, makes research and drug tests extremely complicated. A proposed treatment may work on some cases and not on others, or it may appear to work on some cases that have, in fact, simply gone into remission. One consequence of this uncertainty is that the sufferer is constantly hearing anecdotes of "cures" that have had no real effect on MS but are based solely on experiences of long remissions.

Where there *has* been progress is in diagnosis; magnetic resonance imaging (MRI) and other new tests can now provide positive evidence of the presence of the scar tissue that indicates MS. In Myrna's case, a diagnosis could only be made from her two-and-a-half-year history of irritating, but hardly alarming, transitory symptoms.

A month after we got the diagnosis, on May 25, 1973, we were married among a small circle of friends and family by a renegade rabbi, one of the few rabbis in the metropolitan area who would perform a mixed marriage. Myrna was dressed in a full-length lacy white gown that vaguely suggested a Mexican peasant. She carried a bouquet of salmon-colored roses. A thin gold necklace supported a beautiful garnet intaglio just below her throat, my gift to her in lieu of a wedding ring that she could not wear because of hypersensitivity in her fingers.

During the ceremony, we each read a meaningful passage from a favorite book. My passage was a long quote from Rilke's *Letters to a Young Poet*, and it constituted a promise to respect Myrna's feminist independence. Rilke, writing in 1904, foresaw a time when the feminine was no longer a mere opposite of the masculine, defined and limited by contrast to the idea of masculine. In that future time, the feminine would come to mean something in itself, a new kind of complete human being. When that time came, Rilke said, the experience of love would change. Beyond the man-woman relationship, love, "infinitely considerate and gentle, and kind and clear in binding and releasing," would come to be a human-human relationship in which "two solitudes protect and border—and salute—each other."

Myrna's brief passage, from Lewis Carroll's *Through the Looking Glass*, was more obscure in its meaning but carried a much more active message:

> "When I use a word," Humpty Dumpty said, in a rather scornful tone, "it means just what I choose it to mean—neither more nor less."
>
> "The question is," said Alice, "whether you *can* make words mean so many different things."
>
> "The question is," said Humpty Dumpty, "which is to be master—that's all."

The passage meant two things. First, it was a warning comment on my annoying habit of turning words and ideas upside down and inside out to see how they fared. Myrna could get quite frustrated when I popped up with something like, "But if you turn that idea around, then . . ." or "But maybe the real issue is the reverse. . . ." It must be terrible to think you're talking about one thing and your partner apparently believes you should be talking about something entirely different.

The second meaning of the passage was very positive. Like Humpty Dumpty and his words, Myrna and I would make our marriage whatever we wanted it to be—neither more nor less. It was a challenge: Could we master our marriage and make it full of meaning?

When the words were over, the vows said, the kiss demonstrated, and the traditional glass broken with a good stomp, a tape recorder struck up with the Beatles' "Will you still need me, will you still feed me, when I'm sixty-four?" The absence of rings, with their intimations of chains and ownership, also signified our commitment to our individualities, our separateness, our lonerships. Myrna kept her last name, a sign of her family loyalty and her independence that I could easily honor now that she had accepted me.

We sat down to a good meal with friends and family, with much laughter, picture-taking, and joy. Most of Myrna's immediate family was there: Anne, her mother; Ronald, her big brother; Beverly, her big sister, with her husband Bob and daughter Alison; the three maiden aunts (Ethel, Zelda, and Lillian); and two cousins, Zelda Keller and Charlotte Liebov, and Charlotte's husband, Ben. One of the guests was an old college friend of mine who had been maid of honor at my first wedding nearly eighteen years earlier. She had recently lost her young husband to a heart attack. Two other friends of mine who attended were an artist and his wife, soon to be separated and divorced. Other guests included Myrna's former roommate and her new husband. We hadn't told anyone yet of the MS.

For our "honeymoon" we drove the next morning to western New Jersey where we stayed for the Memorial Day weekend, visiting a crafts mall and specialty shops in Flemington, checking out the Delaware Water Gap, and trying to stay dry during three days of heavy rain. We bought an antique apothecary's chest to serve as a food preparation center in the tiny kitchen of Myrna's apartment, which otherwise lacked counter space. I kept my salmon rose boutonniere on the dashboard by the air vent. By the time we returned to the city, it had completely dried out, perfectly preserved. We kept it for years, along with the stem of the wine goblet I had smashed underfoot at the end of the marriage ceremony. An overzealous cleaning lady finally threw them both away.

Altogether, the honeymoon, in locale and weather, was not worth writing home about. But it didn't really matter where we went, we had arrived where we wanted most to be—in each other's company.

6

The Good Years

I moved into Myrna's apartment at 83rd and Broadway, bringing my best new furniture with me: a sofa, a kitchen table and chairs, and a large area rug. I also brought window drapes, only to discover at that late date that Myrna did not like drapes, an irrational antipathy that I never questioned and she never explained.

We lived in that apartment until 1977, when my daughter, Anna, announced she was coming to New York to go to Hunter College. Myrna, exercising her amazing serendipity for finding good apartments, found a very nice two-bedroom with a bathroom and a half on the twelfth floor of an older building only three blocks away at 85th and Amsterdam. Unlike many New York City apartments in older buildings, this one did not have a long dark entryway or small rooms made smaller by small windows. The rooms were airy and open, the ceilings high, and the windows, especially on the south, unusually large. Those southern windows looked out on a magnificent view of upper and midtown Manhattan, including the Empire State and Chrysler buildings.

We went on an "antique" buying spree, acquiring an old cherry bedstead, circa 1890, and a cherry gateleg dining room table from the same period. Two small chests of an earlier period served as our night stands. We bought most of this stuff on holiday forays into Massachusetts, Vermont, and Pennsylvania.

One day Myrna came home to tell me she had seen and wanted to buy a Victorian chaise longue that was in the window of an antique store on Columbus. I was skeptical; it would probably cost too much and would hardly be appropriate for our otherwise modern living room. Besides, I was thinking of something in the way of a Barcalounger for myself. I walked over to the store to take a look at it. I was flabbergasted! It was outrageously ornate and had been reupholstered in a bright burgundy velvet. It would be completely out of place in our living room. But it perfectly expressed Myrna's ironic playfulness, and I bought it on the spot. We never used it much; it was too "delicate." It just sat there in our living room, a conversation piece, a burgundy elephant.

We went out to California for Anna's graduation from high school, before she came to New York. Not long before Myrna and I were married, I had been out to the small community in the mountains of central California where the children grew up, and the Christmas after our marriage, both Anna and Conrad had come East to visit us. We had a great time showing them the historical sites of the Boston area, where I had once been a tour bus driver.

This latest trip was the first in which all four parents—my ex-wife and her new husband, Myrna and I—were together. We got on without friction. If there had been any bitterness between my ex and me in the past, it had evaporated. We had remade our lives to our own satisfaction.

Anna, now an intense and very independent eighteen year old, only stayed with us a year before returning to California where she finished a pre-med degree in physiology. While she was in New York, she had taken dance and yoga classes and become very interested in the latter. Back in California, she took up the physical discipline of Hatha yoga as taught by B. K. S. Iyengar at an ashram in Poona, south of Bombay. She made several trips there, became a master in her own right, and taught yoga in the Los Angeles area to a client list that included some celebrity names.

In the first years of our marriage, Myrna and I faced a persistent area of conflict. Myrna was often a hesitant speaker, choosing her words carefully for precision and clarity and presenting them slowly and cautiously. I, glib and opinionated, would rush in impatiently to finish her thoughts and sentences for her.

This made Myrna very angry, justifiably. Myrna's anger came and went like a bolt of lightning. Her eyes would narrow and her lips draw in to form the tiniest possible aperture from which her words would emerge like bullets aimed at the heart: "Do. Not. Tell. Me. What. I'm. Saying."

The bullets hit their target, and I slowly began to learn to hold my tongue and wait, a wait that always proved worthwhile. I learned that if I let her complete her thoughts, they were usually much better than mine, both more insightful and more sensitive. It took her nearly two years to fully train me in patience. The discipline proved very useful years later when Myrna's speech became even more hesitant because the MS affected her memory.

Other than the training in patience, Myrna and I experienced little friction. We shared the housework, the cooking, and the dish and clothes washing. I didn't care for house cleaning, but I enjoyed cooking, and Myrna was an appreciative audience. I introduced her to chili served on a bed of Fritos and to *spaghetti al pesto*, both of which became favorite dishes. I also introduced her to corned beef hash with a poached egg on top; that dish disappeared from the menu immediately. Myrna's specialty was chicken dishes, everything from the simplest roast chicken to fancy Chinese and Near Eastern concoctions. Later, when we had moved to the larger apartment, we frequently had people for dinner on the weekends. On Thanksgiving, I gloried in showing off my mastery of the traditional roast turkey with all the trimmings, including an unusually tasty cranberry relish.

By and large, we didn't bring the office home. Myrna rose from simply writing for *Facts on File*, the leading weekly news abstract, to become managing editor of the European and Near Eastern sections. Sometimes we talked about her problems managing a couple of male writers who thought they were overlooked masters of the language.

My job expanded from simply managing the almanac to producing other books as well. One of these involved working with an expert on games and required a familiarity with backgammon. I learned the game and brought it home to Myrna. We became backgammon addicts, often playing two or three hours at a stretch and keeping score over months. Most of the time Myrna was way ahead. My job also involved quite a bit of travel to check on typesetting and print runs and to see contributors. Every year there was a tour to promote the almanac on television and in the press.

Observing the political scene occupied a great deal of our time. We followed both foreign and domestic news closely and became experts on the people and events of Vietnam and Watergate. I was a longtime Nixon "anti-fan," never missing one of his television appearances. I watched him with the same gruesome fascination one brings to auto racing, waiting eagerly for him to break down, crack up, fly to pieces. We watched as much as we could of the Senate Watergate hearings.

In the summer of 1975 most of the Almanac staff migrated to Memphis, where we used the facilities of the local Scripps-Howard newspaper to do an "instant" book on the Nixon impeachment hearings. I had great hopes for a big success with the book, but then the president who said he wasn't "a quitter" quit, and the book disappeared. Richard the Wretched had added a personal betrayal to my list of his crimes.

Of all the books I did at the Almanac, I was most proud of *The World Almanac Book of the Strange*, a compendium of short articles on strange things and theories, from the truly miraculous and awesome to completely bogus "mysteries" peddled to the gullible at a handsome profit. Arranged more or less in order, from the most common unrecognized mystery, the effectiveness of aspirin, to the silliest myth of our time, the Bermuda Triangle, the book tried to point up the wonder-full in the commonplace and the ridiculous in the fabricated nonsense. As I put it in the introduction, "If you want to see a real miracle, look in the mirror." The book appeared as a paperback under the Signet imprint of New American Library. It sold about 240,000 copies and was considered a great success.

Another major activity for Myrna and me was planning and enjoying trips together. These ranged from holiday weekend outings, usually to see fall foliage in Massachusetts and Vermont; to short breaks in the Caribbean; to two-week vacation trips to visit

relatives or friends or to foreign climes. These longer trips were
our happiest times together. We were perfect travel companions,
easily agreeing on where to go, what to see next, where to eat, and
all the other details of traveling that can lead to disagreement and
argument. We made a trip to Portugal in August of '73, to the
Yucatan in the spring of '75, to Ireland in '78, and to the Riviera
in '80. Our last trip, made almost in desperation, but also in cele-
bration, was to Israel in 1990.

The three European trips were plagued by bad weather. In Portugal, in August, we had to buy heavy wool sweaters to stay warm.
On the Riviera in late April, rain and mud made us give up camp-
ing, which we were trying out to save money. We did not get to
swim nude at St. Tropez; it was too cold to even think of going to
the beach. And in Ireland, also in late April, we had to give up
our plans to do an article on Irish gardens. The spring had been
so cold that nothing but rhododendrons had bloomed. We joked
that we should write to tourist centers and ask them to pay us to
stay away.

On many of our trips there was occasion to gamble. We gambled
in Portugal; in Monte Carlo; on Saint Martin; in Atlantic City; and
in Laughlin, Nevada, on the Arizona border. Myrna loved to gamble and usually won small amounts. I, on the other hand, found
gambling boring and usually lost. Myrna emerged a loser only in
Atlantic City. Earlier, before we met, she had gambled in Puerto
Rico and won enough to pay for an extra week there, just long
enough to lose it all again. Later she became a lottery player,
spending four or five dollars a week on New York Lotto. In over
twenty years of playing Lotto, she won only $75, but she continued
to believe, until near the end of her life, that "the big one" was just
around the corner.

When we were getting ready to go to Portugal, our first trip
abroad, I discovered something new and surprising about Myrna.
When I noted that we were going to that country at the height of
the European vacation season, that we intended to visit a small city
during a local festival, and that we really ought to get busy and
make hotel reservations, Myrna looked at me as if I were crazy.
One did not *plan* travels in Europe; one drifted as the wind blew.

One relied on bed-and-breakfast accommodations found with the help of local tourist offices. Myrna, who so often planned out her daily routine in detail and worried too much over any snag in those plans, was a free spirit when she traveled. I, on the other hand, quite comfortable with the unplanned and unexpected in my work-a-day life, wanted a firm schedule and security when I traveled, particularly abroad.

Skeptically and fully expecting to say "I told you so" later, I went along with Myrna. But as usual, she was not simply right, she was brilliant. Drifting is the only way to travel. It led us to delightful out-of-the-way inns, unknown fine restaurants, surprising scenery, and unexpected friendships.

The vacation we remembered most fondly was the one in Ireland in 1978. We mushed around Dublin in cold, wet weather for a few days, explored some historic buildings, including the post office that was the scene of the 1916 Easter Rebellion against British rule, and visited the city's quite wonderful botanic gardens. We stayed in a comfortable bed-and-breakfast almost across the street from the city's main synagogue, where Myrna went to Sabbath services.

A couple of days later, we celebrated Passover with a seder at the rabbi's. He and his wife, both Czechs, were Holocaust survivors, but neither spoke of it. It was not a wholly comfortable evening. Myrna and I had never before been to a seder in a traditionally observant household. The only other guest, an American student, was far more knowledgeable than we were about seder customs.

I suspect, too, that the rabbi had never before celebrated a seder with a nonobservant Jew and her goy husband. Nevertheless, I found it a moving experience, marked not by the seder's traditional joy of liberation from bondage, but by the sorrows of the past, of memories of childhoods in strong Jewish communities, of crowded and vibrant seders, of a security that could never be recovered.

The next day we drove south and west into the countryside, stopping at this or that garden site and finding only rhododendrons. Finally, on a particularly cold day in Killarney, I told Myrna that I was sick of rhododendrons and never wanted to see another. Myrna agreed that the garden idea was a bust. So, on the spur of the moment, we sped north, aiming for the wildest part of Ireland, Connemara, west of Galway town.

But we were waylaid by the Burren in County Clare, where we spent several days wandering that terrible waste where, millennia ago, an Ice Age glacier had stripped away the topsoil leaving behind bedrock so furrowed that a visitor can clearly see the direction of the glacier's flow. The area is dotted with dolmens, great slabs of stone, some placed atop others, marking the sites of ancient graves.

When we left the car at the roadside and walked into the Burren to see a dolmen close up, we felt we had stepped back in time to an era of bleak existence, without history or culture, when life was truly "mean, nasty, brutish, and short." This was particularly true when we visited the site of a prehistoric "fort," little more than a stronghold for perhaps fifty people at the most and now no more than a vague outline of grassy tumulus on a promontory looking out over a beautiful valley. It was easy to imagine the half-savages huddled there in the cold wet of Ireland, now and then making bloody forays on people in the valley below before retreating to their stronghold to defend themselves and their poor gains against the inevitable retaliation.

On our first night in the county seat, Ennis, we went to a pub where we were entertained with great Irish music. Among the musicians was a former all-Ireland champion fiddler, Vincent Griffin, a dairy farmer who lived a short distance from Ennis near the village of Feakle. We were told that if we stayed at the tourist hotel in Feakle one evening, we might be able to persuade Mr. Griffin to come over and play for us for no more than the cost of a couple of brandies. We planned the rest of our stay in western Ireland with the idea of doing just that.

After three days in the Burren we drove north to Galway, around the desolate coast of Connemara, and farther north to Westport in lush County Mayo. From there we explored old churches and monasteries and searched out and climbed a great cairn overlooking Boycott country—the area where Captain Boycott so mistreated his Irish tenants that the surrounding population "boycotted" him.

A few days later, as planned, we pulled into Feakle and stayed at the very pleasant, almost empty, little tourist hotel there. Vincent Griffin did come, and he played for us for over two hours in a tiny bar with scarcely room for the four of us—Vincent, the innkeeper, Myrna, and me. Vincent at first would play only gay jigs and reels, not the dirges and laments that express the other half of the Irish soul. But when I pressed him with a quote from Yeats's "Lapis Lazuli" about old men listening to mournful tunes as their eyes glittered with gaiety, he reluctantly gave us some mournful tunes. The man could draw the sorrows of all Ireland and the ages out of his fiddle, and in that beauty, we were gay. It was a grand evening.

The next morning, on the way out of Feakle, we watched Vincent move large milk cans from his truck to a larger truck that would take the milk to market. Myrna commented that she would like to do PR for the town. She already had a slogan: Feakle matters!

We left Ireland a few days later, stopping off in London, where we went to the theater. Myrna had left *Facts on File* in January, planning to take a year to explore the possibility of writing fiction. So I left her in England to return to work on the almanac, while she proceeded to Yorkshire to spend a week in the countryside of the Brontë sisters and another week traveling in Scotland.

During these early good years, from 1973 to 1980, the MS had little effect on Myrna. Occasionally she would become exceptionally fatigued, a kind of nerve exhaustion peculiar to MS, but this was easily overcome with a few minutes or few hours rest. There was a sense of creeping numbness in her legs, occasional discomfort from "tingling," and infrequent bouts of double vision and vertigo. But nothing really slowed her down.

The pleasure of relaxed and unplanned travel was one of the less important things I gained from Myrna. I profited immensely from her capacity to enjoy things in a very simple and direct way, to be totally caught up in the pleasure of the moment like a child. Her enjoyment of houseplants displayed this simplicity perfectly. Beginning with only two or three, bought to liven up her new apartment in the early seventies, her garden grew to well over a hundred plants of perhaps two dozen varieties.

Sunday became gardening day, when she would spend four to six hours watering, repotting, snipping off dead leaves, pruning, and doing whatever else was necessary—all the while raptly engrossed and contented. Later, when she became too handicapped to do all of this herself, she carefully supervised me or her home health aide as we did the work. I, born with a natural "black thumb," learned a lot about plants I didn't really care to know.

Myrna was also a person of natural moderation; she did not indulge in any pleasure to excess. On the contrary, she was remarkably abstemious. Her idea of a nosh was a piece of fruit in the afternoon—Granny Smiths and pears in winter, peaches and plums in summer. Self-indulgence consisted of more than a couple of handfuls of potato chips or a few spoonfuls of chocolate chocolate-chip ice cream. Other than ice cream, there was seldom any dessert in our house. Perhaps Myrna believed that future pleasure is increased by its prior absence. To her, less was, in fact, almost always more. This trait meant that she could never become jaded, never reach the point where she had to seek out more complicated, exotic pleasures to stimulate a satiated appetite.

Her capacity for simple pleasure extended to reading, to movies, and to theater. To each of these activities, Myrna brought a mind for details and a sharp critical sense. She could let herself sink into the mood of a film or book, turning off her critical faculties for a time. But afterward, as if emerging into the bright afternoon sun after three hours at a Saturday double-bill matinee, she would ruminate on the experience in the glare of reason and esthetics. Her critique of a film or play was nearly always penetrating and on the mark. She improved my taste immensely.

We were not "high culture" purists. Like much of the country, we stayed home on Sunday nights for the larger part of two years to watch *Upstairs, Downstairs* on PBS. We did the same with the PBS *I, Claudius* and *Poldark* series. Even further down the cultural scale, we were habitual watchers of the *Barney Miller* and *Cheers* sit-coms, *Hill Street Blues*, and later, *L.A. Law, Law & Order*, and *N.Y.P.D. Blue*. Myrna had a "thing" for David Caruso, the first lead in the latter series.

Even in the theater, despite her critical faculties, Myrna was no purist. She detested the harsh *New York Times* reviews of Shakespeare in the Park, one of our favorite summertime activities. These excellent renditions of Shakespeare often took considerable liberties in the staging and even the text of the Bard, liberties designed, in large part, to entertain and instruct an audience much like the one Shakespeare himself appealed to. Myrna hated the critics' pretentious refusal to see these performances for what Shakespeare would have wanted them to be—pure and simple entertainment. On occasion, when a play (seldom Shakespeare) was irredeemably bad, Myrna would deliver the ultimate critical comment on the spot—she would fall asleep.

If I was enjoying a performance and looked over to find her asleep, I knew I should take a closer look at what was really happening on stage. Usually I would have to agree with her. I would nudge her awake, whisper "Let's go," and at the next opportunity we would slip away. We did not believe in sitting around being embarrassed for the performers; nor had we paid to be insulted or bored.

That drift into sleep illustrates another of Myrna's natural virtues: Although she could be very critical, she usually would not openly condemn any honest effort. Going to sleep was her way of avoiding the outright statement, This is trash. Myrna, without effort, without keeping a watch on her tongue, never spoke evil of others. She knew evil and the meretricious when she saw it, and she avoided it, but with rare exceptions, she never condemned it. She would listen to my ranting about the perfidious Nixon, the willful ignorance of Reagan, and other crudities of politics, and add only a comment of mild agreement or doubt— her way of expressing distaste for my "Christian" desire to see the wicked in Hell.

On rare occasions, she would condemn a movie—e.g., *Sleepless in Seattle* was "brainwashing, a bubble bath." A new highrise apartment building that rose up at 79th and Columbus, blocking our view of the Chrysler Building, was an abomination, the "Sore Thumb," condemned often and openly. One of the Shakespeare productions was "sloppy," another play was "flat."

Where people were concerned, Myrna's criticism was often numbed by shock. When a street tough calmly and arrogantly took my beret from my head and walked off with it, giving me the finger in recompense, Myrna was speechless. When Myrna, by then on crutches, hailed a cab only to have it roughly preempted by a woman with a briefcase and the excuse that Myrna was obviously not working, Myrna was simply stunned. A few years after that, when bus passengers complained about the time it took to load her, on her electric scooter, aboard the bus, Myrna was silent. There was no place in her understanding for this sort of callousness.

On the other hand, she was lavish in praise of kindness. Once, her scooter's electrical system got a little wet as she was crossing Central Park on her way to a class at the Alliance Française. The scooter would only move in reverse. A stranger helped her maneuver her way through the park and a friendly policeman escorted her to the Alliance building. By the end of the class, the scooter had dried off, and Myrna was able to get home without incident. She immediately wrote a letter to the captain of the precinct, praising the policeman by name for his kindness.

On many other occasions when her scooter broke down for one reason or another, she was full of praise for the kindly strangers who helped, usually by pushing her to a safe spot and calling me to come "rescue" her. Frequently these people waited patiently with her until I arrived. Myrna was always much heartened by their kindness and effusive in her gratitude. These incidents remained firmly lodged in her mind, even when her memory of other events began to fade, and she often remarked on them. They became signs of God's concern for her safety.

7

A Time of Faith
and Good Work

Yes, "God's concern." For the biggest event in these good years, the one with the most long-lasting consequences for us both, was Myrna's return to the faith of her ancestors. A few months after we got back from Ireland, and after her annual trek to New Haven to attend High Holy Day services with her mother, Myrna expressed an interest in learning more about her Jewish roots. I was both surprised and pleased; I had always worried a little about Myrna's apparent lack of a spiritual life. I immediately got on the phone to the rabbi who had married us and asked if he could recommend three synagogues in our area, specifically requesting that they be genuine religious institutions, not social or political clubs. He named three, two of them Orthodox.

Again to my surprise, Myrna was soon settled into a Wednesday night class in Torah learning at one of the Orthodox synagogues. The rabbi had been teaching this continuing class for many years. Having begun with Genesis 1:1, he had got no farther than Exodus 32, giving each verse, each significant word, a thorough and dynamic analysis. Myrna loved it. Her training in history had made her appreciative of the pleasures of close reading, and here was close reading in spades, combined with the adventurous convolutions of rabbinical thought.

She would come home from the classes full of enthusiasm, insights, and questions. Often between classes she would bring up some point made by the rabbi and talk about her understanding of it or of her doubts. For she did have very grave doubts. Perhaps her enjoyment of plants was so great because they were simply there, immediate unquestionable realities, while ideas and moral issues were always subject to her critical review.

I went with her to one of the classes and emerged amused at their similarity to the Wednesday night Baptist "prayer meetings" I had attended as a teenager. In both cases analysis of the Bible text hid an underlying homiletic (moral teaching) purpose. I was so superior!

Sometime in 1980, Myrna began to go to Sabbath services on Saturday morning and soon afterward said she wanted to join the synagogue. "Should it be an individual or family membership?" she asked. "Family," I said without hesitation, eager to support her. I started going with her to lectures at the synagogue and to Sabbath services as well. The latter were all Hebrew to me; I had only the vaguest idea what was happening.

But certain events struck home. One morning a man with a six-month-old son touched the little boy's hand to the Torah scroll as it was passing by on its way back to the ark. The infant appeared to me to follow the scroll from that point until it was hidden by the ark's curtain, a feat of concentration that I thought astounding in a baby. In another incident several months later, the rabbi announced soon after the Sabbath morning service began that the main synagogue in Rome had been bombed that morning, and four lives had been lost. The congregation gasped, but no one stirred.

It seemed to me that every person in the sanctuary was subject to the same sort of threat, attending as they did one of the city's most prominent synagogues. Whether they were conscious of it or not, and I don't think many were, they put their lives on the line every time they went to the synagogue, which for some of the men was every day. Jews had been doing the same for hundreds of years. These people are serious about their religion, I thought to myself.

I had a strong interest in Jews and Judaism that had begun in the summer of 1945, when I first learned that Jews were not dead and gone like the ancient Greeks and Romans, but a living, and now horribly dying, people who had just seen their thriving Yiddish culture in Europe destroyed by the Nazis. At the time, I was deeply unhappy at home and dreaming of a time when I could emerge into a larger, more rational world. The news of the Holocaust was shattering—the "more rational world" outside my home was a charnel house! From that point on, I identified with the struggle of Jews to establish a homeland in Palestine and focused most of my questions about the value of life and civilization on the Holocaust and its causes.

There was another reason for my interest in Judaism, a reason closer to home. When my first wife remarried, she married a Jew, and when they had a child together, they began to attend a Reform Jewish temple. There, my two kids went through a conversion process and were, by some lights, Jewish, although it would probably take a rabbinical court to determine the Orthodox validity of the procedure they went through.

I had attended my son Conrad's bar mitzvah in 1975. When Anna came to live with us while she attended Hunter College, she was quite active in the Hillel Society, and as we were leaving for our trip to Ireland, she was going through the agonies of preparing our kitchen for Passover. While I had no particular inclination to imitate them, the children's religious affiliation undoubtedly made my interest more personal.

My own long conflict with God came to an end soon after my mother died in 1979. While attending her funeral in California, my born-again Christian sisters asked me what I believed, and I said I would write to them about it. Some weeks later, when I sat down to write, the following prayer emerged unbidden, completely surprising me. Episcopalians will recognize that the first line is cribbed from the *Book of Common Prayer:*

PRAYER OF PRAISE AND THANKSGIVING

Almighty God, unto whom all hearts are open and no
    secrets hid,
Thou knowest the nature of my faith:
that I look to Thee for neither love, nor justice, nor
    mercy;
that I *fear* the breaking of Thy spirit into our lives;
that Thy purposes are not human and not mine;
that Thou hast made nature bloody and unforgiving;
that Thy handmaiden Fortune is capricious and cruel,
and Thy manservant, Evil, torments us at Thy will;
and that in the immensity of Thy creation,
we will soon leave no trace.

Thou knowest also that I worship and adore you,
Creator and Sustainer of all that is;
my life's cup is filled from Thy bottomless bounty;
all my senses take continual delight in Thy creation;
my heart is rapt before Thy awful majesty;
my spirit is lifted up when I glimpse Thy unity;
and my soul is enriched in Thy continual variety.
My body trembles and kneels before Thee in
    thanksgiving,
and my tongue is not still in praising Thee.

Thou art the One Source, and from Thee comes all:
    pain and sorrow, joy and delight,
    fear and anger, peace and love.

And whether in the end, I rise up to eternal bliss
    or sink forever into darkness,
I will go to Thee as a river to its bed,
Oh, God, Thou Blessed Father-Mother,
Ever-embracing Holiness.

                                            Amen.

On completing this poem, I felt a great hunger to pray in a community of people of like minds, but still did not think of the synagogue as that community. Then, soon after the bombing in Rome,

I discovered that the synagogue offered a beginners service to teach those unfamiliar with the Jewish service enough of the basics to get along in a regular service.

I remember sharply the deep relief and satisfaction I felt the first time I stood up with others there to recite the opening blessing, beginning with the phrase "I am about to sing praises to my Creator." A starving prodigal had found a home in the Father's house; he sat at a full table, and his mouth was filled with the sweetness of thanksgiving. Nevertheless, mindful of the rigors of Orthodoxy and not sure of this new relation to my Maker, it took me two more years to decide to convert.

The decision had little to do with Myrna. I wasn't even sure she would be pleased. After all, a Sabbath-observing Jew, which Myrna had become, reaps great advantage by having a Shabbas goy around to turn lights on and off, answer the phone, heat water for tea, etc., all of which are forbidden the observant Jew. She had never expressed any dissatisfaction with my pagan state nor any desire that our marriage be made "kosher." I did not consult her about my decision; that was between me and God, but I did not think she would object. She didn't, but she was surprised.

My decision was made easier by the fact that I knew I would not have to conform my beliefs to a rigid dogma, that my iconoclasm fit within a Jewish tradition that began with Abraham and continued through the paradoxes and ironic tales of the Midrash and the Hasidic masters. In one of the best known of the Midrash tales, a rabbi on the losing end of a debate calls for miracles from heaven to prove him right. The miracles duly occur, but the other rabbis ignore them, saying, "The Lord gave the Torah to man to interpret. Divine intervention in that process is inappropriate and irrelevant." The story succinctly illustrated my own view of the God-man relationship.

I did not have to believe a creed; I only had to obey the mitzvot, the many rules of Orthodox observance The mitzvoth, or commandments, served me as a kind of spiritual discipline, reminding me in the kitchen, the bathroom, at the table, on the street, and at all times of the presence of God, of meaning and value. They served to elevate the commonplace, the mundane, the routine to a higher level, the level of sanctity.

The reader should not assume that Myrna's and my return to religion meant that we had emerged from the Passage, that place where meaning is absent and all is futility. Rather, we were actively attempting, in metaphors of speech and action, to create meaning, futile though the effort might prove to be in the long run.

The first steps in the conversion process were informal: preparing the kitchen to observe the dietary laws, setting up an automatic lighting system for the Sabbath, learning a lot of prayers and songs in Hebrew. Myrna and I loved working on these things together and spent many delightful hours in classes learning the laws and customs, songs and rituals. We loved the Sabbath rituals—lighting the Sabbath candles, saying a blessing for the Sabbath and for wine and bread before the Sabbath meal. It is the custom in most observant homes to sing Ayshet cha-yil, "A Woman of Valor," before the meal, in honor of the Sabbath, personalized as a wife. In our house, I read it in English in honor of Myrna, for it described her well:

> A good wife, who can find? She is more precious than corals. Her husband places his trust in her and only profits thereby. She brings him good, not harm, all the days of her life. She seeks out wool and flax and cheerfully does the work of her hands. She is like the trading ships, bringing food from afar. . . . She is robed in strength and dignity, and she smiles at the future. She opens her mouth with wisdom and the teaching of kindness is on her tongue. She looks after the conduct of her household and never tastes the bread of sloth. Her children rise up and make her happy; her husband praises her, saying: "Many women have excelled, but you outshine them all!" Grace is elusive and beauty is vain, but a woman who fears the Lord shall be praised.

The conversion process did not go quickly. In fact it took me nearly five years to complete it, as Myrna and I struggled with her job, my book projects, and the increasing uncertainty of our lives. In the meantime, however, we became active participants in the life of our synagogue and took ever greater pleasure from it.

One of the major uncertainties was that I was now without a regular job. Getting fired from The World Almanac in 1980 was a great shock. I had never before been fired from anything! The reasons for the dismissal were never made clear because, I believe, they were based on petty office politics that in today's employment rights atmosphere might be grounds for litigation. I had received solid raises every year and never a hint of criticism for my performance either in general or in details. The Almanac staff had met every deadline, produced additional books, and done all their work with a minimum of fuss and bother.

But it was also true that I had come to scorn my immediate superior—her aggressive defensiveness, her constant name-dropping, her bad-mouthing of any perceived competition. And I made no attempt to conceal my disgust. It was true, too, that the leading younger staff member was getting married and lusted after my job. What better wedding present could the company give her? It would even save money, because she could be paid ten to fifteen thousand dollars a year less than I was paid. Another possible factor in the firing was that this was the beginning of the "go-go" years when American business bought into the Reaganite fantasy of perpetual profit growth and greater wealth for all, but especially for the "winners." I was never a go-go type and had trouble even simulating the required "rah-rah" enthusiasm for every little bit of corporate self-congratulation.

So, in July 1980, after eight years at The World Almanac, I was on my own with three months' pay to cushion the blow. I could continue to work for the Almanac on a freelance basis for two years in order to become vested in a company pension. But the freelance work was dull indexing, make-work really, and when a book packager offered me an opportunity to develop a new almanac under a contract with *Newsweek* and Avon books, I jumped at the chance and quit The World Almanac for good.

Unfortunately, after I'd worked for about nine months on the new almanac, *Newsweek* got cold feet and canceled the project. That move bankrupted the book packager and sent me scrambling for other work. This experience with the loyalty and commitment of American business empires left me with little inclination to seek employment with another major firm. Long before the age of downsizing in the mid-1990s, I learned that corporate America feels no obligations to its serfs.

So I freelanced, adopting the hand-to-mouth existence of people I had felt sorry for in the past. I designed two or three books for a couple of publishers, edited and privately published the memoirs of a World War II United Press correspondent who had been present at the German surrender, and conceived and edited a two-volume encyclopedia covering the governmental systems and political parties of every country in the world.

The least likely job of all was a one-hundred-page book on the accounting system used by property-casualty insurance companies. The industry was engaged in a struggle to retain its special tax treatment, a constant problem that became more intense than usual in the Reagan years. I was as ignorant of insurance details and of accounting as the politicians and journalists who might be inclined to believe that insurance accounting, despite the fact that it is fixed by law, is an ongoing tax scam. A friend at the Insurance Information Institute, a nonprofit organization financed by its insurance company members, asked if I would be interested in writing a little book to set the record straight. Who better to do the job than a writer as ignorant as his audience?

I found myself fascinated by property-casualty insurance. Ideally, insurance is the most profoundly moral social invention of the last six hundred years. Its fundamental idea is that we are all in the same boat and that harm to one is harm to all. Therefore, restoring a person or community to wholeness after a calamity is of benefit to everybody. Through insurance we create large pools of money that can be used to make society whole again. Unfortunately, the practice of insurance falls far short of that ideal since both insurers and policyholders use and abuse the system for private advantage.

For all these projects except the encyclopedia, I was paid a flat fee. I was supposed to get royalty payments on the encyclopedia, which was a major success for publications of its type, but the publisher set the price so low that the sales didn't come close to earning out the advance I'd received and spent buying the time and talents of experts.

The uncertainties of our lives also included Myrna's health. The trip to Ireland was the last easy one for Myrna. Hiking in the Burren and climbing cairns brought the first signs that her MS was not going to lie dormant. Two or three times, Myrna "hit the wall," a state of almost total exhaustion very like the one that marathon runners encounter, except there is no "second wind." The "wall" in MS is not muscle fatigue but a strange kind of nerve fatigue that is not yet understood by physiologists. It was only in the early 1980s that the Medicare administration was persuaded to recognize that this kind of fatigue is real in MS patients. There is very little warning of the "wall" and no remedy but immediate rest. Fifteen minutes may be enough, or three hours of deep sleep may sometimes be needed.

Our first encounter with the "wall" in 1978 scared us. What if it happened when we were far from a resting place? What if Myrna suddenly collapsed in the street? But like so many MS symptoms, the "wall" initially proved to be more of an unnerving threat than a persistent reality. We did not encounter it again in any serious way until 1982, when Myrna began to have trouble on the long walks (sixteen blocks each way) to and from synagogue. Near the end of that year, we bought our first wheelchair for use on the Sabbath and any other time Myrna might have to walk a long distance or spend much time on her feet. By this time, Myrna was using a quad cane, a cane with four little feet, most of the time.

About the same time, early 1983, Myrna got a good idea for a book. It arose out of her friendship with a woman who had parlayed her intelligence, energy, and sound judgment into a leading vice presidency in a company where she'd started some years before as a clerk and secretary. Myrna's book would tell other women how to do the same. Another friend, Jody Morrow, wife of Cousin Brucie, a leading New York disk-jockey before the days of the "shlock-jock," was organizing and teaching assertiveness classes for women.

The book promised to fit neatly into her program, and Jody and Myrna decided to collaborate. Jodie would garner personal stories and dig up relevant books and articles; Myrna would coordinate the information and write the book. They were quickly off the mark with a contract from John Wiley for *Not Just a Secretary: Using the Job to Get Ahead,* and they buckled down to work.

Myrna had already written several shorter books. She had done three or four on political topics for Deadline Data and two for her present employer—one on time management and one on personal office organization. Those writing projects had been sheer hell for both of us because Myrna was a perfectionist when it came to putting herself before the public with her own words. And she lacked any easy confidence in her ability. She would agonize over details, rewrite and rewrite, spot holes in the information, stop progress to fill them in, reorganize and rewrite again, and otherwise make her life a torment.

The projects tormented me, too, mostly in sympathy for her anguish. She constantly sought reassurance, which was easy to give, and advice, which was seldom taken because her judgment was almost always better than mine. During these times I did most of the cooking. In the beginning, I would cajole her into doing a little to get her mind off the book, but the distraction simply irritated her. When working on a project, Myrna was a different person— irritable, short-tempered, demanding, and narrowly focused on the job and her problems with it. She would chain-smoke as she worked (quitting immediately when the project was done!), and between typing and puffing, she would bite her nails to the quick. I was her gofer—getting her tea, emptying her ashtray, and generally making myself available to fulfill her needs and demands.

While she worked on *Not Just a Secretary,* she was also working full time as an editor of periodicals on employment practices law and regulation. She generally had trouble sleeping more than four hours a night, so she took advantage of that problem to get up at four or five o'clock in the morning to work on the book for a few hours before going off to put in a full day at her regular job. Ordinarily her office tasks were rather routine, but they suddenly got much harder when the management came up with the idea of a new quarterly journal based on rising interest in the ideas of Dr. W. Edwards Deming and his total quality control theories that stressed teamwork, worker empowerment, and thorough collection and analysis of production process and outcomes data.

Myrna could hardly tell her employer that she couldn't develop the journal because she was writing a book on the side. So now she had two major projects on her plate. She worked herself to exhaustion to do a perfect job on both. Some years later, she would complain that she couldn't nap on Saturday afternoons anymore. I had to remind her that when she had napped easily on Saturday, she had also been working two jobs and getting by on four or five hours sleep a night.

I often wondered later if I should have let her drive herself that way, but I couldn't have stopped her if I had tried. She was determined to do the book and to make the *National Productivity Review* the premier publication in its field. Arguing with her about it would only have tired her more and discouraged her.

Developing the journal involved organizing an editorial board of experts, determining the topics to be covered, soliciting manuscripts from leading figures in the field, riding herd on them to meet deadlines, editing their work, consulting on the design of the new publication, and coordinating all these elements to meet a tight deadline for the first issue.

Never one to hang back when working on somebody else's product, Myrna scored a coup when she persuaded Dr. Deming himself to contribute the lead article, summarizing his theories. But Deming proved more of a headache than he was worth. He was an irascible, arrogant old geezer, and his writing was almost incomprehensible. The irascibility and arrogance were understandable in a prophet who had wandered in the desert for years, his message ignored in his own country until Japan, Inc., took him seriously and scared the hell out of the competition, including the United States.

What was harder to deal with was his refusal to take any editorial direction whatsoever. His words had come down from the mountain; they were divine revelation, meant to be pondered by lesser minds, not trifled with by "lady" editors. Myrna's attempt to make his article readable provoked his threat to withdraw it unless it was printed as written. For the sake of his name alone, Myrna suppressed her editorial judgment and printed the article with only minor alterations to correct sophomoric errors in his grammar.

In the end, the *National Productivity Review* was a triumph, greeted with fanfare by quality control cognoscenti, who hailed it as a major step forward in their struggle to reform American management systems. For a while Myrna's self-doubts disappeared. She basked in the praise and found renewed energy to complete *Not Just a Secretary*, which Wiley published in 1984. Twelve years later, that book remains in print, having sold some 13,000 copies, and the journal is still going strong under new ownership, having been sold by its original publisher for a tidy sum. Their readers today might reflect that a determined woman sacrificed her health over these publications. For the two projects marked the beginning of a precipitate worsening of her MS and led to her retirement at age forty-one only a few months later.

8

The Ragged Years

I call the years between 1985 and 1989 the ragged years because we were never sure where we stood in relation to the multiple sclerosis. That it was progressing, there could be no doubt, but there was still hope that it would stop getting worse and leave Myrna with enough function and freedom to enjoy life. In the meantime, the disease made it difficult to look ahead, to plan, to feel even a minimal security.

By now Myrna usually used Lofstrand, or Canadian, crutches, the kind with a cuff just above the elbow. Soon after she retired, we bought a three-wheel electric scooter, a Rascal, to give her maximum independence to go where she pleased. She could still do pretty much what she wanted, by herself, if she acknowledged it was going to take a little longer or might require a bit of rest in the middle. She was still doing about half the cooking and some of the shopping. She kept busy with swimming, classes at the Alliance Française, visits to museums and galleries, and occasional volunteer work.

One of the most difficult aspects of MS or any degenerative disease is adjusting to new losses. A spinal cord injury establishes a new set of permanent limits to what the injured person can do. Accommodations can be made, work-arounds developed, and the future of the disability is relatively predictable, enabling adaptation in the confidence that, once accomplished, the achievement will be permanent.

In MS, however, nothing is predictable. For Myrna, a body function lost today might be regained in a week or a month, or the loss might come and go in the space of mere hours, seemingly depending on the ambient temperature or how rested she was. For example, Myrna sometimes found it difficult now to lift her legs high enough to get them over the edge of our old-fashioned bathtub. At other times, chopping vegetables for salad took more hand strength and coordination than she could muster. In both cases, these little disabilities would come and go, slowly coming more frequently and lasting longer, and finally becoming persistent.

There seemed to be no reason for a loss or a recovery of a function. Not knowing if a loss was permanent, Myrna had to continually try to do things she hadn't been able to do yesterday or last week. Occasionally she would be successful. Too often, she was frustrated. And success gave no particular cause for joy—the function could be lost again the next day.

Just recognizing deterioration can be a problem, a problem compounded by not wanting to acknowledge that something has become more difficult and needs accommodation. For example, we waited too long to shift from a quad-cane to crutches and to use catheterization to alleviate Myrna's anxieties over bladder control, a problem that arose only at the end of this period.

Far worse than these physical problems were the emotional ones. First and least was the problem of remembering that certain things were no longer possible. Myrna, sometimes both of us, would make plans to do something only to be brought up short by remembering that some essential part of that plan was no longer feasible. How many times did we plan to go here or there in the city before remembering that Myrna could no longer use the subway system because of the stairs? How many times did we have to put aside a desire to do something away from the apartment because of the threat of temporary incontinence?

And, unmentioned, tucked away in the back of the mind to be forgotten if possible, there was the increased threat of worse to come. It seemed that just as we adapted to the last loss and were beginning to feel comfortable with it and secure, a new loss would present itself. In the long run, this constant slow slide downward, the constant disappointment of hope and the readjustment to new needs and limits, induced a resigned fatalism in me that contrasted with Myrna's determination to conquer the dragon within. I sometimes thought of her as Don Quixote and of myself as Sancho Panza, her faithful squire.

In the early stages, Myrna would accept no limits on her freedom to move about as she pleased, while I held my breath as she teetered around on a quad-cane or dragged herself about on crutches. At the slightest word of caution from me, her lightning flash of anger would inform me that it was her responsibility and she could take care of herself. I soon learned to let her push herself to her limits and beyond. I accepted the idea that one of my new tasks was to create circumstances that gave her as much freedom as possible, to remove potential hazards, and to pick her up when she fell, which happened with increasing frequency.

We found that the disease itself, by lengthening the time it took for nerve messages to travel to their destinations, provided protection from serious injury—she no longer had the normal tensing-up reflex when she lost her balance. She fell limply and loosely, sustaining a few bruises at worst.

Getting all 130 to 140 pounds of her back to a standing position was not easy. I never found a way to do it that a safety engineer would approve of, and I developed the beginnings of a hernia. The process of getting her back on her feet was made more difficult by the fact that we were never sure how much help she could provide.

Finally we settled on a method that assumed she would not be able to help at all. She would lie on her back on the floor, legs together, while I stood over her, straddling her hips. Half bending over and half squatting, I would reach down to get my forearms under her armpits, while she would reach up to clasp her arms around my neck. Then I would straighten up and step back, pulling her up and pulling her legs out from between mine. Upright, her task was to tense up, preparing her legs to take her weight as I handed her her cane or a crutch.

Successful, we would sometimes celebrate with a triumphant kiss. Failing, with both of us ending up on the floor, which was not often, we avoided tears by laughing at our clumsiness. Once, we didn't bother to get up right away. A kiss of consolation became something more, and we made love right there on the floor. Afterward we cuddled and talked of how lucky we were to be in love.

As Myrna began to lose control of her hands and started to drop or knock over glasses, spills of water and juice became another constant problem and minor irritation. From the mid-1980s until the early 1990s, when her physical therapist gave her a runner's bottle with a cap and plastic straw, there was probably at least a spill a week, some minor, some quite messy. I took the clean-up problem in stride most of the time, under the rule that if one decides to climb a mountain, one may not complain that the path is steep and rocky. Myrna, on the other hand, sometimes fretted about these spills and her falls, blaming herself for the extra work they created. For the most part, we used lighthearted joking about clumsiness and my own time-wasting to finesse our way past any ill-feeling about these kinds of problems.

From the time of the diagnosis, before we were married, Myrna had done everything possible to combat the disease. The first treatment she tried was acupuncture, then just beginning to attract the interest of Western doctors. Myrna went for several sessions to a very pleasant Chinese doctor at New York University Hospital. There seemed to be no immediate result, so both the doctor and Myrna called off the experiment.

Not long after we were married, the British medical journal *Lancet* published a study that indicated that a sizable daily intake of linoleic acid might inhibit the progress of the disease. Myrna researched the acid and found that sunflower seed oil was a prime source. From that point until nearly the end, sunflower seed oil became a staple of Myrna's diet, a part of her morning orange (later, cranberry) juice, her lunch and supper salad dressing, and the primary oil for cooking in our house. Over the years, Myrna also tried yoga, transcendental meditation, Feldenkrais exercise, biofeedback, and a variety of other treatments outside the medical mainstream.

She kept careful track of ongoing scientific research into the disease, largely with the help of publications of the National Multiple Sclerosis Society. When a new drug was authorized for clinical tests, she was quick to try to get into the program. She was able to join in two of these clinical trials—to no effect. She tried to get into another in the late 1980s. We made several trips to the New Jersey hospital where the doctor in charge of the tests was examining possible candidates for the experiment. We were shocked when Myrna was turned away on grounds that her memory was failing and she would not be able to present adequate accounts of the effects of the experimental treatment. As late as 1994, Myrna tried to get into a clinical trial being conducted in Boston, but in that case the distance to be traveled was too great to permit her participation.

She also underwent, in the late 1980s, an experimental chemotherapy procedure overseen by her regular neurologist. The theory behind the treatment was that the progress of this autoimmune disease could be stalled and perhaps stopped by crippling the immune system. So for several weeks Myrna took fairly heavy doses of some murderous chemical that left her weaker, nauseated, and hairless. Knowing I was partial to redheads (my mother, both sisters, and daughter—all redheads), she bought two red wigs, a rather nice one of a modest cut and color, the other in an alarming punk style and color. She loved wearing the latter to disconcert people. Unfortunately, the chemotherapy did no good.

Myrna also maintained a steady schedule of exercise, both at home and in a nearby swimming pool. Every morning, until it was no longer possible for her to do much of anything, she spent half an hour or more going through a regular regimen of arm and leg movements designed to increase both the strength and flexibility of her leg, arm, and torso muscles. In the pool she had another pattern of exercises, but spent most of her time there simply swimming laps, commonly covering as much as a mile or more.

In only one area did Myrna, in these early years of the disease's progress, skimp on cautious management of her illness. She loved very hot showers, and continued to take them despite the fact that heat has an immediate negative impact on the MS sufferer's "nerve strength" and potential bad consequences in the long-term. Cold, on the other hand, will immediately, but only briefly, increase the ability of nerve impulses to get through the damaged pathways. Myrna did not moderate the heat of her showers until one day when she was unable to get out of the shower-tub after one of her steam baths.

Myrna's discipline and determination and her increasingly sophisticated knowledge of the nature of the disease made us both rather short with the helpful acquaintance or virtual stranger who offered advice on how Myrna might better handle or treat her disease. This kind of unsolicited advice began to flow in as soon as Myrna's disability became apparent. At first we listened hopefully on the off chance there was something we had overlooked. But the advice almost always proved to be some enthusiast's offbeat panacea for all ills—a special diet, special exercises, exotic foods or herbs, special massage—all the cockamamie fads of the health obsessed.

These incidents of unwanted advice began to irritate us and then to anger us. We became rather rude to these people and spent some time trying to figure out why their well-meant advice made us angry. We began to examine, for the first time, some common responses to disabilities, including our own. We concluded that many people become uncomfortable in the presence of disability or illness. Sometimes these people simply avoid the handicapped. A married couple who we thought were our good friends before Myrna's illness became apparent, later avoided us entirely. We recognized that the husband was a health nut, a bit of a hypochondriac, and highly anxious in the face of any illness. We could accept his flight from his own vulnerability.

Many of those who provided advice were of a similar sort but with a very unpleasant difference. To cover their anxiety, they had to push their denial onto Myrna. They fended off their own fear with belief in a magic cure. If Myrna didn't share their belief, the disease became her fault and no longer personally threatening. Too often, lurking just behind the advice, was a view that held that poor health reflected a poor attitude. These people are the modern equivalent of Job's comforters, who, to protect their own weak faith, had to believe that Job's misfortunes were the consequence of some secret sin.

This was our first encounter, at a superficial level, with the common American denial of the reality and ubiquity of tragedy, the unavoidable and inexplicable disaster from which there can be no recovery and in which there is no silver lining, no ray of hope. We were made more aware of this denial in the vast majority of people by the contrasting reaction of the few who knew firsthand that circumstances can overwhelm and provide no solution. Time and again street people, the utterly down-and-out homeless, greeted Myrna with "God bless you" and "God be with you." Unlike some of the advice givers, they always spoke directly to Myrna, who needed the comforting, and never to me, as if Myrna could not comprehend or act effectively.

We marveled at these people, mostly black men, who, having nothing to give, gave the greatest gift of all—compassion, the recognition that, whatever our station in life or our accomplishments, we are all finally overwhelmed. We came to believe that many black Americans, drawing on their personal experiences and family histories, have deep wells of understanding and love that are lacking in too many white Americans, buoyed up as they are on the surface of life by inexperience of its darker facts.

These years of Myrna's decline were lightened somewhat by the presence of Conrad, who came to New York in 1985 to get a graduate degree in graphic arts at Pratt Institute after getting a bachelor's degree in Fine Arts at the University of California at Santa Cruz. He was now, at age twenty-three, a very lean six-foot-four and handsome, even dashing. Finding that the courses at Pratt were not teaching him anything new, he got a job as a bank teller and then as a customer service representative for American Express. His girlfriend Joy joined him in 1989.

About once a month, Conrad would come over and cook for us, wonderful meals from recipes he appeared to make up on the fly. Conrad's and Joy's easygoing, helpful concern eased many burdens, and their accounts of their activities brought us news of a New York world that was slowly slipping out of our sight. In the summer of 1991, they returned to California, where Conrad took up teaching elementary school.

During Conrad's stay, and perhaps because he increased our interest in the fine arts, we made the grandest purchase of our lives, a three-by-four-foot painting of daisies entitled *Mid-Summer.* Myrna had seen it on one of her gallery visits with her cousin Charlotte and came home to suggest we buy it. The price was shocking, $5,000. She told me that if that was too much, the same artist, Simon Dinnerstein, had another smaller and cheaper painting at the same gallery. I went across town to check it out.

Mid-Summer was magnificent, depicting over a hundred little daisies, each petal precisely detailed, amidst greenery, growing out of a pot on the floor of a room glowing with sunlight. The very natural white and green of the plants contrasted sharply with the surreal light, which was done in soft, subtle shades of purple, blue, and light green. The mood spoke of fulfillment, of beautiful completeness in the simple moment. The smaller painting (Sorry, Simon!) was a dud. I envisioned *Mid-Summer* on the wall of our bedroom, where Myrna was now spending most of her time, and understood it would be a continual satisfaction in the darker times to come. A week later it was installed, taking up almost an entire wall in the bedroom.

Part of those darker times came to us in the late eighties as Myrna's mother began her slow decline into terminal old age. It began with our sensing in Anne a loss of vitality and a slight confusion during our monthly visits to New Haven and Anne's stays with us in New York.

Arrangements were made to move Anne into a senior citizens complex where several of her friends already lived. The complex consisted of Tower East, for self-sufficient seniors, and Tower One, for those in need of a more protective environment. Initially Anne was to move into Tower East, but it quickly became apparent that her deterioration had progressed so rapidly that she would have to live in Tower One. I remember most clearly that Anne was much slower on the uptake and tired more easily when she came to New York for our Orthodox wedding at the beginning of June in 1987.

I had finally completed my conversion in May after an amusing contretemps with Myrna over my circumcision. Usually a male convert gets only a token nick on his already circumcised penis. Because I was born in the boondocks long ago, I was uncircumcised and had to undergo the procedure in a doctor's office under the watchful eyes of two rabbis. This event did not particularly bother me, but Myrna was very concerned. A few weeks after the circumcision and before the final steps of conversion, Myrna wrote a letter to our rabbi that says a good deal about us both and is terribly ironic in light of the end of our story:

> George was very calm about the whole procedure. I, however, was crazy. I was very anxious about the risk to his health and the probable pain. In fact, three days before the circumcision, I reminded him that he could still back out. But he was determined. . . .
>
> I don't know why I felt so anxious, other than to attribute it to concern for George's physical well-being. I have been thinking about this now for two weeks, and I have identified two other key reasons for my sudden burst of hysteria: 1) jealousy and 2) fear of permanence. . . .
>
> Why jealousy? . . . Since our marriage, and even before, I have felt certain of George's undivided loyalty and love. But now, with his impending conversion, maybe I feel threatened that I will have to share first-place honors with God. You see, George never had to mutilate himself to prove his love for me; but for God he did. . . .
>
> So, if I trust George's love for me [without requiring circumcision], why couldn't God trust George's love for Him?
>
> [If Myrna had told me this at the time, I could have told her that the circumcision proved nothing but my willingness to submit to divine whim, however crazy. I could also have told her then, instead of later, that the great transcendental "sin" of my life is that I loved her more than God.]
>
> And what about fear of permanence? Circumcision is an irrevocable act. I can't think of anything else that has the same degree of permanence.

Perhaps my unwillingness to accept functional losses caused by MS also reflects my refusal to admit that these losses are permanent. I still feel that maybe this new physical therapist, that new medication, this new exercise, that new prayer offers the path to regained health for me. I just have to find the right path.

But circumcision is a whole different ball game. It is final, really final. No turning back. I guess that is where commitment to transcendent values comes into play. Some values *do* deserve permanence.

In any case, the day came when I entered the mikvah, or ritual bath, to answer three questions about my faith and to say the blessings that would make me a Jew. The first two questions were easy to answer with a simple "yes"; I don't even remember what they were. The third question, however, brought the process to a dead halt: "Do you believe that God is just?" In fact, according to the common meaning of this human term, I did not and do not believe that God is just.

After a very long silence, the rabbi gave me a clue about how I might respond. I said, "Yes, but not in any way that we can understand." The attending rabbis' sighs of relief were audible. The blessings were said, and I was, irrevocably, a Jew named Micah Nachshon ben Avraham *avinu.*

The next evening, June 4, 1987, Myrna and I were remarried in the rabbi's office in a lovely quiet ceremony that was, coincidentally, attended by some of the leading lights of the synagogue. Coincidentally, because it was time for evening prayers and they were there to make a minyan. We signed the *ketubah,* or marriage contract, and the chupah, or wedding canopy, was unfurled and held up by the synagogue president, Conrad, a close friend, and one other person. The cantor, our beloved "Chaz," began the ceremony with a sung invocation. We did not stand for the ceremony, because Myrna could no longer do so for more than a very few minutes.

After the wedding, Anne and Conrad "strolled" four blocks with us (we strode, Myrna rolled) to a restaurant for a quiet wedding dinner. The short walk and all the excitement were an obvious strain for Anne. We took a cab home instead of the usual bus.

During her few months in Tower One, a series of "cerebral accidents," or ministrokes, continued to take their toll on Anne's capacity. We arranged for her to visit us a couple of times, and it was heartbreaking to see this once vibrant and jolly lady lost in confusion and helplessness. I remember one evening at the dinner table when I had to keep turning her plate so she could eat all her food. A ministroke had temporarily closed down her awareness of one side of her visual field; turning the plate brought the remaining food into sight. On another occasion, this always modest woman wandered half clothed from her room out to the foyer between our dining area and the kitchen. The worst of this incident for Myrna and me was that Anne was not at all embarrassed, only befuddled.

That was probably Anne's last visit with us. She had reached a point where she needed help taking a bath, taxing Myrna's own capabilities to their limits. It was simply dangerous for Anne to be with us when Myrna's mobility and strength were so severely limited and my attention must, necessarily, be so divided.

Not long afterward, it became necessary to put Anne in a nursing home, the Jewish Home for the Aged in New Haven, which, as nursing homes go, is exemplary in every respect.

By this time, Anne was barely functioning. She still recognized Myrna and me and her friends, she could still feed herself with a little help, and she could, on occasion, respond appropriately to questions and circumstances. For the most part, however, she was extremely passive—silent, slow-moving, unexpressive, and needful of the most detailed direction to get through the motions of daily life.

I think the last time we saw Anne alive was Thanksgiving, 1988, when we took her out of the nursing home for a real Thanksgiving dinner. I handled this "operation" by myself, loading and unloading Myrna's electric scooter, and Myrna, and Anne's mechanical wheelchair, and Anne at the Home, the restaurant, and back at the Home again.

Anne was very nearly absent, not relating much to Myrna, or me, or her food. She briefly mistook me for Ben, her husband, dead nearly twenty years. In the restaurant, she saw a portly man walk by the table. For the first time that day, a spark of animation lit her face. "Ben?" she called out weakly. "Ben?" The portly man and the moment passed, and Anne fell back into absence. Was her mind slipping back to olden days? Or was she already looking ahead to a desired reunion?

A short time later, Anne contracted pneumonia, which was once known as "the old folk's friend," because it killed rather quickly and mercifully. Today, pneumonia can be easily defeated with antibiotics, and that is what the doctors did. They saved her life, so she could strangle to death on her own vomit a few weeks later. Anne was, one could hope, again in the company of her beloved Ben.

We went to New Haven for the funeral, which was gracefully put together by Beverly. Anne was buried next to Ben in a peaceful, uncrowded cemetery shaded by lovely young trees.

In late summer of 1988, we spent a week in Los Angeles, where I attended a conference on database programming and Myrna relaxed, reading and swimming in the hotel pool. At the end of the week, we moved to Studio City to attend my daughter Anna's wedding. Anna and Art, who works in the television industry, had been going together for several years and suited each other well; his calm, easy-going manner serving to dampen Anna's intensity. I liked Art and was very pleased with their marriage.

It was a grand affair at an old house once owned by a big movie star of the silent era. The ceremony and dinner afterward took place in the house's garden. Anna was escorted down the "aisle" by both her fathers, her gorgeous alabaster skin aglow with delight. After the ritual, Myrna and I posed for a picture with Anna and Art. Myrna insisted on standing. The picture shows a smiling foursome, apparently in the pink of good health. It does not record that Art and I are straining to hold Myrna up.

Myrna, meanwhile, had been writing letters to our rabbis, a practice she started soon after her retirement. These letters were a way of asking questions of herself, perhaps even a kind of prayer, about her illness and other issues involving God's justice and concern.

In her very first letter she questioned whether her prayers were done right, implying that if she could only pray correctly, God would deliver her from the MS. Did only Christians get personal miracles? She also raised questions about the lack of any relief for the disabled from Orthodox stringencies and the lack of any mention of the handicapped in Torah: "Yes, God parted the Red Sea and delivered the Jews from slavery in Egypt, but were any of those people handicapped? How could they have made the trip? Maybe the handicapped did participate—*that*'s why the trip took forty years!" She asked if the rabbi could make her situation "any easier to understand—or to endure."

Myrna struggled mightily in her early letters over the question of how God could permit this disease to wreak such havoc on her. She didn't blame God for it, though she did question whether it might not be a punishment for her own particular sins as a nonobservant Jew.

Myrna wrote:

> I know this sounds very naive or paranoid, but sometimes I feel that God is picking on me. I made Him very unhappy for some reason—for some *big* reason—so He chose me for a big punishment. Right? No, of course not. That's a very childish way to look at things. I'm an adult, and I should have sophisticated adult ideas.
>
> But deep down, I don't . . . I don't have a deeper idea about God's love for me. . . . Does God love me? . . . Is it a sign of spiritual development that I sometimes feel that God is picking on me. Or is it a sign of regressive juvenility?
>
> I guess my task is to believe that God loves me even if my health does not improve. But that's a very heavy task. I'm only human, and my intelligence is very limited. It's very nice to know that God loves me enough so that He does not ease up on His standards—He doesn't insult me by expecting less of me—but I wonder if He isn't really expecting a bit too much. Or does He know something about me that I don't know?

A year later, Myrna was reflecting on sin and repentance: "Should I regard my marriage to George as a sin? Should I feel regret that I married him? Is *that* what would constitute proper repentance for me? I understand that our marriage was impermissible, in terms of Jewish law. Does that mean the marriage was a sin? I can say that, but I don't feel it. Nor do I feel any regret for having committed this 'sin.' Hardly the stuff of true repentance. [To regret the marriage and many other violations of Jewish law before I became observant] would be to disavow much of my life. I can't do that, at least not sincerely."

Myrna felt no need for false piety. In another letter she questioned God's good sense in forbidding Adam and Eve to eat of the fruit of the tree of knowledge of good and evil. He had given them reason and intelligence, she wrote, and a serpent that appealed to those talents. What did He expect? "The cards were stacked . . . from the very beginning."

Was God punishing her? What had she done that was so wrong, as terrible as what the disease was doing to her? Was there anything she could do to avert the evil decree? Did God intend that she learn something? Greater humility, perhaps? Or was she supposed to surrender her fierce drive for independence? And if she learned humility and gave up her independence, would God abate the disease, perhaps even restore her to full health, work a miracle for her? Or maybe there was some spiritual growth to be gained here, and if she learned her spiritual lessons, better health would indicate a passing grade?

All of her questions involved the classic problem of theodicy—How can an all-powerful, all-good God cause or condone such tortuous destruction of His creatures? Or: Why do bad things happen to good people? Answers to this question range from the cruelly primitive to the most sublime theological sleight-of-hand. The simplest and cruelest answer is that of Job's "comforters": "If terrible evil has befallen you, search your heart for the terrible evil within, for God is just. A terrible pride in your own righteousness, a deep complacency that ignores the sufferings of others, a refusal to submit your will to the Creator's—any or all of these could be the cause of God's wrath."

In the book of Job, however, the afflicted one demands that God Himself explain His actions. His wife, early on, urges Job to "curse God and die," but by his actions Job asserts that the human creature and his relationship to God are too important for that kind of cop-out. So Job sits in the ruins of his home, covered with sores and bereft of all happiness, and dares God to answer him. "Why are you doing this to me?"

The courageous and wonderfully wise writer of Job does not flinch from the task he has set himself. Nor does he *apologize* for God! He has God speak to Job in thunder out of the whirlwind. God asks, "Who are you to question me? Stand up, like a human being, so that I may question *you*. Did you create the universe? Did you set the billions of stars aglow? Did you draw life out of slime? Have you any idea of the eons of time and the vastness of space in which My wonders move and will continue to move for eons to come? Can you even begin to imagine my purpose in all this? No? Then why do you suppose that My aims are yours, that your idea of justice is Mine?"

The lesson of Job appears to be that God's justice is very much defined by His purposes, and because we cannot understand His purposes, we cannot understand His justice. So from our limited perspective, God is very unjust, even malignant. Unless one has personally heard the voice out of the whirlwind, the story seems to ask our approval for a coldhearted despot who would rather pull rank than sit down and reason with us. Part of the agony of being human is that we are and will probably remain too ignorant and self-centered to understand "the big picture." It does seem that, whatever God's aims are, they involve a good deal of human suffering beyond even the great deal that we inflict on each other and could avoid if we chose.

But all of these are my views and of no comfort to those who suffer. Nor was Myrna much comforted by such ideas: "It sounds so vast and vague and incomprehensible. At least it's beyond my capacity to comprehend."

But she did begin to comprehend a little as the crippling worsened. In late 1988 she wrote: "It's strange isn't it that when misfortune strikes and I *could* feel that God has abandoned me, I am more aware of my dependence on God to see me through. In fact, when I was healthy, I was not at all aware of my reliance on God. [Even when] I had already been involved with the synagogue for five years ... I still did not feel how absolutely I depended on God."

And shortly after that, she wrote: "I guess what I'm saying is that in God's scheme of things, people matter, one to another. Perhaps that is a simple truism, and I should have known it all along. Perhaps I did. But I see it now with greater clarity. And I see the direct connection to my own personal reality."

The letter breaks off there. I wish she had been more explicit about how the person-to-person relation connected to her own reality. Perhaps she made that clearer in a later letter, when she wrote: "George is here for me when I need him. Is God?"

The sad fact was that she was already beginning to experience a decline in her mental abilities. Reviewing the two dozen or more long letters she wrote between 1985 and 1990, it is easy to see a change after 1988. There is less care with the grammar; the comments are less trenchant. There is less capacity to bring an issue into focus. More ominous, some of the letters are quite repetitive, clearly displaying a decaying memory and, worse, the beginnings of the terrible mood swings from euphoria to despair that would become more severe and rapid as the next years passed. Unaware, she had begun the long, slow slide into serious debility.

9

Down, Always Down

During the good years, between 1973 and 1985, Myrna was hospitalized almost every two years for intensive treatment with corticosteroids to help defend her nerves against a flare-up of the MS. Corticosteroids sometimes have the side effect of inducing mild euphoria or depression. Myrna was lucky and became euphoric during her first hospitalizations. She thought of her hospital stays, which lasted about a week, as little vacations, giving her time to read and think about things important to her. She was still fully mobile and roamed the halls, sometimes pushing her steroid drip along beside her, to chat with other patients or read in the ward's sunny dayroom. Later corticosteroid treatments, however, sometimes threw her into mild depressions that lasted several weeks.

In late 1985, soon after emerging from one of these hospital stays, and in mild euphoria, Myrna wrote a nine-page single-spaced letter to her various doctors in which she discussed, very cogently, some of her concerns about patient treatment. She focused on problems of communication and distrust between doctors and patients, noting that both feel a degree of powerlessness—the patients because their bodies are betraying them, and the doctors because they don't always know what to do for the patient and fear the consequences of poor outcomes.

But Myrna pinpointed an added, unnecessary element in the atmosphere of powerlessness and distrust—the doctors' pose of absolute confidence in their superior knowledge. Too often, Myrna said, the result is that doctors feel threatened by patients' questions. "The patient's desire to know might strike the doctor as a lack of trust—and the doctor may long for the good old days of blind faith. But it's not really a lack of trust. The patient knows that the doctor doesn't know everything. And the doctor knows that, too. . . . The doctor could look at [the questioning patient] with *relief.* The doctor is freed to be a little less than perfect."

Myrna's first lengthy hospitalization, nearly four weeks, came in the fall of 1989, sixteen years after the MS was first diagnosed. She was forty-six. She had been having increasing difficulty walking with crutches, her memory was noticeably deteriorating, and she seemed more tired than usual. Dr. Petitio, her neurologist, put her in New York Hospital for steroid treatment and then had her transferred to Burke Rehabilitation Center in White Plains for physical therapy. As was usual now, Myrna hated the "infantilization" created by hospital routine and the sharp limits on her freedom created by her new handicaps.

At Burke she brightened up a bit, partly a steroid euphoria. It was a new environment, and compared to most of the other patients, many of them victims of spinal cord injuries, she was more able and healthier. She enjoyed the "basket-weaving" classes and, at first, responded well to the physical therapists. But the second week, boredom and frustration set in again.

The most frustrating thing was Burke's lack of a cold-water swimming pool. We both knew that swimming was the best possible therapy, but she couldn't use the warm-water pools designed for heart patients and people with hip replacements. (Remember, any unusual heat immediately diminishes the "nerve strength" of an MS patient.) We later found that no physical rehab facility in the metropolitan area had a cold-water pool.

It is difficult to convey the importance of swimming and aquatherapy for MS patients. The buoyancy of water diminishes the pull of gravity and provides a degree of restfulness, while permitting the muscles to exercise slowly against the denser medium. The lower gravity provides the severely disabled MS patient with a feeling of freedom not available outside the pool. Ordinarily Myrna swam regularly at a private swim-and-exercise club atop a high-rise apartment building about twenty blocks from our place. In Burke, the four weeks without swimming was like a jail sentence.

She also tired of her bubbly, positive-thinking physical therapist. Myrna simply couldn't do some of the things the therapist suggested. By and large, physical therapy at a rehab center is aimed at restoring as much function as possible to patients whose condition is stable or improving. Rehab centers and their therapists can become as frustrated and discouraged as their patients in dealing with a progressive disabling condition.

Burke's greatest utility for us was the education it gave in adapting to and managing serious disability at home. Through Burke we got a bath chair and grab bars for our bathrooms. I got some instruction in lifting Myrna and in helping her with passive exercises. Myrna learned to catheterize herself, a necessary procedure now to avoid public embarrassment if her increasingly spastic and uncontrollable bladder decided to act up.

The following spring, understanding that Myrna's decline might soon make a major trip almost impossible, I suggested to Myrna that we go for broke and fulfill our desire to visit Israel. I proposed that we go for a month, because we could only do half as much in a day as the able-bodied and healthy. She agreed. I took the last of my pension savings out of the bank, and immediately after Passover we were on our way to Tel Aviv.

Using a van with a hydraulic lift, provided in return for a contribution to the Israeli disabled vet's organization, we drove to Efrat for our first Sabbath and weekend. Efrat is a prosperous West Bank town south of Bethlehem where several present and former members of our synagogue have homes. After a peaceful Sabbath, we spent a day sightseeing in the arid Judean Hills. Then it was off to Jerusalem and all the regular tourist sites. A week later we were in Tiberias on the Sea of Galilee.

From there, during the second week, we traveled all over northern Israel, right up to the Lebanese border and the Golan Heights.

At the border with Syria, we had trouble grasping that we were only forty miles from the storied city of Damascus. Then it was on to Tel Aviv and all the tourist sites there for our third week.

Finally, we went south to Arad, northwest of Beersheba. From there we explored the Dead Sea region, taking the obligatory slimy and dirty dip. We drove deep into the Negev, where we saw the Maktesh Ramon, the Giant Crater, one of the biggest wadis in the world and more interesting than the Grand Canyon because of its more complex geology.

We were astounded by the lush greenness of the north and the incredible aridity of the south. The Negev makes the Nevada desert look pleasant and comfortable. The view from the Golan Heights over the Huleh valley and the Galilee shows a land made rich by years of care and hard work. But Israel is not a rich country by Western standards, and therefore lacks the resources to create easy access for handicapped people.

Many tourist sites and museums lack adequate access for wheelchairs. Masada, the site of Herod's castle above the Dead Sea, was totally inaccessible. Many streets in the Old City in Jerusalem and in the ancient town of Safad are impassable for wheelchairs. And many little conveniences, such as disposable diapers (for use as panty liners) are unavailable. On the other hand, Myrna had two wonderful swims, one in an Olympic-size pool for disabled veterans and their families in Tel Aviv and one in Arad. The water in the Arad pool was so cold that Myrna, with only my arm for balance, was able to walk out of it and up two steps to her wheelchair.

The trip to Israel gave Myrna the idea of turning her letters to the rabbis into a book. This project became an enduring theme of her euphorias during the next five years. I arranged all her letters, even those to family and friends, in chronological order on my computer and printed out several copies. Still not fully aware of her deteriorating mental condition, I exercised my editorial experience to warn her that there was a great deal of repetition in the letters that would have to be cut, that explanatory transitions between the letters would have to be written, and that new letters would have to be written to more fully develop some of the questions raised. I suggested that she needed to do a good deal of this work before showing the letters to a publisher.

Myrna ignored this advice and proceeded to write many more letters expressing her enthusiasm over the idea of a book and asking rabbis to comment on her letters from the point of view of Jewish law and lore—comments to be added to the book. It was a good idea, but Myrna refused to do any work on the letters herself. This insouciance was completely contrary to Myrna's normal approach to a project. I failed to perceive its meaning, shrugging it off as a natural result of her focus on the practical problems of daily living. If I had paid more attention and thought about the problem more, I might have perceived early on the extent to which the disease was ravaging her mind and judgment.

In the middle of the night of August 16, 1991, disaster struck. Myrna had gotten up to go to the bathroom, managing the now rare feat of getting out of bed and onto her feet by herself. Halfway through the ten steps required to get to the bathroom, she fell and was never able to walk again. Unwilling to accept the idea that the disease had finally completely disconnected her brain from her leg muscles, we hoped the fall itself had damaged something that could be fixed. So Myrna went off to the hospital again, for X-rays of her lower body, steroid treatment, and more rehab. Myrna was now forty-eight and had been struggling with ever-increasing serious disability for over six years.

This hospital stay was almost five weeks long, two in New York Hospital and nearly three at Burke. This time Myrna found no pleasure at all in any of the routines. Like a prisoner in irons, her spirit was constantly and severely chafed by her total dependence on nurses and aides for virtually every need. She particularly hated the fact that she could not have a shower every day and the embarrassment of peeing in her diaper because an aide could not spare the time to move her to the commode at her bedside.

The physical therapy at Burke was relatively useless. The therapist tried to get Myrna on her feet and walking with the aid of a walker. Myrna could stand for a short time and could, with great effort, take a few agonizingly slow steps, leaning heavily on the walker, but the effort was immense compared to the result. And as subsequent days passed, the effort required was greater and the result more meager. Myrna was wheelchair bound. We could only give thanks that she experienced no pain, only numbness.

Other Burke innovations were more helpful. I learned to catheterize Myrna, and we were put on a strict schedule of four catheterizations a day, four to five hours apart. These catheterizations were now required to empty Myrna's bladder. The sphincter that opens to allow urine to pass out had become so spastic that it was more or less permanently closed, leaking a little urine at a time if the bladder was full. If Myrna wasn't catheterized, the urine could accumulate, posing a danger to her bladder and kidneys. I also learned the routine for sterilizing the catheters. My lifting techniques were again examined by specialists, and I was given some pointers on how to make them more effective and less strenuous.

Burke also added more medications to Myrna's regimen—a pill for decreasing urine production and another for decreasing the growing spasticity of her legs. Myrna was now taking eighteen pills, five different medications, every day: Oxybutyinin to relax the bladder muscles; Colchicine to slow down the MS (maybe); Baclofen for spasticity; Elavil (amitriptylin) for depression and to help her get to sleep; and Hiprex, a mild medication to guard against urinary tract infection. From time to time, other medications were temporarily added to the list: Prednisone, a corticosteroid; sulfa medications to fight urinary tract infection; and later, a pill to loosen her stool in order to avoid bowel compaction; and Paxil, a mild antidepressant.

On one of Myrna's last days at Burke, the social worker for her ward questioned me about Myrna's care at home. I assured her that I was present at all times, that I had already been handling all the cooking and household chores and details of Myrna's personal care that she could not see to herself. The social worker was relieved and gave her approval for Myrna's release.

We both, the social worker and I, erred in this interview. I was too sanguine about the tasks ahead; the social worker was too ready to accept my assurances that I could manage alone. The social worker should have questioned me more closely about my

own health and strength. There should have been some professional evaluation, perhaps, of my state of mind, my ability to bear
up under the strain of providing daily care for possibly years to
come. The alternative of Medicaid assistance should have been
suggested and explained. Nevertheless, had the social worker done
all of this, I might still have put her off with bland assurances. At
the least, however, I would have been given some serious idea of
the stresses I would experience as a full-time caregiver and some
clue about how to cope with them.

Hospitals, physical therapists, social workers, visiting nurses, and
psychologists have generally ignored the plight of caregivers. It is
almost as if, hearing that a loving caregiver is on the scene, they
are relieved—of further responsibility and of sorrow. There is little
recognition, let alone study, of either the physical or psychological
burdens of caregivers—no recognition that family members who
care for the handicapped become handicapped themselves,
sharply limited in their freedom and laboring under burdens little
noticed by society and understood even less.

Above all, there is no recognition of the onset of early grief, continuing and unresolvable grief, and, in the case of a progressive
disease like Myrna's, ever-deepening grief. It is as if the "helping
professions" believe the caregiver should be "happy" that the
patient is still alive, however severely handicapped. From the
"helpers" it's all "Rah! Rah! You can do it! Think positive!" And
they ignore the negative.

In December 1991, about six weeks after Myrna returned home
from Burke, I wrote a letter to the advice columnist of *Jewish Week*
that illuminates my state of mind, girding myself for the task at
hand. The letter was a comment on someone else's complaints to
the columnist about an unrectified injustice of some sort.

> I have thought long and hard about the issue of God's jus-
> tice and have not found any pleasant answer. The story pre-
> sented by your reader . . . illustrates the adage "Be careful
> what you ask for; you may get it." The brothers asked for
> God's justice; they should have asked for man's justice and
> God's mercy.

God's justice is whatever Malkenu (our Creator King) wants. Period. Often, it is quite unsatisfactory to our own sense of justice.

To those who question God's justice, I have a simple response. Care for the victims of God's creative process, seek the answer from them, and give praise and thanksgiving to the One who gave you the opportunity to ask. Then, and only then, is your question meaningful. Only then is it answerable.

But the answer is simple: In this small piece of Creation, *you* are God's justice. That is, you were created to be God's caring, God's mercy, God's compassion; you were created to be God's own labor and time here and now, and only you can help create a just world.

Don't ask about God's ultimate justice; God is making a whole universe. Ask about your own justice, here and now in the little time you've been given; ask about your mercy and compassion and labor. Ask the "image of God," yourself, to create what it desires with your whole heart and energy.

Not that I was without help at home. Since the 1989 hospitalization, we had hired assistants to come in a few hours a week to help us with some daily tasks, particularly cleaning. Two of these helpers stand out in my mind. Carolina, who had worked at the Metropolitan Opera as a costumer, hairdresser, and makeup artist, was a Holocaust survivor, having been hidden as a child by a Catholic priest in Riga, Latvia, for the duration of the war. An intense woman, Carolina brought a degree of operatic glamor into our bookish lives.

Claudette, a tall, rangy woman originally from Trinidad, came on after the 1991 hospitalization. Claudette is a powerhouse—strong, confident, energetic, and always upbeat. There was the constant refrain on her arrival: "How are you, Claudette?" "Oh, Goooood!" in a voice of rising affirmation. She would immediately bear down on the task at hand or seek one out if neither Myrna nor I had anything pressing, all the while keeping up a lively patter about people, places, and things of interest.

In early 1992, not long after Myrna's release from Burke, Myrna and I went to see our new rabbi with a difficult question of Jewish law: Is suicide always absolutely impermissible? After watching her mother's decline, Myrna had frequently brought up the question of suicide and, on asking if I would help if necessary, had always been assured that I would. Now she raised the idea again, "trying it on for fit," so to speak. She did not, at this time, seriously contemplate ending her life in the immediate future.

I promised again that I would help, but I suggested it would be good idea to talk to our rabbi about the issue. Myrna was not enthusiastic about the idea, fearing that he might pronounce an absolute proscription that would only further complicate her problems.

A young man with a slightly mystical bent and wisdom far beyond his years, our rabbi was not shocked by the question or dismayed. He patiently explained to us that while, yes, suicide was absolutely forbidden, a person who committed suicide was traditionally considered to be of unsound mind and therefore not to be blamed. Further, he ruled, in certain circumstances, if the suicide was not done in despair and anger with God, if it did not deny God and His love and mercy, then it could be considered "as natural a death as any other."

We were relieved by this response. I have since found in talking with people and in newspaper accounts of people seeking judicial approval of their own suicide, that the free grant of permission to escape gives the prisoner of disease a new lease on life. Empowered with real choice and knowing he can leave whenever he chooses, he chooses to stick it out. That is, the sense of powerlessness is rescinded and the despair is lightened. People are much more likely to wait for a "natural" death when they are not forced to live an "unnatural" life. (The words "natural" and "unnatural" are in quotes because, in today's technological world, I am not clear about what they mean, if anything.)

So it was with Myrna. Although beset from time to time with strong considerations of suicide, Myrna continually sought out and found reasons to continue.

Oddly enough, I did not think of asking the rabbi about the status of a suicide assister under Jewish law. The reasons I did not think to ask are simple: If Myrna wanted to leave, I was going to help whatever the law or the consequences. Furthermore, it was inconceivable to me that if suicide could be condoned in some circumstances, a person who enabled that freedom could be condemned. Nevertheless, I was only a little surprised to find out afterward that many in the traditional Orthodox community saw me as a murderer!

Soon after our meeting with the rabbi, I drew the following fanciful parallel to Myrna's and my situation. Myrna and I are in Auschwitz. Myrna is the object of a fiendish experiment conducted by the infamous Dr. Mengele. Supposedly with the aim of learning something about human responses to extreme conditions, but really out of the same idly curious brutality of a child clipping the wings from a butterfly, Mengele is slowly destroying the connections between Myrna's brain and her body. I am a *kapo*, a prisoner-trustee, responsible for seeing to it that the object of the experiment is otherwise as comfortable and entertained as possible.

The experiment has progressed to the point at which paraplegia (loss of function below the waist) is complete and signs of quadriplegia (loss of function above the waist) have set in. Worse, Mengele is now beginning to destroy the mental abilities of the brain. I did not carry the fantasy any further at the time or raise the obvious question in the context of the fantasy: What were the moral choices of the experimental object and the kapo in this situation?

In Auschwitz, suicide was absolutely forbidden. After all, the Nazis *wanted* the inmates to die, so staying alive was the best way to defy them. But in the fantasy Myrna is an exception. Mengele does not want his experimental object to die and bring his sadistic pleasures to an end. Should either Myrna or the *kapo* or both in concert defy the evil doctor by seeking Myrna's death? Are either of them obligated to act?

In reality, the half-maddened kapo turned to drink. My drinking had begun to get out of hand in 1990, interfering with my work and my general functioning. I had known for some years that I was an alcoholic, but until that year, the booze had always been an occasional thing, something I could overindulge today and do without tomorrow. I thought that pattern was fixed; I failed to appreciate the progressive power of the beast. Later, when I had learned more about alcoholic patterns and that any consistent overindulgence is a sign of the disease, I found I had displayed classic alcoholic behavior from the very beginning.

My first encounter with alcohol was in the spring of 1950, at age seventeen, when I attended a party thrown by my marine corps reserve unit to celebrate the founding of the corps. The beer was free and served in big pitchers; I drank it as if it were soda pop. I felt no ill effects until I walked outside, when I suddenly became staggeringly drunk. I thought it was fun, even when the driver of the municipal bus that would take me home refused to let me on. I had to walk about four miles in the middle of the night through one of the roughest sections of south Oakland.

I drank fairly heavily and regularly during my eighteen-month stint on active duty as a marine brig and gate guard on a couple of navy bases in the San Diego area. But once I got out in 1952, I scarcely had a drink for the next five years. Then, from about 1957 on, I only drank at parties when the booze was free, sticking to beer and wine until a professor introduced me to the pungent glory of fine scotch in 1961. I discovered brandy in 1963.

Brandy and wine were my drinks of choice until 1968 when my boss at Deadline Data introduced me to martinis, and I found that vodka produced much more bearable hangovers than any other spirit. That kind of development (from beer to wine to whiskey, and from rare to occasional to frequent overindulgence) over about twenty years is very common among alcoholics.

By 1980 I was drinking regularly, a cocktail or two a day, at least. There were still false signs of moderation; that is, I could stop at two martinis. On the other hand, I would also get completely blasted in the evening if the booze was free, or I had no obligations the next day. I called these little benders "vacations in place." This pattern began to change in 1989.

Whether it was the natural progression of the disease, my grief over Myrna's deterioration, or exhaustion, or a combination of all three is not important. I began to drink steadily every evening. The alcohol numbed the heartache and, for a while, gave me extra energy. But when, by the end of 1990, I was killing a pint of vodka, neat, between five and midnight every evening, I began to worry. When I realized I was drinking out of necessity and found it impossible to get into the evening without a drink, I knew I had to quit.

So I did, totally—for almost six months. Then, thinking I had the beast tamed and that a return to moderation was possible, I had a martini during lunch with a friend. Within a matter of weeks, I was drinking more than a pint a day. A year later, it was a fifth a day. I had reached that point when I needed a drink to get started in the morning. I despaired. I wondered how much longer it could go on before I did something that could harm Myrna.

I was a quiet drunk, like the dutiful housewife filling hours of hopelessness with a soft fog of unfeeling. I still got the shopping done. I managed the items of personal care that Myrna needed. I continued to get my free-lance work done. I still got tasty, nutritious meals to the table on time. But things were perceptibly disintegrating, including my body, which had shed twenty excess pounds and was now living off needed fats and muscle.

Myrna, of course, was aware of the drinking and as worried about the future as I was. But *she* acted, appealing to my daughter for help. Out of the blue, I got a call from Anna. She did not discuss the situation with me. She commanded: Find a thirty-day detox and rehab program, sign up, and go. She would come to New York to oversee Myrna's care while I was away, and she and Art would take care of the costs. I said, "Yes!" Three weeks later, thanks to about $30,000 worth of Anna's and Art's generosity, I was in a rehab hospital in south New Jersey and Myrna had round-the-clock care, supervised by Anna. I had my last drink the morning of September 16, 1992.

Early in the rehab process, it occurred to me that perhaps I had gotten so sick on booze as a kind of sympathetic reaction to Myrna's disease—we both had a chronic-progressive illness that was killing us. Whether fact or fiction, this idea was a major factor in my recovery. Myrna had fought her MS valiantly for years without success. Could I do any less, when all the treatment I needed was the resolve never to drink again? Going back to the bottle would mock her courage and determination. So, with her example before me, I began to recover. I celebrated my sixtieth birthday in the company of about thirty other admitted drunks and addicts in the rehab center.

When I got out of rehab and returned home for a joyful reunion with Myrna, I found staying dry relatively easy, although I still fantasize about the delicious taste of rich chocolate cake with a brandy chaser. For the first three months, I made an AA meeting almost every day, the recovering alcoholic's "90–and–90," ninety meetings in ninety days. After that I made weekly evening meetings regularly for about six months. By then, however, Myrna's condition had so deteriorated that I no longer felt comfortable leaving her alone for more than a few minutes. I stopped going to AA meetings—with no ill effects.

Drying out had one unhappy side effect. My libido went to sleep. For two years, the alcohol had fueled lust and clouded over the confusion of my roles as both lover and nurse. When the fog lifted, the nurse's focus on Myrna's body squelched the lover's fascination. This was not as serious a development as it might appear. Myrna had already lost a great deal of sensation below the waist— to the extent that I had to keep watch for bruises and little cuts because Myrna was unaware of such injuries—and I have never been able to make love to a physically unresponsive woman. Myrna and I had to be content to cuddle, and we cuddled a lot, usually falling asleep in each other's arms.

10

Losing One's Self

Prior to drying out, I had begun the process of getting Myrna on Medicaid. It was essential that I have help taking care of Myrna so that I could continue to make a living and so that Myrna would have more freedom of movement. Medicaid would also relieve us of the $200–a-month cost of medications and medical supplies.

The first step was to have Myrna transfer all her property to an irrevocable trust, of which I was the sole beneficiary. New York State law permitted the transfer to such a trust of an ill person's assets, up to about $60,000 in such a situation, a measure enabling a family to avoid utter bankruptcy in the face of catastrophic illness and extreme old age. In our case, we managed to stash $28,000 in the trust account. That was done in early 1992. The fact is that we should have applied for Medicaid in 1989, immediately after Myrna's first hospitalization at Burke and long before our money became so seriously depleted. But we were too proud and too protective of our privacy to be sensible.

The actual application for Medicaid was a time-consuming process that involved dredging up piles of documents, mostly bank statements and tax returns, covering the previous three years of our finances. The application process had been interrupted by my stay in rehab but was quickly resumed thereafter, and in late 1992 the first home-health aide—mostly paid for by Medicaid—was assigned to us.

We had been told that there was likely to be a period of adjustment before we and an aide settled on each other; until then, we could expect to see a different aide nearly every day or week. True to forecast, we had to put up with a string of aides who were either too weak, too ill trained, too careless, or too lazy to do the work required.

When Gloria Howard showed up on our doorstep in April 1993, I was disheartened. She was a small black lady, scarcely Myrna's size, and certainly not young, perhaps no younger than Myrna's fifty years. (In fact, I found out later that she was sixty-one, a year older than I was.) That first morning, doubting Gloria's capacity to handle the various lifts required to get Myrna into the shower and out again, I did them myself. Gloria seemed impatient with me. When I lifted Myrna onto the bed for her morning catheterization, Gloria said, "I can do the lifting. It's what I'm trained for."

A certain sharpness in her voice and a glint in her eye let me know I was trespassing on her area of expertise. Gloria was the first of nearly two dozen aides to have obvious professional pride. I was impressed—and a bit intimidated—by her no-nonsense, take-charge attitude. I got out of her way and, from that moment to the end, Gloria handled most of the details of Myrna's daytime care.

Over the ensuing two years, we found that Gloria was a devout Roman Catholic whose family came from New York City. She had raised several children and was a proud grandmother. She was highly intelligent and well educated, and always eager to learn more. A fount of information on black history, especially the Harlem music scene, she constantly added to her knowledge with wide reading. She was almost as compulsive a reader as Myrna and I.

That trait alone would have endeared her to us, but she was also very alert to Myrna's needs and sensitive about Myrna's feelings without being sentimental or intrusively solicitous. Their relationship very quickly developed beyond that of patient and helper, blossoming into deep respect, friendship, and mutual concern.

Gloria came in for up to ten hours a day six days one week, and five days the next week; that is, she got Sunday off every other week.

Her replacement was usually an incompetent stranger, but in the last several months of Myrna's life, we had a regular helper every other Sunday who was both cheerful and able. No aide came in on Saturday, the Sabbath, because we were usually up early and off to synagogue for the morning, and did not go out in the afternoon.

An average day began at seven in the morning when I got Myrna out of bed and onto the commode and wheeled her into the half-bath to brush her teeth. I got her breakfast—almost always a glass of juice, a dish of prunes, and a slice of challah (a Jewish bread made with eggs). While Myrna ate and looked at the newspaper, I took my shower and dressed, had my own breakfast, and started writing. Gloria arrived about eight o'clock and immediately took Myrna to the full bathroom for a shower. My help was required for a particularly strenuous lift that made sure Myrna was seated correctly on the bath bench.

The shower over, I was called on again to lift Myrna and dry her bottom before reseating her on the commode. Gloria wheeled her back to the bedroom, lifted her onto the bed, and prepared for the morning catheterization, which I did when Myrna could no longer do it herself. After the cath, Gloria rubbed a skin softener into Myrna's feet and ankles and put on her elastic antiembolism stockings before dressing the rest of her.

Then, about 9:15, Gloria and I worked to get Myrna properly seated on her electric scooter. If it was winter, we also worked together to get Myrna into a coat. Off they went to the swimming pool or wherever, while I buckled down to get some real work done and grab a bite of lunch before they returned about one o'clock.

On their return, I brought the commode out to the foyer and lifted Myrna from the scooter seat, holding her up while Gloria pulled down her pants and took away the usually soaked panty liner before I sat Myrna on the commode. One or the other of us wheeled Myrna into the bedroom to the card table where she usually ate. Gloria brought her lunch, typically a large green salad with feta cheese.

After lunch it was time for the midday cath. Sometimes, afterward, Myrna rested in bed; other days she sat up at the card table and read or used the computer. Sometimes she watched a video.

On days she didn't go to the pool, she and Gloria often went out in the afternoon to a museum or art gallery.

Late in the afternoon, around four, I went out to do whatever shopping was necessary. Gloria usually left sometime after five o'clock. Myrna and I listened to the national news while we did the evening cath. Then I got supper ready. I almost always cooked with the idea of four servings in mind, so that about half the time preparing supper was simply a matter of warming up leftover lasagna or chicken curry or stuffed peppers, one of Myrna's favorite dishes. Supper was always our best time of day, when we talked most and shared our day's experiences and feelings.

After supper, we might watch a TV program or a video. Often we took care of our own interests— reading, writing letters, watching Monday night football, talking on the phone, whatever. At eleven, we listened to the local news, with particular interest in the weather forecast. Rain or snow meant Myrna would not be able to go out. After the forecast, I got Myrna back on the commode and into the half-bath to wash up and brush her teeth. Then I lifted her onto the bed and undressed her before doing the last cath of the day. We usually listened to *Nightline*. I got Myrna settled comfortably and quickly did my own washup before turning out the lights and coming to bed shortly after midnight.

I have often been asked why we did not request assistance for more hours to relieve me of the evening chores. There were several reasons, the chief of which was that we very much valued this private time together. Because we kept a kosher kitchen, I did not want anyone else to do the cooking, and besides, I enjoyed doing it myself. It was, most of the time, a welcome break from writing and the strenuous tasks involved in Myrna's care. Finally, I enjoyed taking care of Myrna—the exchanges of tenderness, the embraces that came with lifting her, simply the sound of her voice near me. Caring for her was a pleasure I did not want to give up entirely.

When Gloria first came, in April 1993, Myrna could catheterize herself, needing assistance only to arrange her body on the bed, collect the equipment (catheter, cleansing wet-wipes, K-Y jelly, and urine tray), and to carry away and empty the tray when the cath was done. As time went on, Myrna needed help exposing the entrance to the urethra and guidance in inserting the catheter. Gloria was infinitely patient and not at all squeamish about helping.

When Myrna reached the stage, about a year later, when she could no longer manage the cath at all by herself, I had to do it. Medical work rules define catheterization as an "intrusive procedure" that can only be done by a family member or a licensed nurse, not by a health aide. Gloria nevertheless learned to do it and, in Myrna's last three or four months, broke the rules and did most of the morning and midday caths.

Sometime in 1993, Myrna's sister, Beverly, visited Myrna for an hour or so in our apartment. It was a memorable event because it was so unusual. In the ten years between Myrna's retirement and her death, Beverly may have spent, at most, three or four hours in our apartment visiting Myrna. When she came to our apartment to meet Myrna to go to a restaurant, she would only hesitantly step inside and wait in the vestibule while I got Myrna into her coat and onto the electric scooter. When they returned, Beverly would usually say a hurried goodbye in the hall outside our door. I never understood her aversion to our apartment and never asked her what was wrong.

Throughout the ten years I cared for Myrna after her retirement, Beverly's attitude toward me developed from indifference to suspicion to hostility for reasons I have never been able to fathom. She never tried to discuss the causes of her dissatisfaction, any more than she volunteered the slightest hint of gratitude for or approval of my care of Myrna. There was never a family discussion of the problems we faced or how Beverly and her husband might help other than financially during the last year.

Early in 1993, Myrna became fully aware that her emotions were going awry. In January she wrote our rabbi, "I have the time for thinking and learning and writing, but instead I wallow in depression and self-absorption." She was blaming herself for her mental state.

Two months later, her perspective improved. She wrote her sister: "I'm sending you these letters [a string of short letters she had not previously sent] to give you an idea of where I am these days: in deep depression, *the prey* of terrible mood swings between euphoria and despair." The added emphasis draws attention to her partial realization that her mind and emotions were no longer functioning as they should, but not from any fault of her own.

There is some controversy over whether these extreme mood swings, technically known as lability and sometimes seen in cases of late-stage MS, are a symptom of the disease or a psychological reaction to its burdens. I am convinced that it is a symptom and that it is closely related to the loss of short- and medium-term memory.

At the risk of stepping on professional toes, I would suggest that memory plays an important role in helping us maintain a relatively consistent emotional tone. In recalling a recent event or a dream, what we are likely to remember most clearly is how we felt, not details of what happened. When that memory of feelings is limited or erased, there are no restraints on inappropriate feelings that may arise without objective cause and without links to the immediate past.

Further, I want to suggest that the mood swings of late-stage MS can occur with a periodicity of several weeks rather than the, at most, several hours usually associated with lability. This possibility would reveal a major failing of modern medicine, the fact that doctors nowadays almost never observe a patient in a natural setting over a long period of time. Drawing conclusions about patients' behavior on the basis of office and hospital visits is like trying to discern the true behavior of wild animals by observing them in the confines of a zoo.

Having observed one late-stage MS patient hourly for three years, I can attest that Myrna clearly displayed much poorer memory when she was in a period of euphoria or dysphoria. (I want to use the word *dysphoria* here in an attempt to distinguish this MS symptom from depression with a clearly psychological origin.) I can also attest, and demonstrate from her letters, that her moods, when the volatility first began, lasted weeks at a time.

There was an unfortunate aspect to the mood swings: Myrna blamed herself for her failure to carry through with the unrealistic plans and high hopes that characterized her euphoric periods.

In euphoria, she planned to write book reviews for the synagogue newsletter, transcribe tapes of the rabbi's weekly lectures on prayer, get her "letters to rabbis" published, and do some sort of volunteer work in the community.

She did write one book review for the newsletter and had a pile of books still to read and review; but she only read one more of those books and never wrote a review of it. She tried transcribing the tapes, but found the physical process of turning the tape player off and on and typing too demanding and very tiring. She also became aware that her memory of what she had just heard on the tape was either blank or untrustworthy. She continued to pin some hope on the "letters to rabbis," despite the fact that the project had been turned down by a synagogue acquaintance who was also a publisher's reader. Nor had any of the four rabbis she had asked about collaborating on the book responded positively.

At the time, her memory and sense of continuity were still intact enough for her to recall these ambitions when she dropped out of the euphoria, and she berated herself for having done so little, preferring self-blame to accepting the idea that her mind was showing signs of serious decay.

There was one bright spot to which she clung desperately. After her release from Burke in 1991, Myrna found she had lost the ability to swim, partly because she had no opportunity to do so during her hospitalization. She still went to the pool, did exercises, and tried to swim, but without success. Luye, an aquatherapist who gave exercise classes at the pool, suggested she might be able to help, and Myrna began regular sessions with her in July 1992. With specific stretching and other exercises, to the casual observer often unrelated to swimming motions, Luye was able to get Myrna's arms to reach above her head and move in rotation. By February 1993, there were real signs of progress; Myrna began to swim a few laps on occasion. By April, she was swimming regularly again, as many as thirty laps a session, even though her legs trailed uselessly behind.

To Myrna, this was a miracle, and Luye, the therapist, a miracle worker. To me, also, Luye's work was a perfect example of "God's own time and labor here and now." Myrna wrote about this in a letter to family and the rabbi on April 16, 1993:

Today I am soaring, so let me share the good news with you. I swam (the standard Australian crawl stroke) twenty-four laps and did the back stroke for another ten laps. Yes I did. Isn't that sensational! Whom do I credit for this amazing feat? God, for starters. . . . Then, there is Luye, my incredible water therapist, who was able to help me achieve what I thought was the impossible. . . . Next there is me. I really worked hard at relearning how to swim. In fact, I have never worked so hard at a physical task in my life. I am very proud of my success.

This positive feeling about her swimming became a constant over the next year. When she had a good swim, Myrna was exhilarated. On the days when she couldn't swim, she was disheartened and fearful that perhaps the ability was lost for good. I think she became used, however, to the ups and downs, knowing that one day's inability did not portend a permanent loss. Of course, by the same token, one day's gain did not promise continuing success.

Ten weeks later, Myrna was in the dumps again. She wrote to a childhood friend:

My mood swings are ferocious, ranging from despair to exhilaration. Right now it is despair. If I had any sense of shame, I would not send this letter. . . . Please excuse the blatant self-absorption. I know I shouldn't burden you with my unhappiness, but desperation drives me to it. As do memories of a better time, in youth.

Can you believe it, I think back on our [school days] as a golden time? Yes, I remember the down days, too, but now, from the depths of real depression, I berate myself for not having appreciated what now seems the very best of times. Maybe I never appreciate the good times when I'm actually living them. But what stands out now is the richness of possibilities back then. The options were, indeed, many.

Maybe I'm doing the same thing—not appreciating what I have now. Perhaps in a couple of months, I shall look back on these days as a golden age.

Myrna's output of letters decreased markedly after this—for a simple mechanical reason. Her computer's hard disk crashed irrecoverably. I immediately got her a word-processing machine, but between the new commands and techniques and her mental losses, it was weeks before she could make real use of the new machine and months before she felt comfortable enough with it to resume any major letter writing. By that time, her ability to write had become like her swimming—some days she could, some days she couldn't.

In mid-February 1994, Myrna began to take a newly developed medicine, Betaseron, which, it was hoped, would stop the further progress of the disease. Myrna at first seemed reluctant to begin with it. It involved a subcutaneous injection every other day, and she may have had qualms about that. In fact, however, her sensitivity to pin-prick sensation had so deteriorated that she scarcely felt the injections. Her reluctance may have had more to do with some doubt as to whether stopping the disease at that point was in her best interests, given that she was so grievously disabled. She asked herself, often, if a long life in her condition was something she really wanted.

Technically Myrna wasn't even eligible for Betaseron. Only recently approved by the Food and Drug Administration, the drug was in short supply and rationed. It was supposed to be for patients with the exacerbating-remitting form of the disease, a form Myrna had left behind a decade earlier. Recipients were also supposed to be able to walk one hundred yards. An MS patient became eligible for the medicine by lottery. Without our knowledge, Myrna's doctor had submitted her name, and she won a very low number, about 3000, out of some 60,000 applicants.

There were not supposed to be any serious side effects to the drug, and at first we saw no sign of any effect, good or ill. Given the on-again, off-again nature of MS symptoms, it was, of course, impossible to tell right away if it was going to stop the disease's progress, but we did find, after about a month, that it was going to raise hell with Myrna's strength. Some days she could barely drag herself out of bed; other days she would take long afternoon naps. Her ability to swim deteriorated markedly. In general, she felt uncomfortable and listless most of the time. After three months, she and her doctor agreed that any possible long-term effect might not be worth the immediate problems.

I wrote to my oldest and best friend at about this time, early 1994:

> Most of the time her spirits seem fairly good. The mental deterioration caused by the disease helps a little bit to keep her from fully grasping how pitiful her situation really is. But at times, she sees it clearly. Last night she said "I am so terribly unhappy." Today, she seems cheerful enough.
>
> My spirits, on the other hand, are very poor. I feel we're at the end of the road in health, money, freedom. I may be only weeks away from personal bankruptcy; it depends on how long I can borrow from Peter to pay Paul. I'm pretty much bound to the apartment. I can get out a little during the day, but evenings are catheterizations, cooking, getting tea, making sure she takes her pills, and getting her ready for bed. I'm very depressed and have trouble maintaining a strong interest in anything, or even concentrating.

It was about this time that Myrna, recognizing that we could no longer afford Luye's services, appealed to Beverly and Bob, and they began to cover a large part of the cost of Luye's therapy and of Claudette's work getting Myrna in and out of the pool. They contributed about $17,000 over the next year.

The big event of 1994 was the wedding of Myrna's niece, (Beverly's daughter) Alison, in April. Alison and Mike had been together for several years, and they were a good match. Alison was building a reputation as an entertainment journalist, and Mike was a successful young screenwriter. Both are thoughtful, highly disciplined, and ambitious. Mike comes from a family deeply involved in mental health issues. His father is head of psychological services at New York University-Cornell Medical Center in White Plains. An uncle is a professor of psychology at a local college, and another uncle is a noted psychiatrist, a founder of the Hastings Institute, a leading think-tank in bioethics with, I found out later, a strong bias against euthanasia in any form.

Myrna spent months thinking about the wedding and planning for it. It would be no exaggeration to say it was almost as important to her as her own wedding. She pored through catalogs looking for just the right clothes for the big two-family get-together a few months before the wedding and for a dress for her role as matron-of-honor at the wedding. Alison's almost weekly visits to the apartment for an hour or so kept Myrna posted on the wedding plans.

We rode to the two-family gathering in a rented car with Beverly and Bob on a cold February night. Myrna had put together a stunning outfit—a very full, black velour skirt, a white silk blouse with ruffles down the front and great puffy sleeves, and a black satin vest sewn with big squares of colorful velvet patches set off with black braiding. She was beautiful.

It was the first real party we had been to in years, and we found our behavior uncomfortably changed. In the past, we had usually circulated separately, Myrna always eager to stand out in her own right, not as my wife, while I searched out interesting conversation partners of my own. At this party, however, Myrna was not free to move about as she pleased. A large number of guests and small rooms made moving the wheelchair very difficult, so Myrna had to wait for people to come to her. Some did; many didn't. No one spent much time with her in direct conversation, in large part, I suppose, because of her halting speech.

Even Myrna, in these days, had begun to complain to me occasionally that we never had a real conversation anymore, because she had trouble following an idea and finding the words to express herself. This disability had crept up on us. Myrna had sometimes been a hesitant speaker, normally, out of caution, so it was not apparent to either of us when she seemed to grope for a word or an appropriate response, that the cause was MS, not personal choice. It was only after a lengthy period of time, perhaps sometime around the middle of 1993, that we became fully aware that her speech was being affected by the MS.

At the party, I spent much more time with her than I would normally have done and was, she said later, overly solicitous. I may have been seeking refuge with her. I found myself distinctly uncomfortable and unsure of myself in the company of so many strangers. After two years of near confinement to the apartment and our immediate small circle of friends, I had become almost as withdrawn and taciturn as an isolated farmer. Nevertheless, we both enjoyed the party, if only because it was a marvelous break in the routine. Myrna slept for most of the hour-long trip home.

The day before the wedding, I broke down the bath bench and the commode and transported them, the wheelchair, and Myrna to White Plains in a rented car. Once in our hotel room, I reassembled the two pieces of our personal furniture, and cathed and dressed Myrna for a dinner for members of the wedding party at the hotel. It was a quiet, pleasant evening, but I was exhausted before it was over.

The wedding itself was a gala affair in neighboring Tarrytown in a mansion that was once Mark Twain's home and is now a full-time wedding factory. During the afternoon before the ceremony, the wedding party spent nearly two hours getting formal pictures taken. Myrna wore a lovely, long lilac-colored dress with lavender earrings provided to all the bridesmaids.

The wedding itself went smoothly. Myrna did not participate in the wedding march, which was played by a string quartet. Once the bridesmaids and ushers were assembled at the front, I wheeled Myrna into position among the bridesmaids awaiting the entrance of the bride. There were at least a hundred guests.

The officiating rabbi, a Sloane family friend, had been flown in from Los Angeles. He led the bride and groom through their paces, the rings and kiss were exchanged, the ceremonial glass was broken underfoot, and the deed was done. After another round of picture-taking, the guests adjourned to another room for a reception, which Myrna and I skipped to rush back to the hotel for the early evening catheterization.

The process exhausted me. Overall, it meant ten full transfers of Myrna from one seat to another—wheelchair, car, wheelchair, bed, wheelchair, car, wheelchair—and six lifts of her feet and legs to the bed or the wheelchair footrests. I estimate I lifted some nine-hundred pounds of flesh and wheelchair during that hour. I was somewhat numb from exhaustion for the rest of the evening.

We arrived back in plenty of time for the opening festivities of the evening's dinner. Myrna was scheduled to make the *ha-motzi*, the blessing over bread that begins a traditional Jewish meal. The blessing is one of the very simplest and most common, consisting of ten Hebrew words commonly said at least once a day. But Myrna, whether from stage fright, her cursed memory, or both, froze after the first three words. I wanted to give her time to get it, but the Los Angeles rabbi rushed forward and, instead of prompting her, made the blessing himself. Was that a kindness, saving her and the company a bit of embarrassment? Or was it a greater concern for form than for personal feelings? I don't know.

Throughout the meal, people came to the table to talk to Myrna—old family friends, close and distant relatives, even a few near strangers. Myrna was delighted and delightful, expressive, articulate—her usual, eager, shyly outgoing self. Throughout the evening, many pictures were taken—of table groupings, family groups, friends together. I would guess that in the course of the day, Myrna was photographed at least fifty times.

In the months following, I wondered what ever happened to those pictures. In the normal course of things, families rush to share the evidence of the great event to much oohing and aahing over the bride and groom, the wedding party, and the guests, who are sometimes caught in poses that occasion much warm hilarity. But Myrna and I never saw any pictures from the wedding. Myrna had no immediate way to jog her memory and help her relive those happy hours.

Nearly a year later, I asked Alison about the pictures, and she promised to bring some by on her next visit, but she never did. I began to wonder if there were any pictures. After her death, however, one or two pictures of Myrna at the wedding appeared in the press.

The following months were difficult for Myrna. She had great difficulty writing: applying enough pressure to a pen to get the ink out was hard for her, and her fingers were so curled from creeping quadriplegia that she was typing with her thumbs. She complained of brief spells of double vision.

I wrote to my friend George in California in mid-June: "A couple of weeks ago, she asked if I would help her if she decided to end her life; this was just a request for reassurance that I would stick by a long-standing agreement we've had. If the MS attacks her eyesight, that will probably tear it and send me into the criminal underworld to obtain the necessary potion, a couple hundred cc of intravenous Seconal."

About the same time, I began to become aware that the exhaustion and despair I felt were probably common to most long-term caregivers. One Sabbath evening in late June, I was reading in one room and Myrna in another when I realized the Sabbath was over. But when I took the kiddush cup of grape juice and the spice box into her room, ready to do Havdallah, the short ritual that marks the end of the Sabbath, emphasizing the distinction between the sacred and the mundane and God as the source of salvation and comfort, I found Myrna asleep. She was sitting in her wheelchair, slumped over her book, so sound asleep that my moving around the room did not disturb her. I decided to let her sleep, as I usually did when she was so thoroughly resting.

I went out to the kitchen to make myself a cup of coffee. As I waited for the water to boil, I looked out the window into the darkness and, once again, felt the "emotion that almost confounds us when a happy Thing falls" (Rilke, *Duino Elegies*, X), a feeling that is to poignancy as a saber is to a letter opener. I became fully aware of the terrible, unrelievable, abiding grief that was now our home, where we two wraiths went through the motions of existence, trying to be unconscious of the sheltering solace of our sorrow.

I decided I had to write about the experience of the long-term caregiver, having only recently begun to acknowledge the terrible toll I was paying in that role and concerned that other caregivers might think they were failing in their duty, or going crazy, or becoming unfeeling and heartless.

I would assure them, from the outset, that the gloom, the exhaustion, the isolation and increasing sense of distance from the living world, the lack of hope, the numbing from routine, the loss of concentration, the failure of energy and imagination, the inertia, the creeping coldness, the little fits of self-pity and resentment—in short, a process of sympathetic dying, perhaps—is probably common to all who spend a great deal of their time attending to the elemental needs of a profoundly disabled loved one. We, the caregivers, are unique among humans in having only one ghastly thing to look forward to—the death of the one we love or our own death.

I began to fantasize about the possibility of establishing a foundation for the care and nurturing of caregivers, providing them not only with advice and comfort but with vacations, all expenses paid. It would be financed by trial attorneys who become millionaires on their 30 percent share of personal injury awards. Perhaps the American Trial Lawyers Association would sponsor such a foundation. Imagine lawyers providing a little tender, loving care, not to those who have been hit by a truck and might be worth a fortune but to those who have been run over by God and have no prospects at all.

In mid-August, in the middle of a sleepless night, I wrote Beverly and Bob, asking for help. I did not tell Myrna of this, then or ever; I didn't want to alarm her and, later, I didn't want to disappoint her with a clear view of her relatives.

Much as it shames me to admit it, I am at the end of my resources—physical, emotional, and financial. . . .

I suppose I should not be surprised that a sixty-two-year-old man cannot work fifteen to sixteen hours a day for two years without a break, cannot continually bear the strain of putting on a brave front for his sick wife, cannot live in unending and growing grief, and continue to deal effectively with the constant rigamarole of Medicare, Medicaid, taxes and all the other bureaucratic requirements; shop, cook, keep track of bills; work for money; and take care of the dozen little details of household management, without finally failing on all fronts.

But I am surprised, and I am failing. Bills pile up, taxes are undone, contracts are unfulfilled. I cannot focus or concentrate. I am often near tears and sometimes give up to sobbing. I am short tempered. And angry too at everything and everyone that makes it unnecessarily harder. I am so very, very tired. Despairing. Drifting into the irrevocable.

I haven't the vaguest idea of what I need or where to turn for help, except to you.

Help me! Please.

Beverly called a few days later to tell me only that Bob would call soon. When Bob called, we talked for about thirty minutes. He identified the problem as a need to get out of the apartment more and recommended seeking out a part-time job, even if it only paid a minimum wage. He said he would increase their contributions to Myrna's aquatherapy costs by $300 a month, bringing the total to $900, about 90 percent of the total cost.

I felt his overall message was, "It's your problem; tough it out," and that he did not want to understand the practical difficulties of working outside the home. When I told him about being needed to help with Myrna and to do the catheterizations, he seemed to shrug it off. I got the impression he didn't want to be bothered, and I began to worry about what they would do if anything happened to me. I was quite sure they would just put Myrna in a nursing home.

I'm not sure what I wanted or expected at the time. In retrospect, what I needed was simply some sign that they truly cared, some sign of moral support, something besides their cold, withdrawn indifference to me. If Beverly could have sat down and talked with me, it would have made all the difference. But she lacked the emotional resources for that. Foolishly, I continued to hold onto some hope that they might respond as Myrna's condition worsened. At the time, my basic reaction was anger, an anger that gave me new energy and determination and sustained me for months.

In October, Beverly spent about three weeks in the New York area. During that time, she took both of us to a fiftieth anniversary party of old friends of the Lebov family, and she took Myrna out to dinner three times. Those were the only times she saw Myrna during the three weeks and the last time she saw Myrna before her death.

As the year drew to a close, Myrna's mood swings became more rapid and severe, and an ominous note crept into them. In the past, when Myrna said she was going to win the lottery or write a bestseller and solve all our problems, she always had that twinkle in her eye that indicated she was kidding me and not herself. That same twinkle would appear when I emptied her commode and she commented on how sweet it smelled.

But now, the twinkle disappeared, and statements about lottery winning and bestseller writing were made as if they were virtual facts, needing only a day or two to become reality. In the same way, her dysphorias changed from mental states she recognized as unfounded to states reflecting, in her mind, reality.

In the past, Myrna had never spent money in any quantity, particularly on herself, without stewing about it for days and consulting with me. Now, on the spur of the moment, she used a credit card to buy an unneeded fur-lined and -trimmed winter hat for $270. On emerging from her euphoria a week later, Myrna herself recognized the purchase had been extravagant, unnecessary, and completely out of character. She told Alison about it, and Alison paid for the hat as a gift to Myrna.

This minor event forced me to recognize that, while Myrna's mood swings had not, in the past, cut her off from reality and her normal behavior, this was no longer true. Myrna was losing her mind!

There was one additional incident that demonstrated her severe loss of judgment. One morning, while taking her pills, Myrna spilled a little juice on the table. Then she spilled a couple of her pills, Elavil tablets, which she only took before going to bed to help her fall asleep. The spilled tablets got into the spilled juice and began to disintegrate. Without thinking, Myrna picked them up and swallowed them, exercising her habit of not wasting anything. Wiping up the spill, I noticed the residue of Elavil tablets and asked Myrna what had happened.

She explained, and was shocked when I pronounced that she was going to fall asleep and would not be able to swim that day. She protested angrily when I called Luye to cancel the therapy session. Soon after her shower, she was back in bed and slept soundly until nearly one o'clock.

I began to wonder if the time had not come to face the most awful decisions.

11

Scorn, Lies, and Red Tape

Outside the increasing crisis at home, additional tensions and work were created by inept and implacable bureaucracies—Medicare, the Rusk Institute, Medicaid, and not least, of course, the Internal Revenue Service.

In the late summer of 1994, Myrna began to have real difficulty handling her favorite electric scooter, an Amigo we had bought in 1991 soon after our return from Israel. The controls and steering mechanism require the driver to reach forward at all times to steer and maintain pressure on the drive mechanism switch. Myrna could no longer reliably initiate that forward reach or sustain it for long.

For the time being she switched to her old, less reliable, less comfortable, and more cumbersome Rascal, with steering controls that could be pulled forward toward her lap. What she really needed was a chair with a joy-stick control attached to the arm rest. We found that the Rusk Institute for Rehabilitative Medicine would accept Medicare/Medicaid payment to assess Myrna's needs and write up the specifications for a custom-built, four-wheel "power" chair and place an order for it with a supplier.

During several sessions in September and October at Rusk, Myrna tried out a couple of chairs, the physical therapist carefully measured her in a chair-fitting that took into account not only her size but also her tendency to flop over to one side. Myrna's frail condition and poor judgment were so in evidence that I was required to sign a statement vowing never to let Myrna use the wheelchair outdoors unaccompanied. Sessions over and statement signed, the order was placed. We were advised that it might take three or four months for the chair to be ready.

When four or five months later, we had heard nothing about the chair's delivery, I tried to find out what was happening from the Rusk therapist. No luck. Finally, in early April 1995, the therapist put me in direct touch with the supplier, who, it turned out, did not accept Medicare payment. In other words, there would be no chair unless we paid for it in advance, a sum of about $4,000. Impossible! The supplier was willing to begin work on the chair if he was assured that Medicare/Medicaid would pay their allowable fees and we would pay the difference. However, the Medicare bureaucracy would not even consider committing itself to payment until the chair had been built and delivered. Catch 22! an impasse.

What had happened here? Rusk had done its part and had been paid by Medicare, but had failed to search out a supplier that would accept Medicare payment. Did Rusk know, as I later found out, that no supplier in the area accepted Medicare payment because the payments were too meager and were delayed for months in any case? If Rusk didn't know, how could it be so careless? If it did know, why weren't we informed? What Rusk did, in effect, was collect a piece of the public purse for a wasted effort, and if it knew that effort would be wasted, its actions were a fraud on the public. Did anyone at Rusk, the suppliers, or Medicare, express any concern over this breakdown of services? Not in the least.

Just as the sessions at Rusk were beginning, Myrna's Medicaid eligibility was cut off. I found out about it when Rusk canceled her first appointment, and the local drugstore refused to fill an $80 prescription without cash up front. The next day the mail brought notification of the suspension. A box was checked to indicate the reason for the cut-off.

It took me two weeks to straighten out the mess, with part of the time wasted because the reason given with that check mark was not the real reason. In the process of trying to determine what was wrong, I discovered that a sizable piece of Myrna's file at Medicaid was missing and that it contained documents that had to do with another case. A clerk gave me to understand that this was not at all unusual.

The real reason for the cut-off was that Medicaid had failed to inform the provider of the health aide's services about how much of the bill we should have been paying since an increase in Myrna's Social Security payments at the beginning of the year. Once that discrepancy had been discovered and the accounts brought up to date with a charge of about $200, Medicaid was restored.

Two elements of this contretemps were highly disturbing. When I went back to Medicaid to get reimbursed for the $80 prescription, I was informed that Medicaid had never been cut off, and sure enough, a computer printout of Myrna's account showed that her eligibility had never been interrupted! Technically, I suppose, and in some bureaucrat's brain, there had been only a minor glitch—something like a momentary power outage with no harm done. Except that the public record lied, and I was out $80.

The other disturbing element concerned some of the Medicaid bureaucrats. They not only did not care that we were in trouble, they acted as if I were absolutely stupid for letting it happen. Further, they seemed to think that I should know all the details of the case and how Medicaid's rules and procedures applied to those details. In short, they expected me to know their jobs as well as or better than they did! They were distinctly unhelpful; no, worse— they were obstructive.

Their supercilious arrogance caused me to write a letter to the city comptroller, the office in charge of handling liability lawsuits against the city. I warned that the attitude of the clerks was so gratuitously callous that within the next ten years it was a virtual certainty that some grieving, exhausted, half-maddened caregiver would shoot up the Medicaid offices with an Uzi or AK–47. No action was taken. Six months later, the same clerks were still as arrogant, and no measures had been taken to protect them. I did get a visit from two police detectives, just checking to make sure that *I* was not the type to shoot up the Medicaid office. Typically bureaucratic—do nothing about the underlying conditions, but do question the motives and sanity of the whistle-blower.

My tax troubles had begun back in the Reagan years, although I was not fully aware of that until later. During the eighties a variety of changes in the tax laws caught me unprepared and careless. The possibility of income averaging over a period of five years was ended, a disaster for freelance writers, who may make a large sum of money one year and close to nothing the next, and for people who have to close out pension accounts without rolling them over into new tax-deferred accounts. Interest on consumer debt was phased out, just at a time when my reliance on credit cards was increasing. And these changes came just at the time our status as a two-income family was ending and our medical costs increasing, but not at a rate great enough, thank god, to meet the new, stiff limits on medical deductions.

I kept my nose above the tax waters until 1992 and then began to fall behind. By the end of 1994, I was two years in arrears on both state and federal taxes. But I had more or less planned it that way. Being forced to pay off a hefty tax bill would be the perfect way to get rid of another three-year payout from Myrna's disability insurer and so save Myrna's Medicaid eligibility and keep Gloria's services. The alternative would be a loss of eligibility, direct payment for Gloria's help for a few months, and then the hassle of getting back on Medicaid.

Unfortunately, the IRS did not understand this plan and became impatient for their money. Ignoring my pleas for patience and promises to pay by June, the IRS swooped down on our bank accounts on January 5, 1995, and wiped us out, taking Myrna's January Social Security payment of some $900 and about $1,300 from my account. There was still money in the trust fund, so we were in no danger of becoming homeless or hungry, but the levy did foul up my budgeting, particularly by creating five bounced checks at $15 apiece.

I found out the levied money would sit in the bank for twenty-one days to give me time to try to get it back before it became the absolute property of the IRS. So I called the emergency number of the IRS collections office in Atlanta. Over the next two weeks, I spoke to at least a half dozen different people there, a different one every time I called. They nearly all listened patiently to my story, most promised to look into it, and nothing happened.

One clerk asked me why I didn't get a "regular" job like a "normal" person; two people passed me on to their "supervisors"; two people seemed very sympathetic and eager to help. Only one, one of those who passed me to a "supervisor," was relatively honest and indicated I didn't have a chance in hell of getting the money back. All the others lied with such aplomb and style, with such varied techniques, that when it was all over, I could only conclude that the IRS trained and authorized them to lie. Was I naive to be shocked?

From all these experiences, I concluded that our government does not work well for people at the end of their rope, the severely disabled and their caregivers. Different systems of classifying disability used by Social Security, the armed forces, and the workers compensation system make the very idea of "disabled" confusing. The "total and *permanent* disability" classification used by Social Security seemed to be meaningless to Congress when it enacted a law that forbade Medicare to pay for the purchase of wheelchairs and commodes, permitting only their rental.

If the government and society really cared about us, there would be a "green light" system for handling the bureaucratic problems of those with "extreme, total, and permanent" disabilities and their caregivers who are too tired and too hard-pressed for time to jump through the hoops of red tape like sprightly puppies. Unfortunately, such a system would not work. The idea of severe disability has been so debased by the government, "friendly" doctors, and sentiment that anybody with a missing leg or half blind would soon be on the "green light" list.

12

A Tattered Knight

Myrna and I probably first talked about suicide and mercy killing in 1979 when my mother had a stroke and died soon after. I would have told Myrna then that I had promised my mother not to let her live if her mind was gone or if she was unable to care for herself. I don't believe my mother had suicide in mind, but rather my killing her out of mercy when she become utterly incompetent. Her belief in this course of action was based on altruism toward her family and others.

Myrna, on the other hand, in our talks about her own possible choice of death, never spoke to me of any altruistic considerations. Instead, she always focused on loss of independence and freedom, loss of physical and mental capabilities, and loss of awareness as the things she could not tolerate. "If I'm not really there, what's the point?" was her way of looking at it.

These issues were brought sharply to the fore as we watched Myrna's mother die of old age. Anne's deterioration had been painful to watch and, I believe, embarrassing and frightening to her. In the end, she was not much more than a body that ate and felt pain; what remained of her consciousness seemed little more than a longing for her dear Ben.

By the time Anne died in early 1989, Myrna's own condition had become very limiting. She was virtually wheelchair bound and partly incontinent, and the first signs of memory loss had become obvious. Frequently she said, "Don't let *me* go on like that," referring to her mother's condition. "Will you help me kill myself, if it comes to that?" she would ask each time. And each time I promised I would. Myrna's letters to family and friends, all of which I had seen, also mentioned, sometimes in strong terms, that she wanted to die if she began losing her mind.

So there was an explicit understanding that when she began to lose herself, physically and mentally, she would prefer to move to the end quickly. Let me reiterate that Myrna was not in any physical pain and was by no means terminal in the usual sense. It was her mind that was terminal, and her pain was of the spirit.

It was in that light, then, that in late 1994 I began to think about Myrna's condition and her wishes. Two difficult questions arose: When is it proper to lie to a person about his or her condition? and How can we be sure of a person's wishes and intentions about death?

Myrna and I had seldom lied to each other. Our relationship was that of a team; we felt that each had to know what the other was thinking, and more especially, feeling. Lying to Myrna about her condition would only be justified if she could not cope with the truth. But she had never shown any inability to face facts; on the contrary, she was much better at it than most people. Further, if I began to lie, where would I stop? And if Myrna perceived that I was lying, in what important future circumstance might she, therefore, be inclined to distrust me. It seemed to me both right in principle and a matter of respect for Myrna that I bring to her attention my feeling that she was fast approaching a point at which she might not be able to choose to end her life.

But did she really want the choice? Despite her statements to me that she would want out if things really became hopeless, wasn't it likely that this was an intellectual view, purely theoretical? How strong were her feelings about this issue? Her letters to family, friends, and rabbis over the previous four years suggested it was a continuous and fairly firm conviction, alternating with a continuous and fairly firm conviction that there was still hope. Here are a series of quotes from her letters:

Now my greatest fear is that MS has affected my mind; I'm so afraid of further deterioration. .... What happens if my mind deteriorates to the extent of my walking? I can't imagine myself living in that way. ... It's not just that I can't imagine myself living in that way. No, it's more that I don't *want* to live in that way.

—To a rabbi, October 2, 1990

Will this be a suicide note? I don't know yet. Life has become too awful. I'm thinking more and more of ending it all.

—To Beverly, August 26, 1992

My life is a never-ending journey downhill. Down, always down. I don't like it at all. There's not much life in my life, alas. Should I continue? Do I want to continue? The answer is no. Louder. No! Louder. NO!

—To Beverly, January 26, 1993

I've been thinking a lot about suicide. It seems the only honorable course of action still open to me. Honorable???

—To a friend, March 8, 1993

On the other hand:

Thoughts of suicide were often with me. Not only could I not walk, but now I had lost the ability to swim, too. This was the final straw. ... [But] things are really looking up now. ... Last week I could (crawl stroke) eight laps. ... Wow, did that make me feel happy and proud! I really had never expected to be able to swim again. In my experience these past few years, once I had lost a function, it stayed lost.

[Before this] thoughts of killing myself were constantly with me. I don't know how serious I was about this, since I never actually took any steps to end it all. I just thought about it a lot. I wondered about methods. ... Well, whatever.

Yesterday, in the pool, I swam four laps. ... I was swimming, really swimming. I can, I can. Yay! Hooray! Bravo!

—To Beverly, February 13, 1993

Again and again I asked myself: Why continue? Why? Perhaps because now I think I might indeed be able to learn new things. Or old things in a new way. Maybe I can write a worthwhile book.

—To a rabbi, January 4, 1993

Obviously Myrna was of two minds. The reader should not give too much weight to the fact that the January 26, 1993, letter to Beverly, with its strong negatives, has no real equal on the affirmative side. People generally do not spend much time or effort affirming their lives. We take life for granted and assume without thinking that getting out of bed in the morning is affirmation enough. In that oversight, we make a serious spiritual error that diminishes our lives every day.

Which of Myrna's two minds was real? Or were they both real, a quite natural ambivalence in face of this absolutely final choice? To what extent did they reflect the emotional cycling that she began to experience in 1993? My own view was that the wish to exit was the stronger and more principled one, expressed over a number of years, at times when she was thinking much more clearly and uninfluenced by immediate events or false hopes.

But these questions could only be answered truly by Myrna. Should I raise them? Or should I leave her alone to raise the question by herself—if she could? And there was the problem: Was her mental state now sufficient to focus on and clearly perceive her situation without guidance? I thought it wasn't. Further, it was clear that if I let her drift into incompetence, I would be making the decision for her. That kind of paternalism was simply foreign to our relationship.

I decided that Myrna deserved a chance to make a choice before her mind was too ravaged to do so. So, during one of her normal, rational periods, about mid-January 1995, after dinner, I told Myrna that I had to lay out some unpleasant facts for her. I described our situation, pointing out that she was deteriorating relatively rapidly; her body was close to useless; her mind was showing serious slippage; and her emotions no longer seemed consistently rooted in reality. At the same time, I was exhausted, having worked at making a living and taking care of her without a real break for nearly six years. Now, at age sixty-three, I was so tired I could collapse at any time and was not likely to last more than a couple of years in any case. If I died or became incapacitated, her care would fall to her sister, Beverly, who would very likely put her in a nursing home.

But nursing home or not, it was certain that Beverly would not help her die if she chose to do so at some future time. So, the dilemma: If she wanted to be sure of having help to die, she had to consider doing it sometime in the next year.

If this seems unduly blunt, even harsh, so be it. The circumstances were harsh and it was not my task to sugar-coat them. My job was to cast a clear light on reality, not obscure it. My aim was to give Myrna a choice, not false assurances—a wake-up call, not a sedative.

Throughout this period, the alternative of a nursing home was never an option. Myrna had seen the operations of one of the best of all homes, the one her mother was in, and saw it, rightly, as a prison. There was no swimming, no freedom to go outdoors, only endless institutional routine and restrictions. It was a place for mere existence. The best that could be said of it was that, for most of the inmates, that existence did not last long. For Myrna, it could be a sentence of ten to twenty years.

Those who are unable to accept the normality of death and yearn for any other option for Myrna except death may fasten on the idea of a nursing home as a solution to all our problems. To Myrna, a nursing home was equal to being buried alive; in the end, she preferred real death.

I think my sudden presentation of her critical situation came as a shock to Myrna, or perhaps as something she had been trying not to recognize. She was not hurt by what I said, but rather took it in the spirit it was offered—as concerned, helpful, and empowering. Her fundamental feeling was that the time had not yet come for such a momentous decision. I wrote my daughter, Anna, on January 21, "After several days mulling it over, she's opted, very consciously, to stick with things, regardless." Then Myrna was off again into her mood swings. Would she remember what we had talked about, and if she did, would she change her mind?

Myrna did not return to a normal mental state for a month. I waited to see if she would bring up the subject herself. She didn't, so I did.

"Do you remember what we talked about last month?"

"You mean about dying?"

I was surprised that she remembered. The problem had apparently been on her mind despite the mood swings and memory lapses. But now her view was different. She told me that she had decided she would quit the struggle on May 25, our wedding anniversary, saying, "Then I can avoid another terrible summer." (Summers were hard on Myrna because the heat meant she was more confined than usual while all the world was enjoying the sunshine outdoors.)

I was surprised by the specificity of May 25; to me it indicated a firm decision. But was it a lasting decision? Should I act on it? I waited a few days. Myrna brought the issue up again once or twice, reiterating the May 25 date. I was somewhat puzzled by her choice of our twenty-second wedding anniversary as the target date. I saw it simply as a significant date in our lives; that she might see her death as an anniversary gift to me did not enter my mind. She questioned me about means, and I had to admit that I had to find a source for the right pills.

That raised the issue of exposure. She was very fearful that if someone found out what we were planning, they might label her clinically depressed and have her committed involuntarily. I was less worried about that than she was, but I promised to be as discreet as possible. Then she slipped once again into a mood swing, a downer this time.

Were my own motives pure, unmixed? Hardly. In such circumstances can motives ever be pure except in romantic fiction or *Lives of the Saints*? Besides, I have almost always mistrusted my motives and painted myself to myself in a dark light, lest I stumble overconfidently into some evil unaware, in proud self-righteousness, oblivious to others' feelings.

I *was* exhausted, and I wanted to rest. I could not face the idea of taking care of the shell of Myrna until the end of my own life and, afterward, her incarceration in a nursing home, without choices, for who knew how long. The pointlessness of the entire business was oppressive. I wanted her to escape the horror, and I wanted to escape it, too.

I wanted us to escape the hapless condition so eloquently described by Herman Melville in *Pierre* as an aspect of Heaven's mercy: the fact that "when on all sides assailed by prospects of disaster ... the soul of man ... cannot and never does intelligently confront the totality of its wretchedness. The bitter drug is divided into separate draughts for him: Today he takes one part of his woe; tomorrow he takes more; and so on, til the last drop is drunk."

I began my diary of these last months as a way of intelligently confronting the totality of our wretchedness. It was my way of keeping track of our feelings and thoughts, so that I could never after lie to myself about what actually occurred and how I felt about it. I called it "Countdown: A Daily Log of Myrna's Mental State and View Toward Death." I knew, too, that if I did help Myrna die, I would be in legal trouble, and the diary would stand as evidence that I believed I had nothing to hide: By the same token, it would prevent me from trying to hide anything. If I had focused on that purpose alone, I would have been better off in the long run.

But the diary had a second purpose as well. Over the years, I had become conscious of the immense burden society places on caregivers. In December 1994, I had read a lengthy piece in the *New York Times* on "caregiver burnout" and wanted to document that burnout, in part to say to other caregivers that their mixed feelings of love and grief, resentment, and anger did not mean they were failures in loving but that they were only human. To that end, I was perhaps much too open about my negative feelings, feelings some of the public found unacceptable and the D.A. found useful.

I knew that I could falsify the diary or destroy it or hide it, but then it would hardly be worth the effort. There was an element here, too, of wanting to make a public statement: If you really care for the severely disabled and dying, you will care for the caregivers. If you really care about the hopelessly ill and their caregivers, you will not isolate us in these days of dreadful decision.

Finally, I wanted to be able to remember always the last days of a love that exceeded all my expectations and most romantic dreams. I wanted to sear Myrna and this passion into my memory.

What follows, then, is a narrative of our last four months as reconstructed from the diary, which is liberally quoted. I've also added relevant letters and notes made during that time.

"Myrna's on the lower side of a downswing," I wrote at the beginning, on February 27. "It will get worse before it gets better. She worries about every little thing, even denying the evidence of the senses in order to express worry."

Throughout the next three months, March through May, Myrna's mood swings speeded up and the highs and lows became more intense. Most of the periods of euphoria and dysphoria began with only the slightest signs of abnormality and usually progressed over a few days to an intensity that, at times, was little short of madness. When I first began to track the cycling, using memory and notes of previous months as well as daily observation, I thought I discerned a pattern of about eight weeks in a full cycle: two weeks of euphoria, two of normality, two of dysphoria, and two of normality, before returning to euphoria and repeating the cycle again.

I had scarcely arrived at this conclusion in mid-April when the cycle either speeded up or broke down entirely. By late April, there were single days in which Myrna displayed all the characteristics of all three emotional states, one after another, in a bewildering kaleidoscope of emotions. At other times, she would have a few euphoric days, and then go directly into dysphoria, or vice versa. Abruptly, at the end of May, the cycling moderated, and Myrna, though perhaps mildly euphoric or dysphoric from time to time, appeared to have reacquired a degree of emotional stability.

Myrna's memory throughout this period was highly sporadic, sometimes reliable, sometimes almost nonexistent. She went through a particularly bad period between April 29 and May 26, when she went from euphoria that reached a five-day peak on May 8 through May 12, to a very brief normality, before dropping swiftly into a dysphoria that began on May 17, hit bottom on May 22, and ended abruptly May 26.

On May 15 I wrote: "Her memory is a disaster. She can't remember what day it is, whether she went swimming today (no, it rained). And she accepts it all with a blitheness of spirit that is sweet and sad at once." A few days later, I bought a "whiteboard" on which I wrote the day and date, activities for that day, etc., so that she could keep herself oriented. We only had to use the whiteboard for about ten days; when her moods smoothed out at the end of May, her memory also improved.

Throughout this period, Myrna's perception of what was happening to her was rather vague. She knew her memory was quite unreliable, but that unreliability itself shielded her, in the periods of normality, from awareness of the extremes to which her mood swings took her. She did not remember, for example, how demanding and imperious she could be when euphoric nor how anxious and self-critical she was when dysphoric. She did not remember the uncharacteristic interest she displayed, when euphoric, in buying jewelry and precious metals nor the unrealistic plans she made to improve her situation. And she did not remember her endless dysphoric fretting over the past or over trivial details of the present.

My own moods were less than stable. There was, overall, a feeling of having been abandoned. I experienced Myrna's extreme moods as departures and more than once wrote that she was "off again" and, when she returned to normality, that it was "good to have her back." I felt abandoned by Myrna's sister and niece in their failure or refusal to see and understand what was happening. And I felt abandoned by society, by the lack of guidance and help in dealing with both the mood swings and the possibility of assisting in her death. On specific occasions, I felt irritation and anger, disappointment and despair, passivity and resignation, and desperation or cold detachment.

On a visit to Myrna's neurologist the day after she set the May 25 date, I had tried to indirectly broach the subject of pills to help her die by saying that she was "getting really tired of the struggle." The doctor shunted the idea aside, saying simply, "I'm not surprised." He provided no opening for anything further and, assuming he was Catholic, I did not want to press the issue. That evening

Myrna and I talked some more of a timetable and what had to be done before the end.

I wrote to my daughter, Anna, my sister Maida, and George, my oldest and best friend, all of whom live in California, about Myrna's decision to leave in late spring. In each of those letters, I asked if they could somehow get hold of Seconal or some other powerful sedative. Here is part of the letter to Anna:

> For Myrna has set a date, saying she will take the final plunge in late spring. I will not tell you the exact date, and it may change anyway—in fact, the whole thing is subject to change.
>
> I'm somewhat skeptical of Myrna's follow thru on this. She has lost so much mentally that each day now is almost like a fresh start—firm intentions one day are nearly forgotten the next. Even if Myrna changes her mind about this spring, there will come another time in the near future when she will change her mind again. I want to be ready for that.

On March 1: "Myrna seemed very subdued today. She's stopped worrying about every little thing—I guess she's no longer distracting herself, but looking at her short future head on. After Gloria left, I went out very briefly to get some milk for making corn muffins this evening. When I came back, I found Myrna in tears, sobbing. What could I do but hold her. I knew what she was feeling; I've felt it myself. A deep, deep sorrow, inexpressible, inconsolable. I scribbled these lines yesterday:

> My God! I have loved you!
> with a love that ought to
> overthrow the gates of death,
> set that dark city all aflame,
> and free its shades forever from the cold.

Overall, she seems more resigned, almost impatient to get on with it."

It was at this point, early March, that others began to divine Myrna's possible intention to kill herself. Later, when I knew for sure that Myrna had told Beverly what we were thinking about, I was surprised. If anyone was likely to initiate a forcible intervention, it was Beverly, I thought.

On March 6, Anna called to tell me she couldn't help to obtain Seconal or any other sedative. She also announced that she was pregnant with her first child and that she was to be the matron of honor at my nieces's, Maida's daughter's, wedding in Nashville on July 1.

A week later, I wrote in my diary, "We never spoke of coming events, and I was thinking she [Myrna] was dropping the idea of leaving. But yesterday afternoon, out of the blue, she said she was unhappy about not being able to express her ideas and feelings about May 25. She would like to write about it, but simply can't summon sufficient coherent thought."

During that week, I had sent a letter in common to Beverly, Alison, and Myrna's cousin Charlotte admonishing them to give Myrna her due and permission to quit if she wished. As I usually did, I showed Myrna the letter before I mailed it. Brutal as that may appear, I didn't want to do anything behind Myrna's back. I wanted to be the trusted voice of reality in the midst of wishful thinking and willful ignorance. Here is that letter:

To Myrna's Encouragers:

If one is to effectively encourage Myrna to continue her efforts and find some reason to live, some enjoyment in life, it is first of all necessary to understand just how heroic her struggle has been. Ten years ago, when the MS became bad enough for her to retire on disability, she had a number of ways she might have responded to the new situation. As she became progressively more paraplegic in the late eighties, she again had options. The same was true in 1991, when she became wheelchair bound and her short-term memory began to go.

She could have given up then and there and simply lain around feeling sorry for herself; many do. She could have squandered her energies in simple physical enjoyments and become too fat to move. She could have become an angry person, intent on making everyone around her pay for her misfortune. These and other ineffective responses are not uncommon in the later stages of MS.

She did none of these things. She disciplined herself to a regimen of physical therapy, good diet, and mental exercise. She tried every reasonable thing that might help—new medicines, volunteering for clinical trials, psychotherapy, volunteer work, writing, etc. She carefully followed a complicated pill-taking schedule. She has remained throughout these ten years a kind and gentle person, sensitive to the feelings of others, good humored, self-deprecating, and self-demanding, accepting each new failure and indignity reluctantly, but without complaint.

If one is to encourage Myrna effectively, it is necessary to make clear and explicit to her that you understand what she has already done and to give her great honor. Perhaps you can understand her as a brave knight in a tournament in an Arthurian romance. She has fought many personal combats in the lists today—her lance is broken, her mace shattered in an opponent's helmet, her sword arm aching. She has been unhorsed and kneels in the dust, her armor already pierced in a dozen places, her colors in tatters, her helmet broken half away. She looks up and sees yet another opponent on a fresh horse and in new armor waiting for her to get up and fight again. How do you encourage this hero to go on? And remember, the hero knows that this opponent, or the next one, or the one after that will finally prevail.

If one is to encourage Myrna, one must acknowledge to her that she may justifiably ask if all this heroism is worth it. Acknowledge that she now, after all these years, and without any selfishness, has earned the right to ask, "What's in it for me?"

If one is to effectively encourage Myrna, the very truly independent Myrna, one must also give her a real choice. That is, one must somehow give the hero permission to quit if she wishes. One must assure her that if she chooses not to take up her sword again, she will be no less loved and honored. Otherwise, she is not being encouraged, she is being pressured, and Myrna has never responded well to pressure, however well intentioned.

Only Charlotte responded to the "tattered knight" letter. She was confused about what I wanted. I impressed upon her that encouragement was fine, continue it; but permission was also called for, subtly grant it. As we talked, it became clear to me that Charlotte was not aware of Myrna's deteriorating mental condition. Charlotte is really fairly perceptive, but hobbled by expectations. Like all of us, she generally sees what she expects or hopes to see.

On March 12 we had a little party for Myrna for her fifty-second birthday, with her closest friends—Claudette, Gloria, and Luye, her swimming therapist—those who knew Myrna best and admired her most. The party was a success, with lots of talk and laughter, but Myrna was very subdued—"absent" as she put it later.

Luye had brought a cake and Claudette put two candles on it. We sang "Happy Birthday," and Gloria called for Myrna to make a wish. I suppose she did, and then she blew out the candles. I rose quickly from the table and almost ran into the kitchen choking on sobs. My entire body shuddered, as if I were having a seizure. What could Myrna have wished for on what was probably her last birthday?

Another puzzle about that party was that, as far as I can recall, Luye's attitude toward me seemed warm and friendly. Luye later became a witness against me, supporting Beverly's accusations that I had withdrawn from Myrna emotionally and pressured Myrna to end her life. At the party, there was no sign that Luye distrusted me.

During this time I was casting about for some way to gain access to a reliable sedative. I finally went to the *Physician's Desk Reference* (*PDR*) and read up on all the pills Myrna was taking. I found out that an overdose of her Elavil, amitriptyline, could be fatal. It was prescribed for her as an antidepressant and also to help her fall asleep. I wrote: "Allowing for a certain tolerance because of her long usage, a 3,000 mg dose (sixty pills of 50 mg each, half Myrna's standard monthly prescription and ten times the recommended daily maximum dosage) should dissolve in a quart."

I wrote further about what the *PDR* had to say: "What to expect—seizures, convulsions, coma, death. Not many cases of this kind of poisoning, so actual reactions are unclear and may vary, depending I suppose on random closing down of the central nervous system. Whether Myrna would be aware of the seizures and convulsions is unclear."

Then, checking to see how many pills Myrna had on hand at the moment, I made a major discovery. Her prescription called for her to take four pills a day, but she was only taking three. Her doctor had always given Myrna a degree of freedom in how much amitriptylin she took, advising her to take only what she felt was necessary, but not more than four. Myrna had been taking only three a day for months, perhaps years, on the grounds that any more made her feel sluggish all day. In these last days, it never occurred to me to suggest she take more amytriptalin to combat her dysphoria. Myrna had always been the absolute boss of her medication and very averse to overmedicating herself.

The prescription covered one month's supply of pills at four a day, but because Myrna was only taking three a day, we were refilling the prescription every forty days instead of every thirty days. There were an extra thirty pills a month! I began immediately to set aside the excess pills and thereafter filled the amitriptylin prescription every thirty days.

In my diary, I wrote, "Told Myrna about my discovery; she was not enthusiastic. In euphoria, she is not interested in quitting." In retrospect, I think that Myrna may simply have filed the information away for future reference. The method and means of her exit were my responsibility; her responsibility was far more difficult. Only two weeks later, she expressed disappointment that I had not yet collected enough pills to help her out.

These days were filled with my own second-guessing. I asked myself in the diary: "Would I be justified in accepting Myrna's request for help in dying when I know that a turn in the cycle will lead to a change of mind? Would I have the courage to act if the request came when she was at a low point? What if the request came at a low point, but the act at a midpoint?

"The issue is simply that when Myrna is at the top and bottom of the cycle, she is not in her right mind. It's as if half of her personality has disappeared. Just as her muscles have lost tone, so has her emotionality."

The evening of the March 27, Myrna gave me a letter she had been working on for several hours. After reading it, I wrote in my diary: "I had hoped that the special character of the communication would mean a special content, but I feared it would be the usual thing. It was as I feared: You need a vacation; ask Anna for a loan. The lottery may solve our money problems. Let's work on a book together. I'm going to work on a book, with or without you. Alison will help, etc. The letter ended with a veiled challenge—believe in her or else! The exact image was 'The train is leaving the station. This is your last chance to get on.'

"Myrna's self-centeredness when she's high is very unlike her normal self," I had written previously. Despite knowing that Myrna was euphoric, I was shocked. Myrna had never said anything so unfeeling to me. The veiled threat that I should join in her fantasy or get out, and the failure to recognize our years together was completely out of character. Months later, I realized that the tone of the letter reflected Beverly's attitude, not Myrna's. Beverly, over the telephone, had been playing to Myrna's euphoria, which Beverly wanted to believe was Myrna's normal state. If I had seen Beverly's role at the time, I would have reacted more responsibly.

The letter disheartened me immensely and I began to brood on my options, more to think things through thoroughly than to prepare a course of action.

From my journal at that time:

1. Continuation of the status quo—I doubt I can keep it up for another full year. I will either die or go mad.
2. The easy way out [killing myself]—I have given ten years of my life to Myrna's care, five of them virtually devoted to her needs, the last three absolutely devoted to her needs. I am her arms, legs, and hands. I help her pee and wipe

her bottom. I deserve to enjoy a little rest in the few years I have left and a chance to do something for myself.

3. Walk away—I do not want to leave New York and I have no resources to live on outside New York. Just finding another apartment here would be impossible. I would like to stay here. And if I am going to accomplish anything worthwhile by walking away, I want the computer and all these files—hard to see how that might be done unless the walk away is planned.

4. Kill her—That too remains an option though far more difficult without her cooperation. And the consequences could be ghastly. Nor would a possible book be reasonable, because of the Son of Sam law.

New York's Son of Sam law, named after the psychotic serial killer whose book profits created public outrage, is designed to parcel out such "profits" to victims of the crime. I did not know at the time whether the law applied only to murderers or to all felons (it applies to all felons), and I still don't know if the law, as later amended, aims primarily at depriving the felon of ill-gotten gains or at helping provide support for the victims. I suspect I will find out when this book is published.

This business of setting down all the options, however unreal or horrific some may be, stems from the rules of brainstorming, which require that every conceivable option must be noted, no matter how outlandish. That process, in this case, also conformed to my habit of constant introspection, of considering the worst possible motive to see if it fit, if I could live with it. I am told that many people are unfamiliar with this sort of self-examination and find it very difficult to believe it occurs.

Leaving Myrna, for example, was never really an option for me. I could no more have walked away from Myrna now than I could have when I made my last proposal, twenty-two years earlier. As for killing Myrna, that was as hateful to my imagination as taking care of her body when her spirit was gone.

After all this mulling, I wrote the following letter and gave it to Myrna:

I feel I am not being treated well. I feel that everyone is perfectly ready to see me die for your sake, but no one is prepared to do anything for my sake. And I am dying. I have only a few years left, ten at most, probably, but only two or three if my work load continues as it is. I too have a book to write, two books, and essays also. I have work to do, people to see, places to go. But no one asks about my needs.

I have fallen prey to the tyranny of a victim. You are sucking my life out of me like a vampire and nobody cares. In fact, it would appear that I am about to be cast in the role of villain because I no longer believe in you. Well, one can glower and glower and be a hero.

The last sentence, of course, is a reversal of Hamlet's, "That one can smile and smile and be a villain." Here, too, was the infamous "vampire" phrase, pounced on by the D.A. and the press when they sought evidence of my heartlessness. I never tried to explain that the "vampire" image originated with Myrna, who had begun to use it occasionally sometime the previous year, after seeing something about Ann Rice, the vampire novelist we had never read. Myrna had said she was like a vampire, living off other peoples' lives; I was reminding her of that point of view. It is one of the ironies of the case that those who knew her acknowledge that Myrna was an intelligent and independent woman, but if they need to cast her as a victim, they portray her as unperceptive, defenseless, and malleable.

My note to Myrna continued:

If you write something that gives me some slight faith in your ability to concentrate on a book, I will take what time I can to help you with it, providing that you stick with it. We will set aside one to two hours a day to do nothing but that—*every day*—for as long as you keep at it and are effective.

But first you must write something that will persuade me that the effort will be worthwhile. Suggestion—What is your dominant feeling as you read this note? And what do you think and feel about that feeling?'

Why was this business of writing so important? The issue here was not "write a book or die." Myrna's inability to write was merely one sign of the mental deterioration that was destroying her personality. If she could write, that deterioration was not as bad as I feared. And if she pinned her hopes on a book, she had to write. Otherwise, her hope was a crazy fantasy, a sign of more serious illness, not of health. But, in fact, my offer of help was not made in earnest. Oh, I too hoped Myrna would show some renewal of her writing ability, but I was fairly certain she could not.

I gave the note to Myrna the next morning, March 28, "and we had some straight talk. She's in the midway point of her emotional cycle and seemed to take in what my complaint is." Myrna wrote nothing for the next two or three days.

A couple of days later, I wrote: "We talked in the evening. Myrna is more or less rational. Able to see but not accept the reality of the situation. She is only vaguely aware of the degree to which she is now adrift, with little autonomy left. She will admit in one moment that the situation is bad, that she can't write a book, that suicide might be the best solution, but moments later, it's as if nothing of this was said or was real. We can go through the same round again and again with no change. I doubt that anything will come of all this. The drift will get worse, until she's gone." By "gone," I didn't mean dead, but mentally absent.

The next day, March 31: "We talked clearly of suicide—means and opportunity. Myrna was more alert. She admitted that she remembered very little of having discussed it all before, saying that she put it out of her mind as unreal. There are signs that she's already slipping into dysphoria, mostly hand-wringing, but she remains lucid and able to follow a discussion. Certainly, the arrogance and thoughtlessness of the euphoria are gone."

It was around this time that I began to keep daily track of Myrna's moods. I regretted the harshness of the "vampire" letter and realized I had not exercised a reasonable restraint when I wrote it. I hoped that, if her mood swings were predictable, I could prepare for them and perhaps deal with them better. The ways of relating to each other with love and respect that Myrna and I had developed over twenty-two years of marriage were no longer appropriate. I wondered how long it took the spouse-caregivers of Alzheimer's patients to adapt to their charges' craziness.

On April 2 and 3 we tested the amitriptylin solution at her bedtime; the taste was foul. I wrote of the latter evening that Myrna was "well into dysphoria and by bedtime appeared to recall little of our talk of her suicide [during the previous two days]; most particularly, there was no emotional consistency between her expressed feelings [tonight] and those she had expressed only two days before. It was as if she was starting from the beginning in trying to understand what the situation is."

Two days later I described Myrna as "subdued and more or less rational, showing only a few signs of the downswing. This evening she admitted that she can't read a book anymore, 'can't make connections,' as she put it, and said she doesn't want to stick around. I told her I had solved the drug intake problem. She changed the subject. I think I better get ready." In spite of the fact that Myrna "changed the subject," I felt very distinctly that she had shifted into a new stage where suicide was now not just a possibility but a real choice, and one she might make soon.

13

No Escape?

On April 8, I wrote: "Myrna has been pretty steady for the last three days. A bit glum or sad, but not dysphoric. Able to talk haltingly, think fairly clearly, and stay on a subject. This afternoon we had a long talk. In one breath Myrna said she wanted to die as soon as possible, and in the next expressed astonishment at the idea she might not be alive next week. She said she wanted to write notes to everyone but couldn't think. I offered to write the basics and she could add personal feelings. She said she didn't feel much. She complains of feeling unconnected, distant."

This was the normal Myrna—reflective, introspective. Myrna first expressed this sense of disconnectedness clearly after her birthday party. I have never been able to figure out if it was a part of her mental difficulties or a sign of a slow withdrawal from life. I think it was the former, but exactly what the feeling was I am unable to say.

I made a list of expressions Myrna could use in notes to people taken from her own words that afternoon and on other occasions:

I'm tired of body functions as my main concern. I'm afraid of embarrassing myself.

Mostly, I'm helpless. I can hardly wash my own face.

I can't make connections. Trouble reading. Disconnected thoughts. Can't find words. Forget meanings. I'm bored, but too vague to be bored.

I'm scared, because my mind is failing. Terrified of being mindless in a nursing home.

I feel distant, disconnected. No thoughts to express.

I printed out these notes and gave them to Myrna.

Three days later: "She appears to be adapting to the idea that she hasn't long to live. For example, this morning she showed some concern about the mole growing on her left side, but said, 'I won't do anything about it anyway.' Here again, the real Myrna. When she made the comment about the mole, she smiled at me with that glint of 'wickedness' in her eyes that said she was being bold and 'breaking the rules.'"

Passover came and went. We had a small, short seder with only two guests, friends we often invited for Thanksgiving and Passover.

The following two weeks were difficult, with several different problems all cropping up at once: On April 17, Myrna's Rascal, her old three-wheeled electric scooter, gave out; I was engaged with the Medicaid bureaucracy, trying to get Myrna recertified for continuing assistance; and I was locked in a moral struggle with myself over Myrna's disability insurance.

When Myrna's Rascal broke down, "I immediately called the repair people; Claudette volunteered to come up here to help get Myrna to the pool three days a week until the chair is repaired." Initially, Myrna appeared to take the scooter setback with surprising equanimity, "but this evening she objected to the idea of paying for the Rascal's repair and said she wanted to check out tonight. She seemed a little miffed and disappointed when I said I wouldn't help on a spur-of-the-moment decision." This was the first occasion on which I refused to help Myrna die because the decision appeared to be provoked by passing circumstances, a momentary setback.

I later found out the Rascal needed about $750 worth of parts and labor to get it into good shape—differential, batteries, tires.

"Should we spend the money? Not if Myrna is going to quit. Further, buying into a repaired Rascal means a commitment to get the best out of it—at least a six-month commitment to live. Myrna is fully aware of the issue and is mulling it over. If she stays euphoric, I know what the decision will be." In fact, Beverly and Bob paid for the Rascal's repair.

In the Medicaid matter, the bureaucracy, as usual, claimed I had not submitted sufficient financial documentation. I tried to find out what they felt was missing. After a fruitless few minutes on the phone with a clerk at the Surplus Income Unit, I gave up. The clerk had demonstrated the standard bureaucratic style—badgering, short-tempered, caustic, peremptory.

I decided to take a chance on a pattern I thought I had discerned in the way the Medicaid bureaucracy operated. That pattern consisted of Medicaid's demand for every financial document they could think of, even if the documents had already been submitted in a previous recertification process. Whatever I gave them was ruled insufficient, and recertification was denied. I would then file for a fair hearing before an administrative judge. At hearing time, no one would show up to argue the bureaucracy's case, and recertification would be approved.

The first time this happened, I thought it was all a mistake. The second time, I began to suspect that this crazy procedure was policy, designed to discourage people from continuing on Medicaid. Now I was prepared to gamble on that suspicion.

On May 2: "Medicaid is cut off. So tomorrow it's off to VNS [Visiting Nurse Service, Gloria's employer] to pay the March bill [our share of the monthly health aide bill] which arrived April 28, and then to Medicaid's Surplus Income Unit where I will probably have to deal with my candidate No. 1 for an Oklahoma City bomb. I think I'll take a tape recorder."

In the Medicaid office the next day, I pulled the tape recorder out of my bag and turned it on. I might as well have pulled a gun. The obnoxious clerk backed away, put her hands up, palms out, toward me, and said "No, no!" She rushed to her supervisor's office, and I was quickly called in. Within five minutes the matter was settled. Myrna was recertified. I have no idea what was going on here, but I suspect it reflected a policy of harassing Medicaid claimants in hopes that only the truly needy would persist.

The moral quandary turned on whether or not to cash a $50,000 check, a final settlement from UNUM, Myrna's disability insurer. In 1992, we had arranged for a three-year advance payout (about $34,000), and stashed most of it in the trust fund. Otherwise, the monthly disability payout in addition to Myrna's Social Security would have made her ineligible for Medicaid. Now, in March, I had written them to arrange for the same sort of deal again, intending to use the money to pay off most of our back taxes, depleting our resources so that Myrna could retain her Medicaid eligibility.

UNUM countered with a suggestion that we settle the disability claim forever with a $50,000 lump-sum payment. That sum would be equivalent to almost five years of monthly payments. It would also mean that all back taxes could be paid off, with some left over to pay the taxes on the $50,000 itself. So we accepted the offer.

But when the check arrived, Myrna changed her mind. She did not want me to cash the check, even though she signed it. I can't explain this change of mind. I supposed that closing out the disability coverage seemed too final, even though I explained that the relatively small amount of money it provided (less than $900 a month) was simply a headache, not a help. It was not enough for her needs but was enough to threaten her eligibility for Medicaid. Its absence in the previous three years had made it possible to have Gloria's help; its absence in future would enable the same level of care.

The check sat on my desk for over a week as I puzzled over what to do. In the end, faced with the facts that the IRS would soon be on us again and that Myrna could lose her Medicaid eligibility, "I cashed the UNUM check today [May 2] against Myrna's express wishes and it hurt very badly to do it—in effect forcing Myrna. A terrible thing, but Myrna was not being rational about the necessity. Otherwise, she has been fairly reasonable, understanding, and communicative. A good high for her."

Of the money, $35,000 went immediately to pay two years' worth of federal and state taxes. I tried to keep the rest intact to pay taxes on the lump sum, but legal and other expenses ate up several thousand more. By the end of the year, I again owed the tax people some $20,000.

During April, Myrna had passed from a dysphoric period at the beginning of the month into a state of near normality with some euphoria during the last two weeks. On April 28, we had watched all of *Hotel Terminus* on PBS, Myrna "apparently taking it all in." It was about this time, nevertheless, that I began to wonder whether Myrna and I were seeing the same thing when we watched a movie. There was nothing definite, but an occasional comment would suggest that she was making up things to force the movie to make sense for her. I think the technical psychiatric term for this is "confabulation."

This period was very difficult for me. I had been having unusual trouble sleeping for several weeks, but on April 24, sleep eluded me entirely. I got up and went to the kitchen, where I made a cup of herb tea and wrote: "Can't sleep. Before she washed up for bed, Myrna said, 'I'm so scared. My mind is a mess. I want to die.' I said, 'You're in a down period. Give it a week or two.'

"As we were falling asleep, she said, 'I wish I could talk.' 'Is it that you can't find the words or can't shape the ideas?' I asked. 'It's self-absorption,' she said. An image. The caterpillar spins its cocoon out of itself and absorbs itself in the metamorphosis to butterfly.

"Is self-absorption a common trait in the dying? It seems that would be the case. It is a solitary journey. Perhaps especially so in our highly individualistic society where common experience and common values are so rare that a lack of common words about this strange experience is to be expected. Death, today, cannot be shared—one of the things that make it appear so horrible.

"Before I got up to write this, I heard from outside the open window of our bedroom a snatch of some aria—Domingo singing, I think. From the bed, I could look out into the glimmer and glow of the city lights. And there it was again—'the emotion.' That sense of the incredible richness and rightness of the world, the variety of existence, the complexity, the disorder, the confusion—our only true wealth if we would but accept it.

"Some few evenings from now, we will face each other across a small table in the room that has been the center of our lives and feelings for nearly eighteen years. Near the bed, with that space on the headboard that we once joked should be inscribed, 'Here lie Myrna and George.' We will look into tearing eyes and know our short mutual dream is ended, our off-key duet sung out to its last note.

"We will say some of the usual things: 'I love you. I will always love you. I'll miss you.' A touch of humor? 'Put in a good word for me. I'll join you in a while. I'll look you up as soon as I get in.'

"But we will be entering on the Unutterable, into the Land of Lamentations, the poet Rilke's image for the wellspring of our existence."

The evening of May 4: "Alison and Mike came by and stayed about an hour. Myrna talked slowly and haltingly, stating that she had decided to live. She and Alison made plans to work on her book. Myrna spoke of the possibility of selling the painting if she needed money after I died. She often lost the thread of her thought. I don't know if my view yesterday [that Myrna's mood swings had abated] was too optimistic or not. Something is a little off today. I don't know if Alison and Mike noticed it.

"I realized something during the talk. Until then, Myrna's death had not been quite real to Alison. For just a moment, something in her posture, a glint in her eye, told me she was seeing the reality for the first time, and the possibility of real grief was opened to her. It made me feel very alone. The rest are just beginning to get a glimmer of what I've lived with for five years."

That evening's conversation solidified Beverly's and Alison's hostility toward me. Failing or refusing to recognize Myrna's mood swings and memory problems, they took Myrna's talk that evening as proof of Myrna's steady state of mind. What was "off" was that Myrna was at the beginning of a euphoric period. She sounded reasonable but in fact was moving into unreality, as the last paragraph from that day shows:

"Afterward, Myrna rode me for cashing the check, going against her wishes, stealing her money. And I couldn't talk to her, because I felt bad about having to cash the check against her wishes and couldn't say again, when she was feeling so confident in her new hope, that her judgment was just not trustworthy. The kinds of things she said to me, though thoughtless, are so unlike her that I am afraid she's into a high. Woe, woe, woe."

The next day: "Myrna has definitely moved into a high—planning this and that, talking 'book,' being less than thoughtful in what she says and in her demands."

About this time, Beverly, with Luye's assistance and without consulting me, arranged through Myrna's neurologist for her to see a psychiatric social worker in his office. This was a good idea and welcome assistance, but why wasn't I consulted?

On May 9, the day of Myrna's first visit, I wrote a note for her to give to the therapist to alert her to Myrna's swings, remarking that she, the therapist, was meeting Myrna when she was at or near the peak of a euphoric cycle. I also noted that Myrna's short-term memory was most severely impaired during her periods of euphoria and dysphoria.

Following a pattern established years before when Myrna was in therapy, I did not ask Myrna about the details of her talk with the therapist. I only asked how it had gone. "Okay," was Myrna's listless reply. I believe that by this point Myrna had had her fill of "helpers" and pills and all other prescriptions for trying to make the best of her difficult situation. Or it may be that she felt an obligation to see the therapist as a favor to Beverly. Only that could explain why, in the middle of a euphoric period, she showed no enthusiasm whatever for the possible benefits of therapy.

"As for me, I'm trying to think/feel myself into recognizing my own death in a life given to Myrna. Can I do it? Should I do it? Am I required to do it?" I was here trying to persuade myself to give up on my own life and resign myself to what might be necessary if Myrna decided to live.

Here is a problem without a solution: Most of us, most of the time, understand our lives in terms of some project in hand, and our lives only make sense if we have such a project. But the very sick may have no other project than to stay alive. How is the caregiver to understand his life and projects in the light of only existing? I don't doubt that it can be done; I thought about it and tried to feel my way into that situation, but I failed.

On May 11 I decided that I would have to sleep in the single bed we had for guests if I was going to get enough rest. I wrote: "That way I at least won't be awakened unnecessarily. I believe that my getting enough sleep may be the most important thing I can do now." This move was hurtful to Myrna, who laid great store by our sleeping together as a sign of our union.

On May 18 Myrna's niece came by for her first visit since the night of May 4, when Myrna had expressed her decision to live. I wrote: "Myrna is definitely down from the latest high, showing increased depression over her handicaps. This depression increased following a visit from Alison, when Alison mentioned her impressions of the long conversation Myrna had with her and Mike on May 4. Afterward, Myrna told me she had no recollection of that conversation, nothing at all!" Nevertheless, Myrna showed more stunned surprise than despair over this failure of memory.

One of the interesting puzzles is whether Myrna revealed to Alison that she remembered nothing of the conversation. It would be like Myrna to keep this kind of thing from her. But if Myrna was silent about her forgetting, it had the ill effect of permitting Alison and Beverly to believe that a decision to live had been made once and for all.

The next day I wrote: "My problem: if she asks for the poison now but seems very depressed, should I comply? Is she still autonomous? If I comply, I may be serving my own interests more than hers. If I don't, she may be losing her last chance to make the decision. She's mentioned July 4 as 'independence day,' a possible suicide date, but at the rate her mind is deteriorating, she may not still be a whole, autonomous person by that time. I believe I will comply—on the rationale (rationalization?) that I will be saving her from a fate worse than death. (What an ironic cliché in this context!)"

In fact, the cliché was not at all ironic. Myrna's mind was being ravaged by MS. As the situation deteriorated and the likelihood of suicide at some point became more real, my concern for my moral position became more focused. I was not particularly concerned about my legal position, because there was nothing I could do about that.

Just before lunch on May 20, "Myrna said she wants to kill herself tonight. She was very serious, asking me detailed questions about how the process would be handled, how long it would take, whether I would make sure she is dead, how will I know, etc. Then, as the afternoon wore on she became less and less certain, fretful, slowly verging into the dysphoric. A great part of the problem was that she worried over Beverly's reaction. Now, about 9:30, she just got off the phone with Beverly, telling her how her body was betraying her, coming apart. She said Beverly advised that she should seek out nurturers.

"Nurturers. Or torturers? I simply do not understand how well people with all or most of their faculties can advise people in Myrna's condition and worse to stick it out. What is their motivation? Are they afraid? Are they insensitive? Deliberately insensitive? What is this insane valuation of meatloaf life at any price—a price to be paid by others, of course, particularly by the one who wants to die."

"Meatloaf life"—life without awareness, memory, and hope; life as body only. This phrase was not meant to apply to Myrna as she was at the time, but as she might well become. The phrase was later picked up by Beverly and the press as more evidence of my insensitivity. How easy it is for some people to fixate on one phrase that allows them to condemn another person and bask in their own refinement and virtue!

"Myrna showed a bit of cleverness after lunch. Speaking of the poisonous concotion I've made, she said 'That's a real solution.'

Later in the evening, Myrna was very needy for attention. She said over and over again that she wanted to die, but at the same time she went over and over details that were generally trivial or irrelevant. "Two things stand out: she feels that everyone expects her to live, would view her leaving as cowardly, or defeatist, or unnatural, or a betrayal. The other thing is that she is not yet ready for the act itself, although intellectually and emotionally she is prepared."

She was so conflicted that I had to tell her to forget it, go on with the routine. But she also wanted so much to die at that point that "I had to almost force her to wash up and talked to her hard to get her to put her weekly pills together. Her view: If I'm not going to be here, why make the effort?"

I believe this was the closest Myrna came to the act before she actually did it. Why didn't I urge it on her? Fundamentally, because it was fruitless to urge her to do anything significant. But also, because it was not the pre-set date, which indicated that she was acting on the spur of the moment. And also because she was so ambivalent and focused on trivia.

On May 22, after showing it to Myrna, I sent a letter to Beverly with a complete rundown on Myrna's disabilities and the requirements of her care. It ended with an estimate of the incredible cost (about $145,000 annually) of maintaining Myrna at home without help from Medicaid and a family member to do the catheterizations.

I intended to impress Beverly and Bob with the seriousness of Myrna's situation and to try to jar them into paying attention. What I wanted to hear from them was that they were taking steps to find out if Myrna could get Medicaid in California if it became necessary for them to take care of her. At the end of the letter, I told Beverly it would be wise if she spent several full days here to observe what was involved in Myrna's care and to learn what was required.

I didn't really expect her to take me up on the idea, but I had to try. I felt that a display by Beverly of a realistic interest in Myrna's future would give Myrna a greater range of choice about that future.

May 25, our twenty-second wedding anniversary and one of the dates Myrna had picked for dying, came and almost went without the subject coming up until the very end of the evening. Alison and Mike came by and stayed about ninety minutes. We had some laughs and then some serious talk. I asked Alison if she had received the earlier letter—the "tattered knight" letter. Yes, but she didn't know how to respond. Had her mother gotten it? Yes. I told her I had not received even the minimal courtesy of an acknowledgment. She did not respond.

It was in this conversation, too, that Alison later reported I had called Myrna a "burden" in Myrna's presence. Oh! what horror!

Were we all adults in the room that evening, or had one of us become a child?

Myrna had long been aware that caring for her was a burden. As far back as December 1991, a few months after she became wheelchair-bound, she had written to a friend, noting her hopes that I could find a job outside the apartment, "away from me, away from the myriad tasks he has to do for me." Generally, I tried to hide the strain, but occasionally I failed. Once, returning home from the long wheelchair push from synagogue on a hot summer's day, I muttered, "I'm getting too old for this." Myrna noted this in a letter to a rabbi and commented, "And he is!"

Many times during the last year of her life, Myrna commented on the toll her care took on me and said frequently, "George, you deserved a better life." To which I always replied that it was she who deserved a better life and that mine was rich and wonderful beyond my dreams because of her. She never seemed entirely reassured, no matter how many times the mantra was repeated or how many times I read Ayshet Cha-yil to her with feeling before Sabbath dinners.

Alison's assumption that Myrna did not know she was a burden reflects the idea that the hopelessly ill are easily duped by solicitous lies. That is part of the too common tendency to see and treat the hopelessly ill as mentally compromised, deserving of our pity but not our respect. Only the hopelessly ill who want to be duped can be duped; most may appear to go along with the lies only to comfort the liars. Myrna's and my habit of candor did not permit that kind of mutual deception.

At a street fair the previous Sunday, I had bought an anniversary present for Myrna—two white, yellow, and brown butterflies mounted in a Plexiglas box, wings spread. I gave it to Myrna and explained its meaning—self-absorption leading to transformation and beauty.

After Alison and Mike left, "Myrna spoke to me in great earnestness about killing herself. I told her I was very reluctant to help when she is dysphoric and that to do it tonight would be a very heavy blow to Alison. She seemed to accept this, but reluctantly, later speaking again about doing it tonight. She also wanted to know more about the details: the taste of the solution, the use of honey, the after-effects, what I would do to guarantee her death."

I wrote: "I am right about not helping her do it tonight, but I do hope there's still another window. She is so close to losing herself that each time she asks now may be her last chance to get out while she still can." Myrna's talk of suicide that night was, I believe, serious, because her focus was on exactly the same thing as it was on the night she actually did kill herself—would the solution work?

In the meantime, Myrna's condition continued to show signs of deterioration: "For the second time in a few days, Myrna complained of a lack of oil in her salad dressing—when there was the usual amount—a lot. She has lately, too, complained that her Granny Smiths are tasteless. She attributes this latter to the change of seasons, but I'm wondering if her sense of taste is being affected." She also complained about double vision in the top half of her field of view, a complaint that made no sense to me because I thought there could only be variations between right and left fields.

May 27: "Myrna's mood was erratic today. Subdued in the morning, focused and realistic in the afternoon, rather more assertive in the evening—all definitely forward-looking and without any indication that she wants to die. On the contrary, this evening she suggested that I was the only one who wanted her to die. She spent some time exploring options for getting out more and being more active, until I pointed out that she had only one afternoon a week in which to do such things and usually did do something."

At times I *was* the only one who wanted her to die—because it was the only solution available to her—but when she was normal, I was the second person who wanted her to escape. She was the first. I had the most to gain from her death, but also the most to lose. Someone will say, No! Myrna had the most to lose! But that is not true. Myrna's life had become a nightmare.

On May 28 we went to see the Cirque du Soleil, "a wonderful experience. Before we went in to see the show, we strolled [I strode, she rolled] around Battery Park City." Myrna made the first part of this outing most unpleasant. She had ordered the tickets to the circus over the phone, using a credit card to pay, and fretted over and over about my possibly paying for them again. I couldn't persuade her that I wouldn't do that. Once we had the tickets, and I hadn't paid for them again, she began to worry about getting home. It was as if she had to have something to worry about.

"I said it was a shame she couldn't enjoy the day, and she became quiet. Not dysphoric. As we sat waiting for the show to start, she said, 'If I can't even enjoy a day like this, I might as well be dead.'"

The Cirque du Soleil was wonderful, magnificent, glorious. As circus, it was very small; as masque, it was grand. It cleverly set the grotesque, old, deformed, and ugly against the beautiful, perfectly proportioned, strong, and young, all with great color, lighting, and music. The ringmaster was a Cochineal and his cohort a gaggle of fat men/women, garishly dressed and wearing grotesque masks— satyrs in a commedia del'arte form. But there was, as well, another band of handsome and beautiful young men and women, most of them the performers of the acts.

The fact that Myrna could get out and enjoy something like the Cirque du Soleil might strike some readers as reason enough for her to choose life. And it might have been—if Myrna had assurances that she could exit any time she wanted to in the future. But Myrna lived in a society unwilling to grant such assurances, a society that makes no provision for dealing responsibly and openly with the possibility of chosen death. So, losing her mind and without recourse to any assistance but mine, she was deprived of choices a less fearful society could have provided. In short, the ban on assisted suicide and mercy killing can lead to deaths that might otherwise be postponed.

On May 29 Myrna talked to Beverly on the phone. "I asked Myrna if Beverly had gotten the letter about Myrna's condition and costs of care. Yes. Had Alison spoken to Beverly? Yes. And . . . ? Myrna says Beverly continues to feel that the only thing wrong here is me and that Beverly implied that Alison agreed with that assessment.

"Myrna has expressed a strong desire to end her life tonight [May 29], but also expresses doubt and fear over the process. If she remains determined, I will do the final mix of honey and the "solution" and let her have it. I feel very, very alone. And I think

Myrna feels the same way. A half-remembered refrain from a child-hood song keeps running through my mind—"Babes in the woods; poor babes in the woods."

Later, the same day: "Myrna is reviewing her life, trying to find a way to exit with an affirmation. But she does tend to slip into blaming herself for everything, even the illness! She is still waver-ing. Also she tends to think of others' reactions—Beverly's, Ali-son's, her parents'. I tell her to think only of herself here, her wishes, and forget about pleasing anyone else.

"She worries about the consequences for me. I tell her I have only two things to fear: an ambitious, self-righteous D.A. and/or a vengeful, self-righteous Beverly." (I wish I hadn't written that; it could only serve to challenge a D.A.) In the end, Myrna's desire to die that night was not as strong as it had first appeared. She took her pills, washed up, and went to bed as usual.

On May 30, at the therapist's request, Myrna and I went to see her together. I commented: "I think the therapist is very good, with her feet on the ground and her heart and head working in tandem. For example, she said that, ethically, she is required to proceed in a certain direction [i.e., to promote a choice of life], but that is her task; Myrna's may be something else. She may be a little too impressed by some New Age stuff, but if that's all there is in the field of thanatology, one must use what may be helpful. (Thanatology, the study of dying and death, ought to become a recognized specialty relatively soon.)

"The therapist made only one mistake—a shortfall in under-standing the severity of Myrna's mental decay. When Myrna said that her mind is 'just wandering,' the therapist suggested that was a metaphor for a kind of 'walkabout' [a practice of the Australian aborigines that connotes dreaminess]. But Myrna meant it literally, that she could not retain a focus or concentration for more than a few minutes.

"The therapist gave me a good lead on a couple of books. And she had a lot of suggestions, including the idea that both Myrna and I need a vacation from each other, a change of scene." We made appointments for further sessions for Myrna and one for me alone.

If I had believed that Myrna had the mental resources to profit from the therapist's work, I would have discouraged her desire to die until that therapy was worked through. As it is, I almost wish she had continued, although I thought there was little chance that it would do much good, because of her mental disabilities.

That evening we watched Mike's first successful feature film, *No Escape*, on video. The film had to do with conflict and escape plans on an island prison colony in the near future, and its plotting and dialogue were superb.

"Myrna has seemed down all day," I wrote, "in reaction to yesterday, I assume. But she seems to have perked up this evening. The session with the therapist helped a lot, and the movie kept her mind off herself."

I was quite wrong about the movie; it did make her think of herself. To Myrna, it was a parable about the forms of freedom and a call to seek freedom. The next day, Myrna surprised me by saying, "I'm going to end it tonight or tomorrow night." I wrote: "She went on to say that she didn't see the point of going to see the therapist again, she is tired of not being able to do anything by herself, of not being able to go out by herself. She said everything is a chore. She said she is tired.

"She said the Lebovs are supposed to be fighters. I told her she had put up a hell of a fight.

"She said not being able to read a book is shocking.

"She said that she's been told that other people are much worse off than she is. She said, angrily, 'I know that!' with the implication that it was irrelevant and disrespectful of her," which it was.

"She is very worried about Beverly's reaction, recalling how Beverly had howled when she had first mentioned the possibility. 'That wail!' she said, remembering. She is now trying to write a goodbye note to Beverly." And apparently she did write a note. Months later, parts of it were published after the D.A. released it to the press.

"I think it will not be tonight, but I am afraid her mood is very strange. I believe it is a possibility that she has passed the point of no escape into a condition in which she thinks about death, wants it, but is unable to will the act. I hope that is not the case. She could spend the next twenty years in that grim twilight.

"We also spoke of the past. In relation to Beverly's being able to get to the funeral with a broken foot [Beverly had fractured her foot in April], I pointed out how far and often we traveled with Myrna in a wheelchair. We talked of the trip to Israel and her walking out of the pool in Arad. We spoke of St. Barts and how she would swim for an hour, and people would comment on her strength and then gasp when she crawled out of the little bay and I brought her crutches and helped her stand up. We spoke of the pleasure of our trips. She thanked me—'It all would have been impossible without you.'"

June 1 was a difficult day. When I asked Myrna that morning what she wanted for Sabbath supper the next night, "She said she might not be here. I said I had to plan anyway, and would Swedish meatballs be okay. Yes."

At noon, Myrna called to set a time for an Access-a-Ride van to take her to see the therapist the following Tuesday—"in case I'm still here."

In the afternoon, "Myrna spoke to Beverly about the possibility of her having a short vacation [at Beverly's in California], something I had suggested, following up on the therapist's advice that we needed some time apart. Beverly said Myrna would find the physical circumstances too difficult."

Myrna had this trip all lined up. Claudette had agreed to accompany her and take care of her. Beverly wouldn't have to do anything. Beverly's large, roomy single-level home would have presented no physical difficulties.

This rejection was, I believe, one of the precipitating elements in Myrna's final decision. Beverly's failure to support the suggestion of the therapist she herself had arranged for must have seemed like a betrayal. It also indicated that Myrna would probably not be taken into their Arcadia home if anything happened to me.

Beverly's sole concession was to promise Myrna that, when her foot healed, she would come East and take Myrna to New Haven to visit family and old friends. To me, Myrna scoffed at that proposal. She recognized that the plan was part of Beverly's pattern in times of crisis—to travel and talk of trivialities with unthreatening relatives and friends. Myrna also recognized that the idea of a trip to New Haven demonstrated that Beverly had no idea how difficult travel and hotel living was for Myrna.

The odd thing here is the fact that I was not brought into this conversation with Beverly, did not even know it occurred until after the fact. It illustrates the dilemma Myrna was in, a dilemma created by Beverly's inability to discuss realities, and by the rules of secrecy she imposed. An example: When I gave Myrna a speaker phone because she had trouble holding a telephone receiver, Beverly refused to let her use it for their conversations.

Later that afternoon, Myrna called the Lincoln Center library about the possibility of checking out French films. I commented in the diary: "This indicates a renewed interest in life. It also means that she has forgotten that the last time she tried to watch a French film with subtitles hidden, she couldn't understand it. Is she moving into a high?"

The next day, Myrna did go to Lincoln Center. There she got a library card and a copy of Truffaut's *Wild Child*. The planning and persistency in that action showed a consistency of purpose I had not seen in months.

Again, the reader might see such action as inconsistent with Myrna's suicide a month later. The question ties in with one consistently raised in discussions of this issue: How do we know a person really wants to die and won't change his or her mind the next day? The simple and correct answer is that we can't know such a thing. But the reverse question is equally valid: How do we know that a person really wants to live and won't have a change of mind the next day? Again, we can't know such a thing.

What we do know is that the latter question is seldom asked, which suggests that the former question arises not from an objective ethical concern but from the personal death anxieties of the questioner. The question says a great deal more about the needs of the questioner than it does about those of the chooser.

In the same vein, we will not honor a person's decision to die because of a string of negative events, but we are eager to welcome a decision to live because of a single isolated happy event. There is no rule that says a person at the end of her rope cannot have moments of enjoyment and anticipation of pleasure at the same time she contemplates death. The idea that a person who decides to die must be absolutely forlorn and despairing does not arise from any real knowledge of such decisions but from a need to believe that it is madness to choose death.

The reader may raise the point that the concern about the decision to die is extreme because the act is irrevocable. Many of our decisions are irrevocable and their consequences permanent; those facts alone do not invalidate a decision. But more important, it should be noted that there was only one alternative to death in Myrna's case and that alternative was also irrevocable: further years of hopeless illness. The objection to suicide on grounds of its finality is valid only when the chooser has several real options and some cause for hope. Myrna did not.

On June 6 I bought some of the books the therapist had mentioned, books by Stephen Levine, who ran a Conscious Living/ Conscious Dying program in California. I commented: "The books are shot through with Eastern philosophy mush, but they also contain a great deal of good stuff." The reader should not suppose that I have any objection to Eastern philosophy as such; my objection is to its simplification and sterilization for American consumers.

Besides these books, I got several others, including Herbert Hendin's *Suicide in America*, an antisuicide study. This collection of books became the basis for the prosecutor's later contention that I was obsessed with death and suicide. By the same reasoning, I'm obsessed with cosmology, ethology, evolution, and mythology, and absolutely psychotic over computer software.

On June 9 I saw the therapist alone: "She advised that I must get out more and establish some life for myself. I'm seriously thinking about trying to make [my niece's] wedding in Nashville. She made it clear that she felt Myrna was not ready to kill herself now, and might never be. She also indicated that I had the right to walk away if necessary. I explained as well as I could about Beverly's detachment." It's odd, isn't it, that my leaving Myrna would have been more acceptable than Myrna's leaving a life she could no longer truly live.

That evening I got angry and almost yelled at Myrna. "She was leaving a message [on Alison's answering machine], saying that 'everything is wonderful, now,' 'things are looking splendid,' etc. I blew up! Shouting into the phone that everything was just the same, it was simply Myrna feeling different. I told Myrna that she had hurt me very badly, not my feelings, but physically. 'Now what will Beverly think? That I'm lying about how things are tough here?' I put it to Myrna bluntly—'If you won't take care of me, I can't take care of you.'

"Later, Myrna suggested I invite Beverly to see for herself. I reminded her that I had already done that and suggested that we invite Beverly together."

This was the first time I realized how Myrna's gentleness with the others was supporting their desire to see no crisis, or at least confusing them about the true situation.

Sometime during these last weeks, in a moderate euphoria, Myrna came up with a really crazy plan, the substance of which I did not record and can no longer remember. I know that I immediately refused to go along. Myrna persisted, rejecting all my explanations for why the idea was impossible, so I asked Gloria for her opinion. She, too, told Myrna that the idea made no sense.

In the past, when this sort of impasse arose, Myrna's standard response was to shrug it off and tell me I would soon find out how wrong I was. This time, however, she slumped in her seat and bowed her head. The air just went out of her. I could almost see her struggling to grasp this situation in which her ideas, her wishes, meant nothing to anyone else and would be ignored and she was helpless to do anything about it.

On June 13 I wrote: "I've been very tired today, I find it hard to work. The despair is deep. It is largely because Myrna is wholly out of it. Her memory is terrible. She seems to have no connection to yesterday or tomorrow, living wholly in the moment. She shows no emotions, no apparent feelings about much of anything, unless it's irritation over some little frustration. She saw the therapist today; said she talked all the time, but can't remember what it was all about.

I'm essentially living alone." What that entry displays is that the sense of isolation I felt for the two of us earlier had become more focused on myself. There was now just one "babe in the woods."

On June 14 I told Myrna that "I felt entirely alone and that no one was concerned about me, pointing out that I had not seen a dentist in over a year, or had this year's medical checkup for lack of funds, and suggesting that some of the money for Luye could help take care of me. Myrna suggested that I take $90 a month for myself and that she would not tell Beverly about it. I immediately made an appointment to get my teeth cleaned. Myrna has also informed me that Beverly was ready to provide a vacation for me, so I've begun to plan and cost out attenting the wedding in Nashville and taking a week in California or elsewhere afterward."

The next day I wrote: "I've done more work today than in any day for the previous two weeks. It's amazing what a ray of hope will do for one's energy." The hope had two elements. First, that Beverly was awakening to the fact that things were in crisis, and second, that I would have some real time off to renew my energies and spirits. The hope, it turned out, was short-lived.

14

The Decision, the Act

One of the things that most disturbed people about the case was that I not only made no attempt to stop Myrna from ending her life but clearly wanted her to end it. In the spring of 1996, during the filming of an examination of the case by *Dateline NBC*, the show's anchor, Stone Phillips, asked, "Did you try to talk her out of it?" And I replied, "I didn't want to talk her out of it." My diary and Myrna's letters make it clear that we foresaw only a future of pointless misery for us both and that we very much wanted to avoid such a future.

The unthinking, emotional reaction of many people is to imagine that death is always to be averted if possible. Failure to do so is, in their eyes, callous at least and probably depraved. Putting aside the emotional reaction, however, could reveal death, in some circumstances, to be preferable to all other options. I am sure that many of my emotional critics could, with a little imagination, conceive of circumstances in which they would prefer death and be exceedingly angry with anyone who tried to stop them from dying.

About mid-June, Myrna told me something I did not record in the diary, because I did not see its significance. She said she was not going to buy any more lottery tickets. I had always believed the lottery was a waste and had merely indulged Myrna's pleasure in the "gambling" on a sure loser. So I chalked Myrna's decision up as a sign of good sense. It was only months later that I saw its larger significance: Myrna had recognized the irrelevance of one of her dreams of rescue.

There are those opposed to assisted suicide who object to any consideration of financial circumstances in the decision. They argue that more money ought to be made available for the care and comfort of the seriously disabled and hopelessly ill and that to approve assisted suicide before providing that money is tantamount to forced euthanasia. This objection, however well intentioned, is not realistic. No society can afford the kinds of care and comfort needed or wanted by the ever-increasing numbers of the utterly incapacitated kept alive by medicine's new powers.

In Myrna's case, money could have meant greater freedom and independence, more help, greater convenience (e.g., a swimming pool of her own) and other comforts, but her giving up on the lottery was a recognition that none of these things could restore her mind. To a great extent, the prescription of money as a solution to the problem of suicide is equivalent to the prescription of antidepressants: neither can change the underlying conditions that have made continued life undesirable.

By June 20, Beverly and Bob had agreed to pay for me to go to Nashville for my niece's wedding. "They will pay the airfare and for a hotel room and a car, if necessary. This all with some reluctance; they haven't got hold of the idea that if they want Myrna taken care of well, they have to take care of the caregiver." Claudette would come in to take care of Myrna when Gloria was not here; we would have to pay for that.

My initial idea was that I would plan for a real vacation, not just a quick trip to Nashville. But because Beverly and Bob were so reluctant to finance the trip to Nashville, I didn't dare ask for more. The kind of suspicious questioning I got from them about our finances was more unpleasant than what I got from the harridans at Medicaid. There was no family trust here, no emotional generosity at all. Only deep suspicion. Myrna, who heard the whole conversation, said, "I'm very disappointed in them." This was the strongest criticism, implied or otherwise, I ever heard her make of Beverly.

"Yesterday, we talked about decision making and how the decision is in the act, not in its contemplation. I am very fearful, however, that Myrna has passed the point of no return. Certainly, as she is now, she is not capable of deciding to end it. Unless she recovers some control over her moods and some improved mentation, it is too late for her. I don't know what to do." I had more or less settled into the belief that she was not going to end her life.

June 26 began strangely. I went to the dentist to get my teeth cleaned and felt a kind of extreme anxiety I had not experienced in nearly thirty years, not since my therapy in the late sixties. Part of it was about money; one of my crowned teeth had developed new caries, so the crown would have to be replaced. But the worst of it was about being with people.

"I've been alone too long," I wrote. My feeling here was one of deep alienation, of being a foreigner in the land of normal living. I was anxious that I might not recover my capacity to be with people—and in truth, I have lost some of that ability. I continue to live almost like a recluse.

Later that day I wrote: "Myrna has been at the bottom the last two days, but still talking about suicide. If she stays in this mood, July 4 will be the date." But the next day, I was not so sure: "Myrna went to see the therapist today. She had nothing to say when she came home, except that it all seemed irrelevant.

"I spoke to the therapist on the phone; she said Myrna's neurologist will prescribe lithium to try to moderate the mood swings. Myrna has no interest in it. She says, 'It will change my mood, but not my circumstances.'" I did not understand how lithium could be of any help if the basic brain structures it was supposed to affect were being destroyed. Myrna's reaction illustrated her frustration with the constant "more pills" approach to her problems.

I began to get things ready to go for the weekend in Nashville. Myrna was in a fret during the intervening days, very anxious about her care while I was gone and perhaps concerned about whether I would return.

The Nashville trip was restful, and the wedding was very pleasant. It was good to see my sister and my daughter—Anna in the glow of the middle months of pregnancy—and to get acquainted with Megan and Ethan, my niece and nephew. But for the most part I felt terribly out of it; a ghost at the party. I didn't think about what the next few days might bring; in fact, I had come to doubt that Myrna would end it on the Fourth of July or ever. But Myrna surprised me.

"July 3, 9:00 A.M.—Returned yesterday about 5:15 P.M. to find Myrna lucid, tracking conversation, and responsive. We talked about the trip and watched a movie.

"This morning, she said, 'George, I want tomorrow to be my last day. Life like this is a drag. Nothing seems very interesting or worthwhile. It's all too much trouble. I used to love Shakespeare, but I can't get up any energy for going to the park. What would be the point?' I asked if there was anything special she wanted to do or eat today or tomorrow. Nothing, except the chicken."

"Apparently, the difficulties Gloria and Claudette had in caring for her the last four days have also influenced her thinking. She sees that, most of the time, it takes two people to adequately meet her needs and desires, and that without someone who knows all the details of her care and the apartment (namely me), the task is difficult and often unpleasant or frustrating for her.

"Whether she holds to this plan or not, I can't predict, but she is more serious about this now than I have ever seen her before. I'll get her medicines [the lithium and more amitriptyline] today, in any case, and if its not 'the solution' tomorrow night, we'll start the lithium."

Because Gloria had worked Saturday and Sunday, Claudette came to help us that day. After Myrna showered, she announced she was going to the library for a book or film, but when she was dressed and ready to go, she looked up at me from her wheelchair and said, with that twinkle of self-amusement in her eye, "Going to the library doesn't make much sense, does it." Instead she went with Claudette to Riverside Park by the Hudson.

It was a beautiful summer day, clear and sunny, with a moderate temperature and no humidity. Later, Claudette told me that Myrna was mostly silent, looking around at the trees, the people walking by, the shimmering river, and the children playing in the playground. Claudette said she seemed very much at ease. I like to think of her as saying goodbye.

They came home about noon, and Claudette took care of Myrna's lunch and catheterization. She waited with Myrna while I went out to get the lithium and the monthly allotment of Myrna's amitriptylin, then she left for the day. Claudette had no idea what was really happening, but said later that she sensed something different.

"3:30 P.M.—Myrna has pushed up the schedule to tonight. She seems mostly concerned about whether she can keep the amitriptyline down and whether it will work. She told me that when she set up her pills on Saturday night, she only set them up for three days. She said she had made an appointment later in the week with the visiting nurse. She worried that this sign of forward planning could get me in trouble. She noted that she's spoken to both Alison and the therapist about her distaste for her severe dependence, but has not spoken to them of her boredom with the necessary focus on bodily functions, specifically the four caths a day."

She was going to try to work on a suicide note, but at the last minute decided instead to watch *Forrest Gump* on a tape lent her by Claudette. While she watched the movie, I began to dissolve the thirty extra new amitriptyline pills and went out again to get the already cooked chicken that I would warm up for supper, some frozen french fries, and a bottle of a dry white wine.

This change in plans, pushing up the time of her death, struck me as eminently and ominously reasonable. It convinced me that she was very likely to do it. I didn't check her pill case to see if it was true that she had not set out her pills for the full week. I should have, as it would have convinced me that she had been holding the plan in mind since Saturday night, July 1. (The police took the pill case with them later, so the D.A. knows how the pills were set up.) When the movie was over, Myrna dismissed *Forrest Gump* with a shrug, 'A fairy tale.' She was not amused.

Sometime in the early evening, I was vaguely aware that Beverly called and that Myrna spoke briefly with her on the telephone. As usual, I put it out of my mind and did not question Myrna about it. Thinking back now, I wonder that I was not more concerned that Myrna might have told Beverly of her plans for that evening. If she had, I'm sure Beverly would have called the police in New York. Myrna must have reassured her sister that all was well. Certainly nothing could provide more convincing evidence that Myrna wanted no interference.

"7:30 P.M. (supper time)—Myrna is now questioning the efficacy of the solution, a sure sign that she will not take it tonight and doesn't want to. So, confusion and hesitation strike again. If she changes her mind tonight and does decide to go ahead, I will be surprised."

And I was. After supper, Myrna demanded to know when we were going to get on with it. I cautioned her that it would be unwise to take the solution on a full stomach. I also told her that if the taste of the solution was still too foul, the little bit she took to test it could serve as her nightly intake. So we should wait until at least 11:00. Myrna was not pleased at this delay.

It was then that I knew Myrna would drink her "solution" that night. Looking back, I am surprised at my reaction to this certainty. I would have expected a degree of relief that she had decided to go ahead with it, perhaps even taken a certain immediate pleasure in her courage. Instead, I felt nothing but dread.

I blended the solution: about a quart and a half containing about 9,000 mg of amitriptyline, with about one-quarter cup of honey. About 10:30 I brought her a teaspoon of the stuff to test. It was too foul, so I added another quarter cup of honey. Another test. The stuff was tolerable.

Myrna did not wash up and cream her face that night. Before getting her onto the bed for the catheterization, I brought her a suicide note I had prepared in case she didn't do one herself. It was a simple statement of what she was doing, not why:

STATEMENT OF INTENTION

Some weeks ago I asked my husband to help me die. At my request, he prepared a solution containing over 4,000 mg of amitriptylin (Elavil) in about 16 ounces of liquid. I am about to drink that solution now, freely and without reservations, with the full intention of ending my life.

This was the closest I came to pressing Myrna to make her intentions clear for public consumption and for my sake, and I did not expect the note to have much mitigating effect on the legal outcome of the case or on public perceptions. In the aftermath, the fact that this note had been created on my computer, not on Myrna's word processor, raised doubts in some minds that Myrna's assent was genuine and freely given. Why, the critics ask, did I not have better documentation of Myrna's intentions; or, more accusingly, why was I *unable* to get better documentation, with the implication that Myrna would not provide it?

For some of these critics, no amount of documentation would be sufficient; there are some people who simply will not believe that anyone can voluntarily choose death. In Myrna's and my case, I did not press her for clearer documentation of her intentions because the idea of doing so made me very uncomfortable. How could I press her to increase my safety when she was facing death? If she did produce something, fine! If not, I could deal with the problems later. She had problems enough of her own. As for her being concerned about my future, I had assured her frequently that I expected no serious consequences, assurances that I'm sure she finally accepted.

Myrna had seen the "statement of intention" before this. She glanced at it and scribbled a signature as best she could. I transferred her to the bed, propping her into a sitting position against a backrest. She questioned the necessity of a cath. I told her it would keep her from making a mess later. She understood.

I went out to the kitchen, gave the solution a last tweak in the blender, and poured out two plastic cups full, eight ounces each. I brought them and a straw into the bedroom, set them on Myrna's night table by a bottle of cold water, and sat down in a chair beside the bed. I balanced the first cup in my palm, as Myrna steadied it with her curled fingers, and taking the straw into her mouth, began to drink quickly. After a bit, she stopped, and I gave her the bottle of cold water so she could refresh her mouth. We repeated this, moving on to the second cup, until Myrna indicated she couldn't take any more.

I set a basin and a moist washcloth on my night table, in case Myrna threw up, and got up on the bed beside her and held her in my arms. She did spit up a little bit, but seemed to be holding the solution down without much effort. The spitting up, I think, had more to do with the foul taste than with stomach upset. We did not speak.

Later I wrote: "July 4, 12:30 A.M.—Myrna has just consumed about 3,000 to 4,000 mg of the amitriptyline. Her courage was remarkable. Once begun, she went ahead as long as she could before it began to threaten the heaves. About fourteen ounces of liquid, about half of what I had prepared. She said very little. Very direct and businesslike. No tearful goodbyes, no jokes, just a let's-get-this-done approach. All rather anticlimactic.

"Before we cathed and she took the solution, she expressed regret that she couldn't write letters to Beverly and Alison. I said, 'Leave a message with me.' She said, as if dictating, 'I love you both very much. Please don't feel hurt; I know you did all you could for me. I'm bored with my bodily functions and my mind is going. It's better to end it now, while I still can do something.'" I was never able to deliver this message because of their total rejection of me. Beverly and Alison, if you are reading this now, notice that her last words were for you.

Nearly six months later, the district attorney's office released copies of a suicide note dated May 31, 1995, that Myrna had written to her sister. The note was found on Myrna's word processing disk and was apparently never sent, because Beverly denied having seen it and questioned its authenticity.

That note, recovered from the court files on the case, read:

Dear Beverly,
    My life is over. It's time to end it.
    I'm tired of bodily functions being my major concern. Peeing dominates my day. I catheterize four times a day—and *still* have occasional accidents. And worry a lot about having

more. Even worse is my worry that I might have a bm in public, like in the swimming pool. Or on the bus. What a stinking mess *that* would be.

And how helpless I have become! I can't do much for myself anymore. Can't cut my food, touch-type, wipe my ass, turn over in bed, travel by myself, etc., etc.

Translation: No freedom. I've been trapped in my life, with no escape—except suicide. Beverly please forgive this final act. I don't want to hurt you. But I can't go on. I don't want to prolong my days, as I am today. I want my freedom. Try to understand. I *do* love you so very much.

All my love,

I would hope that the very plain language of the note would help authenticate it. I would not have put some of those words in Myrna's mouth.

Obviously, by July 3 Myrna had forgotten she had written this note the day after watching the feature film *No Escape*, with a screenplay by Alison's husband.

Looking back now, from a distance of more than a year, I am filled with regret and guilt over my own behavior during those last hours. I was overcome with anxiety and made nearly mute by the enormity of what we were doing. Would the solution in fact work? Would Myrna throw up? Would she have convulsions soon, or later? If later, would she be aware of the convulsions? Would I have to use a plastic bag? If I did, would Myrna wake up? All the imagining I had done earlier about these last hours was simply that, the maundering of sentiment; now I was overwhelmed by the horrific reality. I was little more than an automaton, going through programmed motions, unfeeling.

I'm disappointed, too, that Myrna was finally so direct and single-minded about it. I wish she had said goodbye. I think there was an element of desperation there that simply blocked out everything else—the kind of total focus she used to have when she was writing. I wish I had reminded her of the apple orchard in West Virginia and noted the strange prescience of that poem's last lines:

> And afterwards, you said
> you thought that
> Adam *found* the fruit
> and offered it
> to Eve.

I wish I had recalled for her the view from Nimrod's Castle on Mt. Hebron in Israel, of the beautiful acrobats in the Cirque du Soleil, Vincent Griffin's fiddle, and the haunting Burren in Ireland. But if I *had* done so, I suspect we would have wept inconsolably.

I think now that Myrna's businesslike manner and my numbness were defenses against a potential failure of will. We could not risk feeling, lest our bodies and emotions betray us. For months afterward I was haunted with regrets about our silence. There was so much to say, and yet what words could have born the weight of what we were doing. We were in the place of the Unutterable, at the Portals of Silence.

Near the end, Myrna asked for a rice cake. I got it for her and climbed back up beside her on the bed. She ate about half of it before she began to droop. I asked if she wanted to lie down flat now. Yes. I pulled her down on the bed and arranged her legs for comfort, kissed her cheek, and said "I love you." I don't know if she heard me; she may already have been asleep. I sat down in the chair by the side of the bed, watching and waiting for what might come. If there were convulsions, I had a moist, tightly rolled washcloth at hand to put in her mouth to keep her from biting her tongue.

At 12:30, I left her side for a moment to make an entry in the diary: "We sat up together on the bed for about a half hour after she drank the solution. She's soundly asleep now." I returned to her bedside to watch over her for almost two hours before I began to nod off. "2:15 A.M.—Myrna is sleeping very soundly, breathing heavily. I'm going to grab an hour's sleep."

There was one fact of that night that the police never asked about and I never volunteered, except to two understanding friends and my defense attorney. When I woke up later, much as I feared, Myrna was still breathing. I was confident that the solution would work sooner or later, but if it was later, I had a serious problem. Gloria was due to arrive at 8:00 A.M. Whether I explained the situation to her or not, I would be placing her in an intolerable moral dilemma—should she accept Myrna's decision on my say-so and become an accomplice in an assisted suicide, or should she call for an emergency medical team? I could not face her with that dilemma or take the chance that Myrna could be "revived" with who knows what kind of brain damage. I had promised the solution would work; that is, I had promised her the suicide would be successful.

So I steeled myself to do what I most feared doing, feared because of the probable psychological consequences and the legal questions it would raise if it were discovered. I went to the drawer where I had put some two-gallon plastic bags (they were right on top of the top drawer and stayed there; I made no effort to hide them later), put one bag inside another, and picked up a piece of ribbon. I went to Myrna and, without changing her position on the bed, slipped the bags over her head and tied off the open ends at her throat with the ribbon.

And I watched—stupefied with primitive terror—as she breathed, the bag moving in against her face with each inhalation, more and more slowly, until, in a few minutes, her breathing stopped. Myrna had not stirred or made a sound. I waited a few moments to be sure. I took the bags off her head, cut them into shreds, and flushed them down the toilet with the ribbon. I went back to the body and opened the eyes. Yes, the pupils were dilated and did not react to light. There was no pulse in the neck. Myrna was gone.

This act was at the base of a primitive, irrational guilt that haunted me for months after Myrna's death. It was not a moral guilt, an awareness of having done something ethically wrong; it was more immediate than that, almost physical. It reminded me of the idea of ritual uncleanness and seemed to me to be related to simply having been instrumental in a death.

I have come to believe that we humans, like other primates, have an instinctual block against killing our own kind, a prohibition that, if violated, sets up strong undercurrents of dissonance;

contradictory feelings about what has happened, what has been done. I'm reminded of the behavior of many animals in the face of the death of another animal of their own kind. In observers' accounts and in films, it appears that animals do not quite know what to make of this strange event, don't know how to behave in its presence, and often go through the most unusual and unexpected kinds of behavior that suggest denial, sorrow, fear, respect for the body, anger—behaviors that sometimes follow one after another quite rapidly.

I do not recall any accounts of the behavior of primates who, in the heat of battle over territory or group dominance or by accident, have killed another of their own species, a relatively rare but not unknown event. But I suspect that after the victorious animal finishes celebrating his or her survival and victory or comprehends the fact of death in an accident, an observer might see some unusual behavior—withdrawal, heightened sensitivity to slights or threats, increased rejection or acceptance of grooming, nervousness, and a host of other possible signs of uneasiness. It was this sort of primordial, instinctual unease that I felt and called "guilt."

In the weeks and months that followed, I often spoke of my guilt feelings, trying to sort out their natures and sources. Listeners misunderstood, thinking I was referring to the act of helping Myrna die. But I had no moral guilt about the act itself, only about how I had handled it, about the silence. And, at other times, I was referring to this primitive guilt, the dissonance of the primate over the violation of a fundamental instinct.

Am I a murderer? Or did I only carry a promise to completion? The answer to that question will depend on one's understanding of the variety of the causes and the natures of death. Whatever the answer may be, I do not think it can be simple. A quick and unequivocal answer, even if not thoroughly wrong, bespeaks avoidance of the issues and denial of the fundamental ambiguities that will always surround a chosen and assisted death, whether the assistance is criminalized or not, whether the choice and the act are public or secret.

"5:30 A.M.—Slept through the alarm. It's over. Myrna is dead. Desolation." I chose the word *desolation* here for lack of any word that could precisely express the numb horror I felt. It was only in the ensuing weeks that I would begin to fully grasp the accuracy of the word and the extent of the devastation.

I have been criticized for what I did next, which was to take a shower and have a cup of coffee before calling 911. It strikes the merciless as callous, cold, and calculating. They want evidence of remorse and anguish, signs of the eruption of the terrible that should destroy daily routine.

But consider this: Myrna and I were intensely private people made even more so by the recent years of semi-isolation. A last time alone together/apart, doing some of the normal daily things, before the descent of the police, before the inevitable body-bag and the medical examiner's knife, felt appropriate and right to me, a way of respecting what was now lost forever.

"8:20 A.M.—Called 911 about 6:30. EMS [Emergency Medical Squad] and police arrived almost immediately. The police are still here, a whole slew of them. Won't let me into the bedroom to water the hanging plants there. I watered the others.

"I've talked to Collens [our family doctor] and [Rabbi] Cohen and Alison. Alison was mostly silent. Claudette . . ."

At that point I had to stop writing and begin to print out the diary for the police, at their request. It was perhaps during the printout that the full realization of Myrna's absence came crashing down on me. Grief seized me and shook me violently for several minutes. It was an "unseemly display," and the detective in charge asked immediately if I wanted to go to the hospital. I was violating the "happiness principle" and perhaps should be put away, out of sight, and medicated. As if there were a pill for grief!

Beverly called. She just yelled at me for the first minute: bastard, son of a bitch, etc. Then we talked very briefly about funeral plans. I told her we had a plot in New Haven and that I wanted the funeral handled by the same people who had done Anne's funeral. We didn't get into specifics.

Gloria arrived for a normal day's work promptly at eight o'clock. She was devastated. We comforted each other. Gloria spent the rest of the day faithfully waiting to give a statement to the police and the D.A.'s office. I'm glad she could honestly say that she knew nothing of our plans and that it all came as a shock to her.

It was about eleven in the morning when I was permitted to go into the bedroom to say a last goodbye to the body that Myrna's spirit had once animated. I was more or less dry-eyed, unwilling now to let my emotional guard down, fearful of an even worse "unseemly display." I kissed the cold cheek, took in once more those peaceful features, and left.

Gloria and I walked with the detective in charge—Sergeant Steve Kuspiel, a good man—to the local precinct station about four blocks away. There we gave statements to Kuspiel and a homicide detective and waited and waited for an assistant district attorney to show up and take more complete statements. Gloria was finally able to leave about six hours later, after what must have been one of the most harrowing and exhausting days of her life.

My interview with the assistant district attorney was videotaped. The two-hour film shows an exhausted man trying to answer the questions as best he can, trying to relax, but strung tighter than piano wire, almost chain-smoking. The interrogation was not intense or aggressive. On the contrary, I felt it was almost too gentle. Perhaps the young prosecutor was too respectful of my age, or my bereavement, or was simply nonplussed by the strangeness of the case. I think if he had read the diary thoroughly, the interrogation might have been a lot tougher.

The tape does not reveal any significant questions or answers. For the most part the questions were about details of time and place. I was surprised that I was not asked if I believed in life after death. After all, a firm belief in an afterlife could be a sign of devaluing the significance of death, something the prosecutor might have been interested in ferreting out. If I had been asked, I would have said that I am completely agnostic on the subject but tend to feel that this one life is all there is and gloriously sufficient. *Dayenu!*

I was asked if I was aware that my act had violated the law, if I was aware of the criminal penalties involved? I responded that I was aware of the violation of law but not clear on what the penalty might be. I also said that I had given only minimal consideration to the issue. While I had been concerned to avoid an unjust charge of homicide, I would not have been deterred from the act by the threat of a long prison term. In helping Myrna escape, I felt the law, the state, government, and society were all irrelevant. I would have helped, whatever the penalty.

15

The Media, the Law,
and the People

On July 7, a sunny afternoon, Myrna was buried in New Haven. The service was attended by close to one hundred friends and family and presided over by the beloved cantor of our synagogue. I managed to control myself, more or less, breaking down briefly only once. After the grave-side service was over, I walked the few yards to her parents' grave and gave a prayer of thanks to them for the loan of their daughter.

A gathering at the home of a relative following the service was made tense and unpleasant by Beverly's rancor toward me, a rancor that had been increased by my refusal to let her dictate details of the funeral service and an angry negotiation over payment of the costs. That negotiation was the last time Beverly spoke to me. Ronald, Myrna's older brother, who had serious financial and caregiving problems of his own, took a very low profile at the funeral and subsequently; he expressed no opinions about the circumstances of Myrna's death to me or, as far as I know, to anyone else.

My grief in the following months was intense. One reason Americans are crazy when it comes to death is that we, more than any other society on earth, tend to live in isolated nuclear families.

When a family member dies, a large portion of one's emotional world vanishes. In other societies, with their larger, extended families, the death of a loved one means that a much smaller portion of the emotional world disappears.

The sum of Myrna and me was much greater than our two parts. With one of us subtracted, the remainder amounted to much less than he had thought. I was astonished to discover how much of my strength was really Myrna's. A week after the funeral, I wrote in my diary: "I simply didn't realize how much of my life she was, how terribly, terribly important she was to me. I find myself wanting to share these days with her—to tell her how many people have spoken of her kindness, good cheer, gentleness, etc., etc., etc.: of how much the synagogue has said they will miss her. I had not allowed myself to imagine how much I was damaging myself in helping her to escape. Grieving for years, I saw no worse fate for myself, but it is so incredibly worse. But I would do it again, even if I knew what I know now."

A month after her death, on Tisha B'Av, a Jewish day of mourning for our lost Temple in Jerusalem and for recognizing our responsibility in that loss, I returned to the cemetery to visit Myrna's grave. It had rained; the sky was dark and glowering, the grass wet. A cool, light wind rustled the trees. The grave was marked by a small green stand with the legend "Myrna Lebov, July 4, 1995." It was peaceful, quiet, beautiful. I came away with some of her spirit, comforted.

But a few days later I wrote: "I feel there really isn't much point in going on. There's no point to me anymore." And a few days after that: "So much of me and my daily experience was focused on communicating with Myrna that now, impulse after intention, so many motions of my mind and feeling just fray off the edge of the torn fabric that was us."

I began to have a recurring dream. A stranger accosts me on the street near the apartment and tells me he just saw Myrna turn the corner over there, pointing. I look, but see nothing. I pull away from the stranger, unbelieving. But I want to believe; I want to run after her. I would awake from this dream angry with the stranger and frightened by the dream's meaning. My simple, sleeping brain was reminding me of something that had always been true before: If you want to be with her, you have only to go where she is.

My grief was assuaged by the gentle and forgiving embrace of the synagogue, so consistent in its emotional support that I likened it to a down comforter on a very cold night. I also found comfort in resuming the round of daily prayers, something I had not always been able to manage while caring for Myrna. In particular, the daily donning of teffilin (phylacteries, little boxes containing passages of scripture, and attached to leather thongs so they can be bound to the head and one arm) became, again, the symbol of my binding with God and of God's inescapable embrace.

Myrna's childhood and college friends were another valued source of moral support. One of her childhood friends lived in our building and knew us both well; his help and concern were invaluable. Myrna's closest college friends, one of them a devout Catholic, were equally unstinting in their care to stay in touch and keep me from harm.

In addition, letters and cards streamed in from other friends and family, including people I had worked with twenty years before and had all but forgotten. Of close to two hundred letters, over twenty were from strangers who had read about the story in the press. The letters all expressed understanding, and several of the writers communicated regret that they had not done the same for a relative—or made quiet, sorrowful, still horror-stricken confessions that they had. One old friend told me how she and her husband had ended his mother's life, on the basis of her statements that she wanted to be done away with when she no longer knew who they were.

I wrote in my diary, which had now become a habit, "I am astonished at the outflowing of support for what I've done. I sense an almost universal tide of public yearning for some guidance and support in the effort to escape the medical machine, for some humane way to effectively handle people in need of a dignified death, for some return to a sense of the spiritual in death." I did not receive a single piece of hate mail or one crank phone call.

By the end of the year, the dream stopped recurring and the smothering pall of grief began to lift. I no longer had to avoid people because I didn't want to cry in front of them. Sleepless nights became rarer, and I stopped taking over-the-counter sleeping pills. The lethargy and listlessness began to lift. Now and then, unexpectedly and without warning, I would be struck by that terrible awareness of loss, but those times became rarer and briefer. Resilience returned. One thing helped a great deal: At the end of October, Anna gave birth to a healthy boy, Jonathan Conor; I was a grandfather at last.

Despite all the comforting, throughout those early months I struggled with the dream's suggestion that I follow Myrna. I might well have killed myself, but for one reason—I feared my suicide would be used as evidence that I was overcome by guilt for having coerced Myrna into killing herself. That fear was created by one newspaper reporter and Beverly.

In the immediate aftermath of Myrna's death, most media reaction was moderate, even sympathetic, restrained perhaps by the conventions of respecting grief. Even the city's major tabloid, Rupert Murdoch's *New York Post*, was relatively decorous. But there was one exception, the *Forward*. Once the major Jewish newspaper in the city, a lively, wide-ranging Yiddish daily, the newspaper was now a dull and obscure English weekly, managed by a very traditional Orthodox group.

The *Forward's* first story on the case, July 14, was mild and gentle, but subsequent stories were viciously accusatory. Those later stories were written by Lucette Lagnado, the executive editor, and were largely based on Beverly's accusations, which fit neatly, I believe, with both Ms. Lagnado's prejudices and those of her employers.

Lagnado did provide one service. Her comments to me and her stories gave me some idea of what was going on in the district attorney's office. By the time of the first Lagnado article, I had a lawyer, Benjamin Brafman, compliments of a synagogue member who had talked Brafman, one of the best defense attorneys in the city into taking the case for a third or less of his usual fee.

Ben Brafman is a human tank, built close to the ground, stocky and compact, brusque, with intense eyes that seem to be looking for a target. He was best known as Sonny "the Bull" Gravano's lawyer, before Sonny ratted out his boss, John Gotti. Brafman and his partner, Brett Gilbert, played "good cop, bad cop" to perfection. It was Brett who quietly told me to stop talking to the press; it was Brafman who told me to "shut up." Ultimately, 60 percent of his bill was paid by friends at the synagogue, with large single contributions, and by small contributions from strangers around the country, most of them members of the Hemlock Society.

Brafman was well known to the district attorney's office and would normally have been in a position to let me know what the D.A. was planning for me. But he told me that the office was being unusually secretive. I learned from Lagnado's articles in the *Forward* that the D.A. was looking at the case as a possible homicide and, at the least, would try to prove "selfish motives" to make the charge of "assisted suicide" at least support a severe sentence. I also learned from Lagnado that Beverly was talking with the D.A. and that the case would be taken to the grand jury. Gloria and the apartment building superintendent told me they had been called to the D.A.'s office for statements.

Lagnado hit the big time on August 4 with an op-ed piece in the *New York Times*. Entitled "Assisted Suicide and Rational Choice," Lagnado's article was relatively rational and fair. Among other things, it informed me of something new—Beverly had told the reporter that she and Myrna had talked about Beverly's getting a small apartment in the city so they could spend more time together. If that was true, Myrna had never mentioned it, and of course, Beverly had not told me about it either.

The piece raised some interesting questions, even if they were not very well thought out. "If someone expresses a wish to die, at what point do we know this person won't change his or her mind later?" Lagnado asked. "And if someone is extremely ill, do we assume that a decision to commit suicide is a perfectly rational one and conclude that a premature death is the best possible ending? Do we somehow value the lives of the disabled less?"

This passage seems to suggest that if we do assume the hopelessly ill person is rational and that death is the best possible option for that person, then we are devaluing the disabled person's life. But the opposite might be equally true. If we assume that any decision to die is irrational or a passing whim, particularly in the hopelessly ill, are we not adopting a very paternalistic attitude toward the disabled, an attitude that devalues their personal integrity and robs them of respect in life *and* in death?

It was this op-ed piece that made me slowly begin to see clearly the threat to Myrna's honor in the arguments of those opposed to assisted suicide, in any attempt to paint her as a victim. Up to this time, I had taken only a mild interest in the discussion of chosen death and assisted suicide. My real interest was in the spiritual decay that follows from the American devaluation of death and denial of tragedy. I was not inclined to get down in the trenches and fight for a right to die. Nor was I much concerned about what the criminal justice system had in store for me. I had broken the law, the penalty was five to fifteen years, and I assumed I'd have to do at least eighteen months in prison. I was prepared to face whatever the system handed me for carrying out Myrna's wishes.

But I was not prepared to tolerate the idea that Myrna was pathetic, or a victim, or anything but her own decision-maker. I was fully aware of the two-edged nature of this concern: By vindicating Myrna, I would be vindicating myself. Up to this point, I had not much cared whether I was vindicated or not. Now I began to care passionately, because I wanted Myrna to be seen in a proper light: I wanted her reason, her will, and her courage to be honored. I would have to begin speaking out as much as possible within the confines of my attorney's command of silence and my own lack of experience with public advocacy.

I had been contacted soon after Myrna's death by a past president of the Hemlock Society USA with an offer of help. Sidney Rosoff, a tax and estate attorney in the city, can only be described as a cherub of a man. With a wide smile below twinkling eyes in a round face atop his slight body, Sidney emanates peace and goodwill, an aura reinforced by his quiet voice and gentle manner. When we first met, I told him up front that I had no desire to become a poster boy for the Hemlock Society, and he accepted that position with gracious understanding.

Now, however, what had been a private and personal conviction was becoming, willy-nilly, a public controversy. I had begun to grasp the absurdities and contradictions in the arguments against a rationally chosen death and to experience the opprobrium of suspicion that falls on those who must help carry out that choice in secret. I wanted to get involved.

To get my feet wet, I attended a meeting of the Manhattan Hemlock Society at the end of August. There were only about twenty souls there, nearly all of them in their sixties or older. The speaker was the legislative aide of a state senator who has, for several years, submitted bills to enable and regulate assisted suicide. The bills have always failed to emerge from committee. The aide made the standard political promise that the next legislative session promised better results.

I was not recognized, at least not noticeably, until the end of the meeting, when during a discussion period, one Hemlock member asked if I wasn't "that man in the news." I acknowledged that I was, and my interlocutor asked why I had not tried to keep secret my role in Myrna's death. I replied that no one who knew Myrna's condition well could have believed that she could carry out, by herself, the various steps required. I could not tacitly ask those friends and neighbors to lie for me.

Further, if I had tried to hide my role and failed—because my sister-in-law would certainly have raised serious questions—the act would look much worse. After Nixon, I should think we would have learned the grim consequences of cover-ups. And finally, I wanted to bring death out of the closet, speak of its natural inevitability, and lift the pall of unthinking sentimentality that surrounds it.

Afterward, Sidney told me I was an inspiration to all those who had been fighting for years for the right to die with dignity. The idea of being some sort of public hero made me distinctly uncomfortable. My own feeling at times like this was that I was just a damned fool who had wandered without thinking into a moral and legal morass out of a habit of service. I felt naked in public. I was embarrassed. But I began to regularly attend the Hemlock Society's monthly meetings.

Bits of information continued to filter out of the district attorney's office, some through Brafman, a lot more through Lagnado. According to Lagnado, the case was definitely going to the grand jury, in spite of the D.A.'s receipt of many letters urging him not to prosecute. My bank informed me that my financial records had been subpoenaed. I assume the D.A. got my tax records and that he was informed when I filed for bankruptcy at the end of November.

Brafman told me that while the district attorney handling my case was a sympathetic man without any political agenda, he was taking detailed instructions from above in this case. I had always voted for District Attorney Robert Morgenthau, the source of those instructions. I felt he handled one of the most difficult jobs in the world with dignity, decency, and common sense. I was rather sympathetic to his dilemma: He would find that I had no ulterior motive in Myrna's death, but I had dealt a direct challenge to the authority of the law. He would have to appear severe.

The grand jury heard the case and indicted me on December 12, five months after Myrna's death. I did not testify; no point in it. I heard about the indictment from Lagnado. On December 14, the acting D.A., Tom Schiels, held a press conference to announce the indictment and to release my diary to the press. He apparently made only the briefest of statements, to the effect that I had planned Myrna's death, and showed self-interest, and therefore deserved to be prosecuted.

The release of the diary ended my honeymoon with the press. The passage that described Myrna as "sucking my life out of me like a vampire" caused reporters to handle the case with a good deal more ambivalence or condemnation. Insofar as the press had wanted to make me a hero, when they found I was only an ordinary person, some now wanted to make me a villain. In his novel *The People's Choice,* Jeff Greenfield makes an interesting comment on this point: "The first instinct of the contemporary American political press is its preternatural fear of whatever lies beyond the security perimeter of conventional wisdom." Calling Myrna a "vampire" was far beyond the perimeter of convention.

Remarkably, Lagnado did not write another critical article. In fact, after a story in November, focused largely on the perfidy of my synagogue for tolerating my presence, The *Forward* dropped the case until the following May, when the case again touched on an issue of concern to the very Orthodox. Perhaps Lagnado and her bosses felt the rest of the media could carry on without them now.

On December 20 the *New York Times* published an editorial endorsing the idea of physician-assisted suicide. It was the first time this prestigious and influential newspaper had taken a position on the subject. The editorial was considered something of a coup for the right-to-die movement. Using my case as a jumping-off point, the *Times* commented that it illustrated "how mixed and ambiguous the motives of both parties [the person dying and the helper] can be." It concluded that "whatever the legal outcome [for Delury] may be, the tragic story strengthens the case for allowing qualified professionals to assist desperately ill patients with no hope of recovery to die with dignity. . . . Medical participation would provide objective counseling and professional support that would reduce the risk that a patient—or an overburdened caregiver—could make an irrevocable mistake."

I could not have asked for a clearer statement of my own views.

On December 27, in court, I again pleaded a formal "not guilty," this time to the indictment, and for the first time saw the district attorney handling the case, a tall, handsome man, with a long face that projected dignity, determination, and a sense of humor. He sported a mane of white hair and a full beard. The judge also had a beard, as did one of the bailiffs. I was reminded of Los Angeles in 1965 when, on three separate night-time occasions, I was stopped and questioned by the police solely because I had a beard and was engaged in suspicious behavior—*walking*. I felt safer under criminal indictment in a New York City courtroom.

The following day, the D.A. released to the press the May 31 suicide note found on Myrna's word-processing disk. I did not know what to make of this disclosure by the D.A. of information that went a long way toward confirming that Myrna wanted to die. Now, in retrospect, I think the D.A. was beginning to soften the earlier picture of me created by the diary in preparation for the plea bargain I was finally offered. Brett had said that the D.A. was seeking a way out of a harsh prosecution and wanted time to let interest die down and tempers cool. Brafman had told me after the indictment that if I stayed quiet he could present the case as "sad" and "isolated" and argue for mercy. He said if I spoke up, showed no remorse, and appeared to present a challenge, the D.A. might not settle for a plea bargain at all.

But I was no help. I wanted people to discuss the issues, and I was naive enough to hope that, sooner or later, some reporter would treat the story with the caution and seriousness it deserved. I gave an interview to *Newsday* on January 4, to *People* magazine on January 17, and another interview to the *New York Times* on January 22.

The two newspaper stories, both rather negative in their treatment of me, broke before January 30, when Brafman informed me that the D.A. was offering a bargain: Plead guilty, get a six-months sentence, and serve only four. Take it or leave it; no negotiating. And don't mention the offer to the media.

I accepted with little hesitation. Why, I am often asked, did I not go to trial and prove my innocence? For one reason: I simply was not innocent. Whatever my motives, I had violated the law against assisting in a suicide, a law that is important but too broadly drawn at present.

There were several additional reasons to accept the bargain: I could not bear the time and expense of a trial; I felt I could only realistically expect a hung jury; and most important, I did not consider an adversarial courtroom, with its ancient precedents and arcane rules, a place to air effectively the fundamental ethical and spiritual issues in the right-to-die question.

On the last point, for example, the D.A., in announcing the indictment, had mentioned that Myrna's death was planned. In criminal law, evidence of planning shows premeditation, traditionally a very bad thing in a real crime. It is far better if one can plead a spur-of-the-moment impulse, that one was out of one's head. A Long Island man who shot his ailing wife a few months later used that quirk in the law to very good effect for himself. He pleaded that he was out of his mind with grief over her condition and would never have done such a heinous thing if he had been normal. He served, I believe, eight days in jail before being reprieved.

My own point of view is that an assisted suicide requires careful forethought, moral care, and rational self-criticism over a period of time. The idea of an impulsive suicide or assistance is, to me, anathema. But impulse is always a mitigating factor in criminal law; premeditation never is.

On February 8 I taped a *Donahue* show with half a dozen other people, all but one supportive of the right to die. I believed that of all the talk shows, Donahue's would be the one most likely to give the issue a fair hearing, and it did. The *People* magazine piece was published on February 19. It was a fairly objective presentation of the case. Then, on February 21, Brafman informed me that there was a snag in the plea bargain procedure: The judge wanted briefs on the case from both sides. That meant the *Donahue* show would probably air before the bargain was accepted by the judge. It did, on March 4, and it was, in the view of the authorities, too favorable to me. Brafman exploded and threatened to quit if I didn't keep my mouth shut.

The D.A. had submitted his brief to the judge on February 21; Brafman submitted his response on March 6. How would the judge respond, considering all the publicity I was generating? It turned out there was nothing to fear. On March 15 we all appeared in court, and in a few minutes the deal was done. I pled guilty and answered a few pro forma questions about what I had done. The actual sentencing was postponed until May 17, pending a probation department report.

New York State law prescribes, but does not mandate, five to fifteen years for assisting in a suicide. A moment's thought will reveal why. Using extreme psychological pressure to induce a suicide would be akin to murder. It would also violate a fundamental principle of statecraft—that the state should have a monopoly on the use of lethal force. But no one can remember anyone else having been indicted for assisting a suicide in the many years of the law's existence.

In the early 1990s, Dr. Timothy Quill admitted in an article in the *New England Journal of Medicine* that he had assisted in a patient's suicide several years earlier. His case was brought before a grand jury, but the panel refused to indict him. My indictment apparently turned largely on the fact that I was not a doctor but a close family member who might profit from Myrna's death, and on the district attorney's interpretation of the diary as suggestive of coercion.

But if the D.A. was convinced of my guilt in such a grievous crime, what can explain the comparatively light sentence of only six months in jail? Conversely, if the D.A. was so unsure of his case that he finally settled for a token punishment, why did he press for an indictment in the first place?

I can't give a definitive answer to these questions. I never met the D.A.; I have no idea what he was thinking or what kind of pressures he was under to be harsh—or to go easy. My attorney never told me anything about his negotiations with the district attorney. Undoubtedly Brafman's canniness and reputation had a good deal to do with the outcome, but he certainly was not the whole story. Despite my ignorance of the details, I think I can piece together the various factors that resulted in the final plea bargain.

First, a serious law had been openly, even defiantly, violated. The D.A. could not overlook that fact any more than I could. In addition, Dr. Jack Kevorkian's activities in Michigan, where he had assisted in about thirty suicides by the time of my indictment, must have raised the specter in the authorities' minds of something similar happening in New York. The new Republican administration in Albany was, I believe, very concerned about that possibility. They feared serious judicial problems similar to those encountered by the Michigan D.A. who had prosecuted Kevorkian twice, unsuccessfully.

And many in the new, overwhelmingly Catholic, administration also shared the personal, superstitious anxieties, nearly a hysteria, with which so many Catholics—and others—face death. That near hysteria was revealed that spring when the United States Court of Appeals for the Second Circuit overturned the New York State law against assisting a suicide. (The ruling applied only to doctors and had no impact on my case.) The state attorney general, Dennis Vacco, was quoted as saying the decision gave doctors "a license to kill," which raised the absurd image of frustrated doctors finally being allowed to do what they had always wanted to do—murder their patients. Law enforcement officials wanted to squelch any idea in the public mind that I was some sort of hero or that assisted suicide was acceptable. The best way to do that was to turn me into a convict.

Their determination was evident in the D.A.'s relations with the press. An early leak was part of a glancing remark I had made to the arresting officer as he escorted me from the precinct to central booking. It was the first time I had seen the streets of Manhattan at night in about two years, and I was stunned by the bright lights and crowds. I said, "If I were still a drinking man, I could go back to the bars now."

It was a crazy thing to say, because I had never frequented bars at night; they're too noisy and usually too dark for reading. On emerging from the D.A.'s sausage maker, the statement was simply, "Now I can go back to the bars," with never a mention that I had been dry for nearly three years. From that I learned never to accept without question anything a prosecutor alleges in the press about a person charged with a crime.

With the release of the full diary to the press at the time of my indictment, the D.A. played the media like a virtuoso. He knew that certain passages would be red meat for the media, and he probably even pointed out those passages. He also knew that the media, particularly TV, would be incapable of conveying the complexities and ambiguities of the diary. All the public would learn of the diary would be the easy, sensational phrases the media love because they simplify the story and heighten the drama.

The most important of those phrases was the statement likening Myrna to a vampire "sucking my life out of me." Neither the D.A. nor the press could have known that the vampire image originated with Myrna, but the D.A. did know that the press would never be able to convey the more complex story of what I had told Myrna immediately after that statement—that I would work with her several hours a day on her book if she showed a real interest in it.

But it was precisely in the "vampire" statement, perhaps, that the D.A.'s case was weakest. For why, the defense could argue, would this intelligent man not only fail to erase this damning phrase but freely hand it over to the police? The diary as a whole screamed this question. It was, on its face, a very thorough exposure of the situation and my conflicted feelings. It had everything—the sublime and the ridiculous, the self-sacrificing and the self-serving, the noble and the base. In short, the diary was complex and ambiguous, and every trial lawyer knows that in the face of the complex and ambiguous, juries become unpredictable, particularly when the standard of proof is "beyond a reasonable doubt."

To make his case, the D.A. would have had to convince a jury that I was such a clever and devious monster that I had kept the diary deliberately to obscure the issues and hide the real—i.e., coercive—nature of the crime. Yet he knew from the tape of my original interrogation that I came across, at worst, as self-absorbed and naive, hardly the sort that would or even could create such an elaborate fiction.

Complexity and ambiguity are anathema to a prosecutor's case. Complexity confuses and ultimately bores a jury. And ambiguity only increases the confusion. It doesn't even take a smart defense attorney to drive a truck through the holes of ambiguity. For a top-flight attorney like Ben Brafman, ambiguity can be a freeway to acquittal.

On top of all this, the D.A., I suspect, came to realize that Beverly's testimony would be worthless, if not counterproductive, and that under sharp cross-examination, she could blow up in his face, dropping her conventional facade and revealing the irrationality of her antipathy to me. Her repeated statements to the media that I should get the maximum penalty of fifteen years could only make my case stronger.

The same doubts would apply to Alison's testimony, though to a lesser degree. Myrna's aquatherapist would be a much stronger witness, but even she only saw Myrna for an hour two or three times a week.

Against that short list of witnesses, the D.A. faced a dozen or more people who knew us well and were eager to testify to our deep, loving relationship. That dozen would be led off by Gloria, who had seen us in all sorts of situations, at all hours of the day, day after day, for over two years.

In short, when the prosecution looked at its case, the best it could see was a hung jury, no matter how often it might be tried.

So why seek the indictment in the first place? Why didn't the prosecution go to the grand jury, downplay the negatives in the diary, and subtly indicate that a "no bill," a refusal to indict, would be acceptable. That way, the D.A. could have shuffled off all responsibility for leniency onto the grand jury. As already hinted, one word explains why an indictment was necessary—politics.

I doubt if the approaching election year was far from the minds of the D.A. and the other elected officials. Any appearance of leniency toward me, particularly if it was followed by another similar case, could only create additional political problems for the Republican administration in the city and the state. To the extent that politicians of both parties do not want to deal with the assisted suicide issue at all and would rather suppress the problem, my jailing can be seen as a political imprisonment.

In the end, the D.A. used his discretionary authority to reduce the felony category by one level. The Class C felony of assisting a suicide became the Class D felony of attempted manslaughter, a purely accidental and arbitrary label that meant nothing. The proffered deal for a guilty plea was a sentence of six months in jail. I have no idea how that term was arrived at, but it seemed to me a reasonable compromise between the facts of the case and the D.A.'s political need to present some appearance of severity.

Standard New York practice is to immediately reduce a jail sentence by one third, holding the suspended time over the prisoner's head as a guarantee of good behavior during incarceration. So unless something unimaginable happened while I was in jail, I would only serve four months. *New York* magazine thought this was such a coup that it named Brafman the "best defense attorney" in its April 15, 1996, edition, dedicated to the Best of New York.

The evening of the day of my guilty plea, filming started for a *Dateline NBC* show on the case. Brafman had been assured that there was no way the show would be ready to air before the sentencing date, and he agreed to do an interview for the show.

Stone Phillips, who conducted the interview, is even more impressive in person than he is on TV. Tall, broad-shouldered, "hunk" handsome, deep-voiced, and articulate, he is intimidating to ordinary mortals, a fact he knows and uses. The major part of the interview took place in one evening in my apartment. It lasted for three hours and is probably the most harrowing interview I have ever been through. My doctoral orals were less intense; the police interrogation in July was a picnic in comparison. Phillips was aggressive and quick with questions. I've never been fast on my feet in such situations and at several points I had to call for a time-out simply to recover my composure.

The show, when it finally aired in late September, accomplished my primary purpose. Many of the people who sent letters to NBC afterward said the interview had forced them to think about the issues and to discuss their own wishes with family members. But if I had hoped *Dateline* would allow me to present a fair picture of my case, I would have been sadly disappointed.

I had agreed to do the show knowing that Beverly, Alison, and Luye would make their charges against me and knowing, also, that Gloria would not appear on it. Her camera-shyness was reinforced by a virtual command from her agency employer that she not appear. I did not expect, however, that Phillips would completely ignore Gloria's viewpoint—that Myrna and I had a loving, supportive relationship and that I did everything I could for her. (Later that year, not long after I got out of jail, Gloria was found to have inoperable liver cancer. She died in a hospice in early January 1997.)

Nor did I expect the show's producers, who had a complete copy of my diary, to make a fundamental error of fact and build part of a prosecutorial case around that error. The show put Myrna's first session with the therapist *before* her May 4 statement to Alison that she had made a decision to live, and concluded that that decision was a result of the therapy session. In fact, the first session with the therapist took place five days *after* Myrna's statement to Alison. This error illustrates the desire on the part of many to believe that there is always something that can be done to avert death, a desire so strong that even a fictional straw will serve to prop up that belief.

But the show's greatest error—its thoroughly unethical error—was not to raise with me the question of the documentation of Myrna's wishes before making it the centerpiece of the show. The show's primary question was: "How could this man, who so meticulously documented his wife's daily moods, fail to document her wish to die at the time of her death?" The implication, expressly drawn by Phillips, was that it might have been impossible because she did not really want to die.

If the question had been raised with me, and if I had been told that it would be the central issue, I would have pointed out to Phillips the many passages in Myrna's letters that showed she had been thinking about suicide for five years. The producer had copies of those letters. I would also have reminded Phillips of the *New York Times* story about the suicide note to Beverly found on Myrna's word-processing disk, written a month before her death and made public by the D.A. at the end of 1995. And I would have asked Phillips just how close to the act itself a documenting statement would have to have been to satisfy him—a day, an hour, five minutes—or would it be rational to assume, as I did, that the verification of her decision was in the very act of drinking the foul-tasting solution. That, by the show's own telling, is what the D.A. assumed.

Brafman had warned me that the media was "not my friend." Jeff Greenfield's book had warned me that TV personalities are terrified of the unconventional. Here was proof. What I was not aware of were the lengths to which the people in charge of the show would go to build drama and make a point by leaving out essential parts of the story—that is, how far they would go to boost audience appeal and ratings. *Dateline NBC*, which began in hopes of competing with *60 Minutes*, has instead begun to stoop to "tabloid TV."

That show had a deleterious impact on some of my relations with others. Those easily influenced by television and those squeamish about any sort of controversy drew away from me. The Westchester chapter of the Hemlock Society withdrew its invitation to me to speak to its members. My own sister, Maida, expressed shock and dismay. And many friends asked in deep concern, How could you have been so imprudent, so straightforward, as to say some of those things on that show?, referring among other things, I suppose, to my assertion that I didn't want to talk Myrna out of dying.

I began to see where my most serious crime lay. I had not been prudent; I had not shown a proper sense of self-protection; I had not shown a proper regard for social sensibilities. I had suggested that some social heroes, the caregivers, were not necessarily noble or happy in their role and that they might need some serious recognition and help. I had created a lot of discomfort.

Above all, I had violated an unspoken agreement among "decent" people that suicide, assisted or otherwise, is a shameful thing and not to be thrown in their faces. In short, suicide, whatever the circumstances, falls into that same "don't ask, don't tell" limbo the military has created for homosexuality. Everybody knows about it, but "we don't talk about that sort of thing!"

This crime seemed particularly heinous to some people in May 1996 when they learned I had been invited to participate on a panel about assisted suicide at the annual meeting of the American Psychiatric Association in New York. The panel had been organized by a liberal Orthodox rabbi-psychiatrist and included an archconservative Orthodox rabbi as well as panelists representing Catholic and Muslim viewpoints.

Lucette Lagnado of *The* (Jewish) *Forward* put in an appearance again, not only in that paper but also on the editorial page of the *Wall Street Journal* (May 1, 1996) in an article entitled "Welcome to the Era of Euthanasia Chic." The crux of her argument was that it was shameful that a felon convicted of aiding in his wife's suicide should be invited to speak at such a prestigious gathering. The implication was that the act of abetting a suicide was so horrible that the public, even a learned segment of the public, should be told nothing about it by someone who knew the details. The other part of Lagnado's critique was that I appeared to be making a career of right-to-die advocacy. Before the month of May was over, Lagnado became a staff writer for the *Wall Street Journal*, a major leap upward in her own career.

Ten months and two weeks after Myrna died came the next grimmest day, the day of sentencing. On May 17, I met Ben Brafman's partner, Brett Gilbert, and two friends in the courtroom. We chatted together for a while before Brett and I moved to the defendant's table. Beverly and Alison came in with the acting district attorney, Tom Schiels.

Before the sentencing, the judge permitted the principals to make statements of their own. Beverly's was read by Mr. Schiels;

Alison read her own. The gist of their complaint was that I had put Myrna under intolerable pressure to end her life because I was tired of taking care of her, that her mind was alert and she was in full possession of her faculties, and that she had many years of pleasurable life she could have looked forward to were it not for me. Beverly's accusations were a good deal more muted than I had expected, but I did not listen closely to either of them. Both statements were fairly long.

In my statement I opted for brevity. I said only, "I regret that my wife's spirit of independence has been impugned and her courage dishonored because society and the government have no procedures to deal with these situations with respect for individual freedom of conscience and personal dignity."

The judge did a double take, not quite believing I was done. Then he said, much too firmly, "I have read the diary. It seems to me a term of incarceration is well warranted in this case." He pronounced the sentence and gestured me toward a door on his right. I picked up the shoulder bag I had packed with a few personal items and walked through that door into the "belly of the beast."

16

Criminal Justice

The mindset of the "perfect bureaucratic soul" is that members of the general public are nuisances who keep the bureaucrat from his real work: career promotion, turf protection, and cover-up. Many people who work in bureaucracies are still human beings, but too many, particularly those who have risen above the lower ranks, have become perfect bureaucratic souls. For those who begin or end their uncivil service careers as perfect bureaucratic souls, a large correctional system is Paradise.

Within a prison the general public is no bother at all, and press coverage is minimal and easily misled. If conditions in the "joint" deteriorate, the public is, as like as not, pleased that the inmates are suffering more. The bureaucrat is thus left quite free to carry on with his or her real business.

A prison can offer considerable emotional satisfaction to some. That is, the bureaucrat not only can shuffle papers, he can shuffle people as well, and if some people, like some papers, get mislaid or destroyed, no one much cares, except "bleeding heart" prisoners' rights lawyers, whose ability to do something has been severely limited by a new law passed by the Gingrich Congress. Further emotional satisfactions can come from the bureaucrat's knowledge that he or she is doing one of those nasty jobs that someone has to do for the greater good and that this sacrifice puts one far above the general herd in social understanding and moral attainment.

Rikers Island is the highest circle of the bureaucratic Paradise. The Rikers bureaucracy consists largely of two ranks: captains, distinguished by their white shirts and starchy manner; and corrections officers, or COs, who range from raw and sometimes frightened beginners, to a good many experienced and corrupted old-timers who relish their daily exercise of power without responsibility. Between these two groups are a few real people trying to do the best they can in a hellish place.

It was my impression that there were far more captains than necessary, a tribute to the career-promotion abilities of the unbridled bureaucracy. By the time I left, I had concluded that few COs were promoted to captain until they had learned to respond to every question or request from a prisoner with scorn and derision, however legitimate the question or request might be.

Rikers is the largest jail in the world, with an average daily inmate population of twenty thousand housed in some fourteen separate facilities on an island at the western end of Long Island Sound, immediately north of La Guardia Airport. A jail is not a prison; it is not a "correctional institution" wholly populated by people serving long sentences and enjoying, perhaps, some rehabilitative services. A jail is a warehouse for defendents (some of them innocent) awaiting disposition of their cases and for people serving sentences of not more than a year. Nevertheless, a combination of completing a previous sentence after violating probation, waiting for the disposition of a new criminal charge, and serving a new sentence can keep a man in Rikers for well over two years. Most Rikers inmates are only awaiting resolution of their cases. This makes for relatively rapid inmate turnover and skeletal rehabilitative services. Rikers provides no comforts for any inmate.

There is not enough work on the island to employ more than a handful of prisoners, probably less than 10 percent. There are no trustees; all prisoners are treated equally as violence-prone, drug-crazed habitual offenders. Most of the prisoners I met were neither drug-crazed nor violent, although my guess is that most were inside on some sort of drug offense. Nearly all spent their days in absolute idleness.

I was housed in a protective custody facility called the North Infirmary Command (NIC), the smallest of Rikers facilities, with some four hundred inmates, of whom perhaps fifty, segregated from all others, were serving sentences. At NIC three-quarters of the inmates were housed in six barracks-like rooms on the three upper floors. A few, the ill or handicapped, were housed in a separate, true infirmary section. Most of the sentenced inmates, never more than thirty, were in the south wing of the sixth floor, or NIC 6S.

Before I went into Rikers, I feared the prisoners, but I was treated with surprising respect and deference, even guided and protected, by the hapless misdemeanor offender and tough street-thug alike. With few exceptions, the inmates I met were poorly educated and impulsive, with delusions of "manhood" of the John Wayne and Sly Stallone variety. In short, they suffered from that endemic disease unique to the United States—chronic adolescence, that state of mind in which everything is possible and death is inconceivable. I soon realized I had nothing to fear from the other inmates, most of whom were harmless. The only threat to spirit and body came from the bureaucrats.

One of the key methods the Nazis used to cow the populations of occupied countries was the erratic enforcement of a panoply of arbitrary regulations, some of which could not be obeyed without violating other regulations. Thus, almost every citizen became guilty of some offense and could be arrested at any time. That situation describes Rikers very well. For example, prisoners were not permitted to have pens. We could use only the short thin plastic refills of ballpoint pens, supposedly for sale in the commissary.

Unfortunately, the NIC commissary did not have any refills in stock for most of the four months I was inside. Any prisoner who wanted to do much writing had to become a rule breaker—generally by swiping pens from guards. Usually the COs and the captains ignored the presence of contraband pens, except during the surprise general searches, when they were confiscated. But if a prisoner with a pen angered a CO enough to do the paperwork required, he could lose "good time" and get ten to twenty days added to the time he must serve.

In other cases the arbitrariness consisted simply in different COs applying the rules whimsically. A visitor who brought me Rosh Hashana greeting cards to mail out had to take them back home; they were ruled "not stationery." An unlined writing pad was not permitted—it was "artist's materials." Visitors could not bring inmates hardcover books, but hardcover books could come in by mail.

I could go on and on with examples of truly crazy rules and crazy rulings. It appeared at times as if the list of contraband items grew longer and longer and was never reviewed for rationality. And as long as guards go in and out of Rikers without being searched, most of the island's security measures will remain ineffective, useful more for harassing prisoners than for increasing safety and keeping drugs out of the jail.

The worst part of my daily Rikers experience was the food. I was eating kosher meals prepared by outside providers and warmed up in Rikers' kitchens. As far as I could make out, on July 1, the beginning of the fiscal year, a new supplier was to start providing meat meals (as opposed to dairy ones), but was not ready to meet the contract. For six weeks before and after July 1, Rikers' kitchens appeared to be scavenging old supplies to feed "kosher" inmates.

Unfortunately, all the good meals had been eaten up by guards and by inmates working in the kitchens. Nothing was left but the two least appetizing meals—chicken "bricks" (barely chewable pressed breast of chicken) in a cloying sweet sauce and fish in a vinegary sauce. Once I was served chicken bricks nine meals in a row; two other times I had nothing but fish for seven days in a row. The printed kosher meal menus created by the kitchens for the delectation of outside regulators were a total fiction.

On protesting to the captain in charge of the kitchen, she explained that I could not expect beef for every meal. But the other, "non-kosher," prisoners were getting beef or dark meat chicken for at least every other meal. The captain felt no need to explain the cause of the problem or to do anything about it. There was only the most feeble attempt to try to feed the "kosher" prisoners properly, and that attempt came only after I went on a hunger strike.

In spite of these problems, the first two months of the sentence went quickly. Contributions from Manhattan Hemlock Society members bought me a subscription to the *New York Times*. Its regular arrival on the day of publication was the high point of the day. A friend in England sent me fifty *London Sunday Times* cryptic crossword puzzles—wonderful time killers. Another friend sent me a commentary on the Psalms, with much food for thought about hard times and faith. There was never a day without a letter, usually three or more. Many people sent me books, and my many visitors brought more.

The visitors came from the synagogue, from the Hemlock Society, and from Myrna's friends and mine. A particularly enlightening book I read in Rikers was Robert Hughes's *The Fatal Shore*, the history of Australia's founding as a penal colony. I learned that while the level of guard brutality had decreased immensely since the eighteenth century, guards' attitudes toward prisoners had not changed in the slightest.

By and large, were it not for uniforms, it would have been hard to distinguish between the guards and the prisoners. They came out of the same neighborhoods, had similar family backgrounds, spoke the same coarse language, and shared many interests. The chief distinguishing feature, I would guess, was that all the COs had high school diplomas.

This similarity of guards and prisoners explains, in part, the general CO view of prisoners as degenerate scum. The guards had to struggle constantly to avoid seeing themselves in the prisoners. It is this need on the part of the guards to distinguish themselves from the inmates that may lie behind the wildly exaggerated stories of homosexual sex in jails and prisons. It probably occurs occasionally, but during my time in Rikers, although I was aware of drug and alcohol use, I never saw the least sign of sexual shenanigans. The only reference to homosexual sex I heard in Rikers came from guards whose comments indicated they believed it was a regular way of life on the inside. Information from inmates with considerable experience of Rikers and of larger prisons confirmed that homosexual activity among inmates, consensual or otherwise, was rare.

The COs' need to differentiate the prisoners from themselves extends to prisoners' families and friends. A single example of unnecessary callousness will suffice. Visitors are not allowed to have anything in their pockets or to carry purses when they enter the visiting room at North Infirmary Command. They cannot even carry in a handkerchief or tissue. If visitors cry or need to blow their noses, a guard does not give them a box or pack of tissues, but degrades them with a roll of toilet paper!

July 3 and 4 found me very withdrawn, spending a lot of time looking at a picture of Myrna from about 1975. I thought of the wonderful days we had spent at the beach on the Fourth of July weekends in some years and of Myrna's childlike delight in the fireworks of other years. July 4 was brilliantly bright and sunny and, from the large windows of the barracks, the waters of Long Island Sound sparkled invitingly. The day should have been dark and gloomy.

Novelty gone, the third month dragged along, but in the fourth month time speeded up, and suddenly it was time to go. It is the routine at Rikers to manage the releasing process at night. I got the call to leave the barracks immediately after supper, about 5:30 P.M. I packed my few belongings hurriedly and hustled off without fanfare. I was taken in a van to the central processing building, where I was put into a holding pen. The next eleven hours were the worst of my entire jail experience.

By 6:30 P.M., thirty-six inmates from various Rikers facilities were crowded into the ten-by-twenty-five-foot pen; only three were not black or Hispanic. Five backless benches could seat only fifteen people. Some of the prisoners, apparently used to this routine, had brought sheets or large paper bags to put on the floor so they could sit or lie there. The single sink was filthy; only a few of the inmates dared to drink from the faucet there. An open toilet was right beside it.

At about eight o'clock we were taken downstairs to get our street clothes. I was the only one who had a suit, now musty and with four months' worth of wrinkles; the other inmates were dressed in varieties of scruffy.

Nothing more happened until after 11:00 when the next guard shift took over. The new boss CO's first act was to warn us all to stay away from the gate and wire mesh at the front of the pen. Of course, that was the only place one could get a breath of fresh air. Otherwise, the air in the holding pen was completely motionless and, as the night wore on, it became more and more fetid. The guard put us through an identification check. Later we were run by a captain for a further identification check.

By that time it was about 12:30 A.M. All we needed to get out now was our personal property (money, keys, wallets, etc.). We told ourselves that we might be out by 2:00 A.M., even though the boss CO said it would be 4:30. Between one and two o'clock in the morning, we got our property back. I got my money, about $50, but my keys and wallet had been moved to NIC and had not been returned to central processing. There was nothing to do now but wait for the bus. And wait we did. Some of the inmates said they thought the bus had come and was just sitting out there. We waited.

I wondered if I was going to make it without fainting. The bullpen had begun to get hot. The air was foul. The place had become filthy. The sink was stopped up and so was the toilet. And we waited.

Finally, a little after 4:30, we were loaded aboard two buses and hauled off to Queens Plaza. I immediately got into a livery cab and came right home, where I had to wait a half hour before getting duplicate keys to my apartment from a friend in the building. I went out to Rikers again the following day to pick up my keys and wallet at NIC. Although I was no longer a prisoner, I was still treated like one: I had to wait an hour and a half before a CO brought me my property. The total trip took over six hours.

What was so maddening about the experience was that the whole routine was completely unnecessary. Directly beside the pen we were caged in were two empty pens of the same size. If even one of them had been used, we would all have been more comfortable and cleaner during the long wait. Further, the wait needn't have been so long—the lot of us could have been processed in four hours instead of eleven and released by midnight. But the guards and/or administration have apparently determined that each shift will cover only part of the release process and that no one will leave before 4:30 A.M. It is irrelevant that the process could take much less time. So, in the end, a simple process was transmuted into a bit of gratuitous cruelty, a parting shot, a reminder to the men who had served their time that they were nothing but dregs.

I had handled the entire jail experience fairly well until that night. I could handle the daily callous disregard of the Rikers guards, the constant disrespect for the humanity of the inmates. I could even see that, to a very large extent, the prisoners created that climate of disrespect—they brought it on themselves. Within a few weeks after my release, Rikers had become only a bad dream that happened long ago.

But this parting shot has left a permanent scar. I had already concluded that no one could spend time in Rikers without emerging with a new load of frustrated anger at "the system." The treatment at the end seemed designed to make sure that every inmate emerged with a bad attitude. For myself, I think I felt very much like someone who has been raped. Even though no one laid a hand on me, I felt physically violated, degraded, shamed.

The reactions of the other inmates in the holding pen varied. A few were garrulous, obnoxiously noisy, and verbally agressive as a way to blow off tension. Others talked quietly on occasion. Some slept on the floor. Some, including me, paced or sat quietly.

There were a few, however, who really worried me—the Stone Men. I named them that because they were alert, watchful, silent, and sparing in action. I had the feeling they were recording everything and filing the experience away in storehouses filled with resentment. Perhaps they were already planning revenge.

The poverty of their condition, however, was clearly revealed by one of them, who spoke just once, to say that the first thing he was going to do when he got out was "smoke the biggest rock I can find," a reference to crack. This was one Stone Man's idea of defiance—to thumb his nose at the law. Most of the others probably had more serious ideas about appropriate retaliation.

I suspect that every man in the room felt the same kind of physical and psychological degradation that I did, but probably less consciously, so that, quite unbeknownst to them, their self-respect was torn down and they emerged even less human than they had gone in. Most would put a good face on it and make light of the experience, but each would transfer the humiliation to his family, his neighbors, his next victims. In short, many would return to Rikers because they had been primed to do so by that last experience. The Department of Corrections sows the wind on Rikers Island; society reaps the whirlwind everywhere else in the city.

Locking me up for four months seemed stupid and wasteful to me. A heavy burden of community service would have been much more effective in keeping me poor, busy, and silent and would have added benefits to society rather than subtracting them. Only a few weeks before my sentencing, I had been accepted into a program that would train me as a volunteer literacy teacher for adults, a program that would require a commitment of two or three nights a week for a year. The jail sentence reflects the poverty of imagination and social concern that afflicts our bureaucracies.

This pattern of bureaucratic carelessness continued in subsequent months as I tried to get back the property taken by the police from the "crime scene"—particularly Myrna's purse and her word-processing disk, which contained the letter that prompted my "vampire" reply. The D.A.'s office, for unknown reasons, refused to deal directly with me, referring me back to my lawyers, Brafman and Gilbert. But since I had no money to pay the lawyers, they were not very active on my behalf. At this writing, four months after my release from Rikers, most of the property has still not been returned, and some of it, including the word-processing disk, seems to be lost. No one in the criminal justice bureaucracy seems to be concerned about this negligence.

To conclude, I encountered nothing in the criminal justice system that gave me any reason to respect it and a great deal that leads me to suspect that it is part and parcel of our crime situation—a bureaucracy cultivating and feeding on the problems it is supposed to mitigate. It strikes me as exceedingly contradictory—and frightening—that the politicians who rail against big government in all other areas are the same ones who place great trust in the efficacy of harsh prosecutors, severe judges, and more prisons.

17

How Will We Live?

If it can be imagined, it can be done. This is America. We never say die.

    —Ad for the CIT Group often aired on PBS

Someday we'll beat this thing called death.

    —A doctor at Johns Hopkins Hospital, circa 1970

We must accept that we now have the potential to do more good than we can afford.

    —Paul Uhlig, M.D.

If you can't get to seventy by a comfortable road, don't go.

    —Mark Twain

Dr. Sherwin B. Nuland, a professor of surgery at Yale and author of *How We Die: Reflections on Life's Final Chapter*, writes of the chosen death issue in an op-ed piece in the *New York Times:* "We find ourselves trying to make sense of an issue that, by its very nature, deals with the most irrational currents of the human mind. . . . As we think about assisted suicide, rather than pretending to the intellectual detachment that we like to say we apply to legal matters, we would perhaps do better to think more about the inner fears that influence our decision-making." (*New York Times,* January 13, 1997, page A17)

It is those inner fears I want to talk about now, both as they relate to Myrna's chosen death and to the general discussion of assisted suicide.

My attorney, Ben Brafman, told me that when he discussed the case with other people, their first reaction was usually sympathy for Myrna's choice and my assistance. But when they learned that Myrna was not terminal and could have lived another ten years at least, many reacted with angry condemnation, particularly of me.

Why did these people assume at first that Myrna was terminal? I believe their assumption was largely self-protective, a way to soften the blow the idea of suicide delivers to the psyche. After all, in the terminally ill, the choice of death is only a matter of timing, of days or weeks, at most, months. Death is in the anteroom, waiting. By assuming Myrna was terminal, the casual observer does not have to consider the nightmare of long and hopeless illness, does not have to think about what makes his or her life worth living right now, does not have to look into the abyss. I believe their subsequent condemnation was, in part, anger over having that first line of defense destroyed.

Myrna's basic problem was that she was *not* terminally ill, she was worse off: severely and hopelessly ill with no end in sight. If she had believed her death was only a few months or even a couple of years away, I know she would have stuck it out. What terrified her was the idea of years and years of a steadily worsening "life" of which she might not even be particularly conscious.

Some people have a similarly angry reaction when they learn that Myrna was not in any physical pain. Intractable pain is commonly accepted as a sound reason for accepting the last anesthetic. A variety of studies cited by opponents of assisted suicide strongly suggest that pain is not the chief reason people seek to escape; pain is not the agony they fly from. I find it almost incomprehensible that so much allowance is made for physical pain and so little or none for psychological pain and the emotional exhaustion of a long struggle with hopeless illness. But here again, it is terror in face of the meaningless, the intangible, the "unfixable," that influences our thinking—or rather, brings thinking to a halt.

Myrna was tired and bored by the endless round of palliatives—the pills, the catheterizations, the exercises, the good advice, the encouragement in face of what experience told her was inevitable—unavoidable deterioration. She was tired of being under pressure to be positive and cheerful for others. She was in deep psychological pain over the way the disease was running her up and down the mountainsides of her emotions. She was in pain over her increasing sense of being "disconnected" from her own words and her inability to hold and express coherent thoughts for any useful period of time.

She said, "I'd be bored, but I'm too vague to be bored." She was shocked by the fact that she could do nothing about her boredom because her brain no longer functioned sufficiently well to let her focus on anything complex enough to be truly interesting. She could watch *Sesame Street* with understanding and enjoyment because everything was repeated. But in another place in her mind, she knew this interest was itself horrible, a terrible symbol of what her mind had become.

I am convinced, from Myrna's example and from various studies I've read, that people do not choose death because of pain or because death is near anyway. They choose death when, after consideration of the facts over a period of time and after casting about for any other alternative, they admit the situation is hopeless and not worth the cost in energy, money, or suffering. There is every reason to believe, however, that most Americans will refuse to admit any such thing right to the end. Not that many of those who would never think of suicide actively choose to live. Instead, they simply drift—passively—toward death.

This hopelessness of those who choose death should not be confused with treatable depression. Many people are dismayed to learn that Myrna was often depressed, and they leap to the conclusion that her choice of death came about because of treatable depression. Some are shocked to learn that she was not taking her full prescription of antidepressant medication. They are even more shocked to find out that she rejected medication that might have alleviated her mood swings, choosing death instead. I think we ought to question our reasons for clinging so desperately to this idea of treatable depression as a cause of chosen death.

I recently asked a psychiatrist, a panelist on a symposium on assisted suicide, if depression appeared to be a more outstanding problem in the United States than elsewhere because it was seen against the backdrop of our socially enforced optimism. Do psychiatrists in other countries agree with U.S. doctors' diagnoses of clinical depression? Have there been any cross-cultural studies of depression? He dodged the questions, but his answer went to the heart of the issue anyway. He said his European colleagues often kidded him with the taunt, "Oh, you Americans; you think you can live forever."

I'm inclined to suspect that the focus on depression in the media, in medical conferences, and elsewhere over the last few years is a fad, or worse, a subtle campaign by pharmaceutical companies pushing their "happy pills," their *soma* for that Brave New World we may be creating. There is, in our "happy" society, a strong tendency to see illness in reasonable sadness and an even stronger tendency among psychiatrists to assert that they can "cure" that illness. I do not deny that there is such a thing as pathological depression, only that it is so widespread. I also don't think that reasonable sadness should be treated with drugs.

The same psychiatrist mentioned above said earlier in the symposium that he had never encountered a patient who, wishing to die, had not changed his mind when properly treated for depression. Of course, one must note, if the patient didn't change his mind, then ipso facto, he hadn't been properly treated. In either case, the doctor is still in business, his optimism and professional pride still intact. For if "happy pills" are not the answer to the horrible question of chosen death, what is? What good is he as a psychiatrist? What does his life mean?

Many people, including experts in health care policy, are also disturbed by the fact that Myrna had no assurance that she would be well taken care of if something happened to me. But what does "well taken care of" mean in a situation in which one is helpless to lead a normal life and is slipping away mentally? Can anyone be "well taken care of" in such circumstances? Oh yes, one can be babied, and some hopelessly ill persons can accept that. But most adults whose minds and bodies are deteriorating are not babies and don't want to be treated like babies. They suffer enormously from knowing they have lost that prize at which all human life aims— responsible self-determination and the respect that goes with it.

Personal responsibility is the hallmark of the socially mature individual. It is one of the chief curses of a severly debilitating illness that it usually involves the regression of the mature adult to a condition of infantile dependency, a dependency condoned and often required by medical professionals and other caregivers. Where an illness is curable and a return to adult function and responsibility is possible, such regression may aid recovery. In the case of the hopelessly ill, however, social support for that regression may have the effect of killing the responsible person at the social level long before physical death occurs.

Besides that loss, those who are "well taken care of" must often bear another, heavier burden. If they retain sufficient awareness, they may be socially required to reflect the cheerful optimism of their determined caregivers. They must be grateful. They must appear to subscribe to the "happiness principle." It is thus that the heaviest burden of all is added, the last crushing weight: loneliness, the lack of anyone to talk to who will accept and respect and join in their sorrow.

Some people are horrified to learn that Myrna may have chosen death for my sake. Her aquatherapist asserted on the *Dateline* show that Myrna's choices of our wedding anniversary and then the Fourth of July as days to die had nothing to do with nostalgia or her own freedom, as I had believed. Rather, according to Luye, they were chosen to suggest an anniversary gift to me or to symbolize *my* freedom.

Why is this so awful? Healthy people who sacrifice their lives for others are considered heroic; why aren't hopelessly sick people entitled to the same honor? Is it because we have already relegated the very ill to the status of "pathetic victims," unable to rise in strength to nobility of spirit? Is it that we don't want our own nobility, our generosity, brought into question by this challenge to our assumption that we might live forever and never have to make such a sacrifice? Or is it simply that a chosen death is so awful to contemplate that there can never be any good in it?

Finally, some people want clearer evidence that Myrna did truly want to die, evidence that would convince everyone to "a moral certainty" that she chose death of her own free will at the time of the act itself. Here, I believe, those who see only horror in a chosen death ask for something that is simply not available—absolute assurance. I doubt if any evidence, including film of the act itself, would be sufficient to allay their need to doubt. (And if there were film, wouldn't the filmmaker be criticized for coldly invading those horrible private moments solely to protect himself—perhaps even for monetary gain?)

We are often unsure of the motives and intentions of many acts, and for acts short of death, we accept a certain muddiness of motive and intention as unremarkable. I think we long for absolute certainty about the choice of death because it is so terribly absolute and frightening to ourselves. More than anyone else, I wish I could be absolutely certain about Myrna's choice of death. To know for sure, without a shadow of a doubt, that she drank the solution without moral hesitation, without regret, with one wholehearted aim in mind.

I cannot know those things; no one, perhaps not even Myrna, could know those things. I can take solace only in what I see as a preponderance of the evidence from more than twenty-five years of knowing and loving her, in my conviction that her decision was in the act, and in my certainty that her choice was brave and wise whatever her motives.

There may be a partial solution to this need for certainty, one that would at least answer legal questions. Let me suggest that each state establish a licensing system that would enable people to record their desire to die under a variety of specified future circumstances. Once the wishes were recorded, an applicant would be licensed to end his or her life, with help from any consenting adult if desired or necessary, when and if those circumstances became real. States would require that the license be periodically renewed. A requirement that a license to die could not be used until it had been renewed at least once would provide further evidence of intention and forethought.

For example, from a preset list, I might choose do die if, at any time after reaching age seventy, I was confined to a wheelchair, was stricken with any disease the treatment of which would not restore an active life, or if at any time before age seventy I suffered a spinal injury that left me quadriplegic, etc. I would be free to use the license or not when the time came. (Such lists of circumstances are readily available.) A waiting period might be imposed in some cases in order to allow time for a person to adapt to a traumatic handicap rather than rushing to the end before the alternatives were fully examined.

Another possibility: require new drivers to apply for such a license. Such a requirement could provoke some serious thought about what they might do to themselves and others.

Contrary to the anxious assumptions of those opposed to chosen death, very few people would use their license to die. The biological instinct to live is immensely powerful and beyond reason. It is not easily overcome even by those who do truly desire to die. Studies have shown that, whatever their expressed wishes in unthreatening times, the majority of hopelessly ill people want to continue treatment, however unpleasant, even if it only provides a few more painful weeks of life. In even the worst circumstances, it requires an extraordinary strength of will to choose death.

Therefore, a license might even provide for a mercy killing if one were to become comatose or suffer severe cognitive losses. With such a provision as an option, Myrna might still be alive, assured that when her mind was thoroughly damaged, someone could provide for treating the empty tomb of her body with the dignity it deserved.

The advantages of such a licensing procedure are many. It would provide a legal cover for the question of "real" intentions. It would help prevent unwanted intrusions on one's privacy and freedom by well-meaning professionals. It would help exclude interference from family members who cannot face the thought of death. It would exempt a suicide assistant from legal penalties, and at the same time place an obstacle in the way of abuse. Above all, it might force people to talk about the issues and prepare themselves and their loved ones for the inevitable.

Would such licensing be abused, with harried caregivers pressuring their charges to get a license and then "helping" them die? Outright murder, out of malice or for profit, could probably be disguised behind a license to die. Such abuse is certain to occur. But it is highly unlikely that it would account for even 10 percent of the forty to fifty thousand deaths that occur annually from abuse of driver's licenses.

Arguing that highway deaths are accidents and not in the same category as chosen death is not effective. When the same toll of death occurs year after year, it cannot be considered an accident. The only thing accidental is who will be killed, not that the killing will happen. If we can accept that kind of highway slaughter in the name of personal freedom, surely we could accept, if we were rational about death and the terribly ill, some abuse of a license to die in the name of the same personal freedom.

Even if a moderate level of abuse was accepted, the licensing solution would still be unacceptable to many people for what appears to me to be a very strange reason: a belief in the certain value of suffering. This need not be a purely religious point of view, as is demonstrated by the peculiar juxtaposition of the ideas of suffering and psychological health made by a psychiatrist adamantly opposed to chosen death. Herbert Hendin, executive director of the American Suicide Foundation, writes in his *Suicide in America:* "We need not believe that suffering is good for the character in order to understand that the capacity to deal with adversity, including illness, is one of the features of psychosocial stability."

I would never deny that there is much to be learned from suffering. But I have been to that school, and I know that the courses are elective.

One can learn humility, the recognition that no one is spared and that disaster can strike even the great immune Me. But one can also learn denial, the assertion that the great Me could never be faced by any but the most minor and manageable adversity.

The student of suffering can learn self-abnegation, the setting aside of one's own needs and desires for the sake of others. Or the student can learn intense self-centeredness and recrimination, blaming his disaster on others, who should be punished.

A brave person can learn resolution, persevering in spite of adversity, struggling to retain as much freedom and dignity as possible. The weak may learn only to abandon their will and drift into passive helplessness.

The wise will learn compassion, the ability to acknowledge and join in the suffering of others. But many will learn only envy, seeing others as unjustly spared.

Are envy, passivity, recrimination, and denial signs of psychosocial stability? The school of adversity and suffering provides no promise of graduation into a greater understanding of the goodness of life. On the contrary, for many it will only promote further moral decay and that despair that denies larger social values. I suspect, too, that it is precisely the kind, the generous, and the bold who are most likely to choose death in face of hopelessness, asserting the value of life, while those who sink into moral decay are more likely to persist in their own life against all odds, sustained by meanness of spirit and of imagination.

Why must we find value in suffering and adversity? It may come from our need to assume that we live in a beneficent universe or under the concerned eye of a beneficent god. If we do live in such a universe, then any suffering must be part and parcel of its goodness, and we require the hopelessly ill to demonstrate that value. It may be that, at a deep subconscious level, some of us require our loved ones to continue in suffering as living human sacrifices to our need to assert that God is just, in a way we can understand.

A slightly more rational religious objection to chosen death is that our lives are gifts from God and are not to be returned until called for by the giver. It is my understanding, however, that the gift is given to be used responsibly. It seems to me that returning the gift when it can no longer be used responsibly is a highly responsible act.

What has happened is that modern American medicine, in its irresponsible pursuit of an unreachable goal, has created an added burden for hopelessly ill responsible adults. They can no longer be comfortably and irresponsilly infantile, knowing that their condition is but a brief prelude to death. Instead, if they are alert to the dynamics of modern medicine, they are forced to take on the added burden, the responsibility, of deciding when and how they should die.

They must take on this burden not simply because no one else can or will do it for them (certainly not the medical professionals, who routinely ignore advance directives and do-not-resuscitate orders), but because, unless they choose and act, the modern medical machine will force them to join in its wasteful pursuit of the impossible. In short, in the context of modern American medicine and its mindless focus on thwarting death, choosing physical death is no longer an irresponsible avoidance of the unpleasant; it may well be the most responsible and life-affirming choice a hopelessly ill person can make.

It is a measure of our illogic that few religious persons who adhere to the idea of life as a gift from God see any contradiction in resisting its called-for return with every means available. A person can no longer be "called home"; God has to send a squad of archangels to wrest the dying from the medical machine.

Finally, in this examination of the irrational in our thinking, let's turn to my case: Was I wrong to help Myrna die? Think back to the parallel I suggested in an earlier chapter of the kapo and Dr. Mengele in the concentration camp. The mad doctor is torturing an experimental human subject; the kapo's job is to keep the subject as comfortable as possible. The last thing the doctor wants is for his experimental subject to die. If Mengele can't be killed and if the subject wants to die, whom should the kapo assist, the human subject or Mengele?

If the kapo, at her request, kills the experimental subject, he is seen to be delivering her from harm, from evil. If I help my hopelessly ill wife die, I am seen to be inflicting harm; I am the evil. In one case, the victim is delivered from harm; in the other, harm is inflicted on her. Same act, similar circumstances, same result—with diametrically opposite moral evaluations. Why?

The answer, I think, lies in an unexamined vestige of medieval religious thought that is still common today: The actions of a Mengele are evil, even Satanic, because they are taken by a supposedly responsible human being; but the actions of a virus are "natural," in some way related to God's will and therefore not an evil from which one should seek deliverance. The fact that medicine is devoted to eradicating such "natural" visitations of the divine is accepted without question and the contradiction goes unnoticed. If a doctor, using antibiotics, delivers an aged patient from the ravages of influenza so she can die some uglier way a few weeks later, he is obeying the first rule of the Hippocratic Oath: "First, do no harm." If a doctor, with an overdose of morphine, delivers a patient from the ravages of late-term cancer, he is doing harm.

What is "harm"? I recently heard a very wise and experienced doctor, who is also an expert in law as it applies to medicine, discuss these issues with great reason and moderation. But he ended his talk with the throwaway line, "I do not see how we can get around the 'harm' problem."

Doctors—whether few or many, I do not know—see death as "harm," and only "harm," in all circumstances. They seem to lack either the intelligence or the emotional strength or the will to distinguish between death as disaster and death as release from disaster. They raise death, any death, to the level of absolute evil and take "do no harm" to be a simple direction to always thwart death and never cause it. In some doctors, I suspect, this view is a form of moral laziness or cowardice. It is so much easier and safer to adopt an absolute abstract principle and so avoid the thought, the anguish, and the courage necessary to deal with the ambiguities of the concrete.

On July 21, 1996, when I was in jail, the *New York Times Magazine* published a long article reporting the views of those most adamantly opposed to legalizing physician-assisted suicide. Some of my friends were upset that these views were so prominently reported. My own reaction was disappointment that the "expert" views displayed were so obviously contradictory, sentimental, and irrational—even hysterical.

What struck me most particularly was the apparent assumption of the medical professionals among the experts that legalizing physician-assisted suicide was equivalent to granting doctors permission to kill their patients. One of the opponents, Daniel Callahan, a bioethicist, put it differently. To him, the desire to legalize physician-assisted suicide represents the patient's desire for his doctor's approval of the choice of death. Both these views are presumptuous. They are arrogant, self-aggrandizing, and paternalistic. Their prevalence among medical professionals is probably the most dangerous aspect of legalizing assisted suicide.

For example, one doctor quoted in the article, Linda Emmanuel, a spokeswoman for the views of the American Medical Association, recognizes that when all options are explained to patients, "they are *very good* about getting their own big picture." (Emphasis added.) At the same time, Emmanuel and other professionals are fearful that other physicians, fed up with handling hopeless cases, will suggest death as a treatment option and, using their prestige and subtle pressure, will persuade the hopelessly ill that death is the best option. That is, when patients are presented with all the options, they are *not "very good* about getting their own big picture." That paternalism, combined with the standard professional pieties, keeps many doctors from seeing what they are really doing. Dr. Emmanuel asks, "If killing you is an option, how can I expect you to trust me to do all I can to heal you?"

But, doctor, that is the whole point—you are not healing me! You are only prolonging my death! And, killing me is not an option for *you;* when I want your *help,* though, I'll ask for it. I would be far more inclined to trust a doctor who can humbly say, "I can't heal you; I can only delay your death. Is that what you want?" I can "just say no" to either option.

In the *Times Magazine* article, Daniel Callahan argues that legalizing assisted suicide would undercut the demand for health care reform and efforts to improve care for the severely disabled. The reverse could be as true: If the medical profession could be persuaded to stop its futile thwarting of death at great expense, more money and energy might be focused on the restoration and preservation of health in the young, the poor, and the severely handi-

capped. There might be more money and energy available for—
and professional interest in—preventing illness and for the mundane management of chronic conditions as opposed to the
excitement of treating acute conditions. That would appear to be
the long-term aim of health maintenance organizations, if they are
not forced by misplaced sentiment to submit to the public's unrea-
sonable expectation of affordable medical miracles.

I hope I have demonstrated that in the discussion of chosen
death and assistance, we cannot rely on our instinctive reactions.
The quick assumption may indicate avoidance of the issues; fine
sentiment may cover up personal fear; traditional pieties and old
ideologies may be irrelevant in the world of high-tech medicine in
a free-market economy. More facts, careful thought, detailed and
imaginative analysis, sensitivity to the realities of suffering, and
acceptance of tragedy as part and parcel of human existence are
all desperately needed if we, as a society, are to reach any consen-
sus on these issues.

This book will be published soon before or soon after the United
States Supreme Court rules on whether physician-assisted suicide
should be permitted. However the court rules, the issue will not go
away. If the court rules in favor of permission, fifty state legislatures
will have to deal with regulating such suicide. If the court rules
against permission, there will be more discussion and more cases
like Myrna's and mine. As the population ages and the power of
medicine to thwart death grows more rapidly than the power to
restore health, the question will become more critical than ever.

An experienced hospice worker quoted in the *Times Magazine*
article, tells the touching story of a young man with AIDS who
asked for help to die. "His religiously fundamentalist family was
appalled with [his homosexuality]. . . . Gradually, the hospice team
was able to bring them together, and to see that father gently
bathing his son's rectal herpes was nothing short of a miracle. . . .
It's all right there, the moment of truth. This man died in peace,
and his family will always know they had loved him, something that
wouldn't have happened if I . . . had listened to his request to die."

It does not detract from that miracle to suggest that the recon-
ciliation could have come years earlier if the family had recognized

that death is always imminent. For it is by facing daily the reality and imminence of the "big death" of the body that we are most likely to be motivated and freed to enact the "little deaths" of the self that reconcile us to each other and the world—apology, for-giveness, atonement, self-effacement, patience, acceptance, vulner-ability, openness to both joy and sorrow . . . above all, compassion.

The author of the *Times Magazine* article concluded by noting that "we haven't begun to give the slightest thought to these issues," and asks, "In dealing with all these decisions about death, how will we live?"

I am convinced that when we begin to deal with the question of death forthrightly and without sentimentality, we will also begin to live more wisely, more compassionately, more abundantly.

Not long after Myrna's retirement in 1985, when she was still able to get around on crutches, she volunteered to work with the Hor-ticultural Society of New York in a program designed to brighten the lives of the elderly with indoor plants. Myrna's first project was to teach a much older woman how to care for a few plants donated by the Society and by Myrna. Coincidentally, the woman had a very mild case of MS.

The older woman constantly complained about everything and treated Myrna like a servant, but Myrna went back to her apart-ment week after week to teach her about the needs of different plants, watering schedules, repotting. Myrna even went shopping for her on occasion. Myrna made the trip across town and down-town every week for as long as she was able, despite the old lady's ingratitude and apparent disinterest in the plants.

Myrna described the woman's behavior with some exasperation, but she also expressed an understanding forgiveness and a sadness that the old lady seemed unable to enjoy anything. She said, "Maybe it's just me. Maybe she feels guilty that her MS never got as bad as mine. Or maybe she's afraid of the future and the fear is ruining her life."